People of God

People of God

A Plea for the Church

Anton Houtepen

ORBIS BOOKS
Maryknoll, New York 10545

Translated by John Bowden from the Dutch *Mensen van God. Een pleidooi voor de kerk*, published by Gooi en Sticht, Hilversum 1983.

Copyright © Gooi en Sticht 1983

Translation © John Bowden 1984

First published 1984 by SCM Press Ltd, 26-30 Tottenham Road, London N1 and by Orbis Books, Maryknoll, NY 10545

Typeset by Input Typesetting Ltd and printed in Great Britain by Richard Clay Ltd (The Chaucer Press), Bungay, Suffolk

Orbis ISBN: 0-88344-402-X

Contents

Introduction
Do We Still Need the Church?

What is faith? Something vague half-way between knowledge and illusion? A powerful longing, restless and unsatisfied, which is always in search of a better tomorrow? Certainty in thought and action, with ideas and practices based on authority? A heritage of rites – words, gestures, tabus – from the multi-coloured past of many peoples? A feeling of sheer dependence, of being supported by an all-encompassing mystery, the source of wisdom and comfort? Remembrances of the words and actions of the founders of religions, men and women of God, who have made a name by their lives or deaths?

It is not easy to say in a few words what faith is, much less to define it in such a way that non-believers, too, feel and understand what one means. A survey carried out recently in Holland showed that only one in ten of the population were prepared to say that they did *not* believe. But what about the other ninety per cent who *did* believe? Why do they believe? What do they believe in? The same survey gave them a wide range of articles of belief to choose from: they could say whether they believed in God as some vague higher power or as a living God who had a personal interest in their lives; whether they believed in a life after death or future salvation for this world. Obviously there were different ways of expressing belief in Jesus of Nazareth: as a model human being; as a man sent from God; as the divine Son of God; as the living guide in our midst; as a liberator, a prophet, a martyr for righteousness and justice. Finally, they could express belief in the church as the movement of Jesus, the instrument of salvation, the medium of the gospel, the way of peace and righteousness, a sign for the peoples, the people of God, God's building and temple.

How we believe and what we believe in evidently depends less and less on any clear connection with a church. Belief is formed and nurtured – or is abandoned and goes to seed – in a completely new complex of cultural influences: breeding-grounds for thought like the media, the trends of the day, literature and the theatre, involvement and action.

Only a few people look to one another to be nurtured in their faith: traditional families, critical groups, parish leaders, religious communities. Apart perhaps from the Reformed Churches and fundamentalist groups, many Christians today have become 'religious independents' (Peters). Among them, Catholics do not come off at all badly!

Involvement in the church, that is, being aware that we are dependent on one another for the nurture of our faith, joining others in making opportunities for new disciples of the Jesus movement, is in decline throughout Europe and in North America. Fine words have been coined for this development, like secularization and partial identification. The reality is that for the vast majority of people in Western countries, the church has disappeared to the very periphery of their lives. It may be true that even today, after two generations of militant atheism and boycotting of the church, a third of all Russians have their children baptized. It is also true that the proportion is almost exactly the same in the secularized Western world, without any form of pressure and despite all the efforts of the church to reverse the trend. In this connection Dorothee Sölle speaks of the 'trivial atheism' of the West. And even if we should not perhaps speak in terms of real atheism – in that case why would so many people still say that they believe in God? – we can say that dissociation from the church is commonplace: it is taken for granted and hardly thought about. Terms like 'marginal' or 'nominal' churchmanship are becoming inadequate. Such terms would suggest that church membership was a norm by which everyone should be judged, or at least that to be a church member was the most natural thing. In fact that is no longer taken for granted. And although many people still seem to find it natural to call themselves believers, it seems legitimate to conclude that they do so more out of a reluctance to come down positively on the side of a consistent atheism than out of a desire really to live as 'people of God'.

My own view – and I hope to provide good reasons for it in this book – is that, given this situation in the Western church, it is impossible to live as 'people of God' without learning to come together again as a 'church'. Here, of course, indirectly I have all the theological support I could ask for: the New Testament, basing itself on the Old, soon began to call the followers of Jesus the Messiah the 'people of God', *ekklesia tou Theou*, those whom God calls out of the great mass of the peoples who do not want to know him, the *gōyîm*, the *atheoi*. In theological terms – i.e. in the language of those who want to begin from a picture of God active in our history – the only foundation for the 'church' lies in the fact that it brings people together as 'people of God'. The theologians of the early church said that God began on this process when he created Adam; he continued with it even when Cain killed Abel – when did he ever stop? He gave himself a new opportunity with Noah's ark and cherished new hope when Abraham came to believe and went on a journey to a land of *shalom*. Only after communicating with humanity in many kinds of ways did God finally come to us in Jesus so that, following and accepting him, we should become children of God, people of God. Of course theological support along these lines does not get us very far in the situation I have just outlined: the very different picture actually presented by those who call themselves 'people of God' contradicts such visionary claims. The 'people of God', like those who built the tower of Babel before them, have split up into countless groups – almost 21,000 of them. Every year this process of splintering produces 200 new small Jesus movements. And polarization is increasing even within the movement of those who are in search of greater togetherness – say, the three hundred member churches of the World Council of Churches and the eight hundred million members of the Roman Catholic Church. The old schisms have not yet been healed and new ones are already appearing. They relate to differing reactions to the distribution of poverty and riches in the world; to nuclear weapons; to equal rights for women; to whether Black people and Jews, aliens and those with different opinions can also claim the same human rights.

Given all this, is there not far more cause to accuse the church rather than defend it? I have often thought so, and the spokesmen of the church usually do not do much to banish such thoughts. The charges against the church have become almost clichés, but that does not make them any less harsh. The two thousand years of the Jesus movement and the 'people of God' has included at least fifteen hundred years of persecution of those with other convictions – Jews, Moslems, and atheists – and power struggles among its leaders: bishops giving themselves airs and behaving as though they were generals; popes acting as despots or prima donnas; pastors playing the part of moralists and killjoys. There has been a centuries-long defence of the *status quo*: the authorities are always right, laws are holy, authority must be respected, patience is better than violence, work ennobles and the nobility does not work, you have the poor always with you, the powers that be are ordained by God and inherited rights count double. And when the revolution came – first the philosophers of the Enlightenment, then the slaves of the proletariat, and after them the technologists and the social scientists – the church of God rejected it. It pronounced anathemas before listening; it did not bring people together but drove them apart; it enslaved consciences and muzzled innovators in the name of natural law, revelation and the teaching office. And although it was written in Scripture that the Spirit of God would lead the people of God into all truth, these people preferred to take matters into their own hands and fixed it in canons, dogmas, orders of service, defended by theologians as the official guardians of the church's authority: the Inquisition, the Holy Office, the Congregation for the Doctrine of the Faith. Here was the department for truth, where faith was kept on deposit. The faith once given to the saints, the riches of Christ, the precious talent, was hidden in folios full of decrees, printed on Denzinger's India paper.

In this respect, Catholics in particular have little to rejoice over in their church history. The more the church identified itself with the kingdom of God through the mouth of its bishops and theologians, the greater became the difference from what Jesus had intended. As the much-quoted comment by Loisy put it, Jesus proclaimed the kingdom of God, but the church came. The original claim to 'catholicity', that is, a call and commission to universality, generosity and openness to everyone throughout the world, came to be limited in 1054 to the West, after 1517 to those who abjured the Reformation, and after 1870 to the true followers of Rome in all things. Had Vatican I lasted rather longer, it would have added to the marks of the true church which are given in the Nicene Creed – the one, holy, catholic and apostolic church – yet one more: *ecclesia* romana *catholica* (Schema on the Church, ch.X, conclusion, in the outline by Kleutgen). But even without this addition, 'Catholics' have become 'Romans' – those who have claimed the church for themselves. For them, the church of God is made up of those who accept the legitimate authority of the bishop of Rome: all other people fall outside the circle of salvation. They are not the 'people of God'. Only after Vatican II could 'Romans' again become 'Catholic'. The process is continuing only with the utmost difficulty. We in Holland have our own experiences; elsewhere in the world there are still cries for a 'new ecclesiological order' in which the ecumenical spirit will be realized in the form of solidarity and hospitality, in which the community will find a place for 800 million poor at the Lord's table, in which women will be given their place so that their gifts and devotion can be made use of in all kinds of tasks and functions, an order in which justice, peace and unity determine the code of behaviour.

Obviously there is good reason for supposing that a plea for the church will not be able to blot out this past. Others have already made the effort often enough, pointing to the church's contributions to culture and civilization, to the *pax Romana* and the Holy Roman Empire, to scholastic universities and Renaissance art, to colonial expansion and the education of barbarians, to the formation of the welfare state and the origin of the United Nations. In one particular period, unbelieving Romantics, attracted by 'the genius of Christianity' (Chateaubriand) and 'the triumph of the Holy See' (Cappellari), found a way to faith through aesthetics and ethics, on the basis of the intellectual order and the impressive unity of Christianity, especially in Rome. But Newman, Maritain and Mauriac could not disguise the fact that their choice of this church on the basis of order and aesthetics was also governed by its 'splendid isolation'; its refusal to face all the searching and questioning, experimentation and struggle on the part of those who live on the underside of history. As will always be the case, their view of the church reflected their view of God and Jesus Christ as the mighty one who sits enthroned on the clouds. Anyone who thinks in terms of power and authority, law and order, will find enough to praise in the church over the centuries. But can anyone in search of liberation and healing, mercy and compassion, also find a hearing among the 'people of God'?

If there can be such a thing as a plea for the church, then it will be a plea which looks towards the future: how the church could be if we could live as 'people of God'. Such a plea for the church can only be a powerful longing for a way to salvation, a Messianic way, a vehicle of meaning, a framework giving a guide to life. The offer – the programme – of Jesus of Nazareth has a place all of its own in the midst of the many systems of meaning on offer. Anyone who continues to choose this way of Jesus, by birth and upbringing, on the basis of a great many obscure factors (some would say chance, perhaps cowardice, but could it be providence?) – and I do that not without prevarication – may and must give an answer for themselves. Yet they must do this without belittling others who opt for Buddha, Socrates, Mohammed or Marx, or who find satisfaction in the God of the universe, the Mother of life, the Father of the people, the Ground of our Being. Without belittling the other systems of religion – the service of God – Christians, *christianoi*, those who have been marked, given a sign, anointed, sent (to outsiders), must bear witness to their calling and mission, in the steps of Jesus the Messiah. For in fact to follow him is to choose a different course in a great many respects.

There has been an abundance of messianic pretenders, messengers from God, prophets of salvation, visionaries seeing life as it should be. They keep emerging every day. They are so many spokesmen for the deepest longings of individuals and peoples. Together they present the cry for redemption, liberation, healing, fulfilment over the ages. They stand surety that human beings are not caught up in despair and that a gleam of hope is not smothered at birth.

Among them Jesus of Nazareth occupies a special place. We believe him to stand in the place of God and we trust in him as in God himself. We have reasonable grounds for that trust: reasons for believing. In the following chapters I want to give a number of these reasons for believing in his movement. I have not invented them, but found them in the beliefs of people across the boundaries of the churches, and especially within the ecumenical movement in which I am privileged to work. So I hope that this plea for the church is at the same time a stimulus towards an ecumenical view of the church.

First of all we must note the facts. The chances for the church in our society are not simply determined by attractive ideals; they also depend on the starting point and the context: our Western, secularized society, in which many people are 'alienated' from any form of religion (Chapter 1).

Next, we must look at the past. We need not invent the church again all over anew, nor is the church the only way devised by God for human beings to come to salvation (Chapter 2).

Anyone who describes the church as a Jesus movement and as the people of God must give an account, first, of belief in God, and then of the way to salvation ascribed to Jesus. How do we know God? How do we experience redemption? Ecclesiology – theological talk about the church – becomes corrupt if it does not attempt to answer these questions, and degenerates into a mere organizational theory of a sacred system (Chapters 3 and 4).

The visible community of the church comes into being as a community of human beings who participate in the same tradition of listening to God – the tradition of Israel and of Jesus of Nazareth – and who on that basis assent to the same faith (Chapter 5). They also celebrate their community in the messianic token of *koinonia*.

They are baptized in the name of Jesus (Chapter 6) and come together at the Lord's Supper, in remembrance of him (Chapter 7). Their conduct is determined by the criterion of God's will, God's guidance, his kingdom (Chapter 8).

In all this, from the beginning the church of God has had the service of guides, prophets, shepherds, teachers, heralds and apostles with a great many names and functions, in a great many contexts. There is increasing agreement about their main tasks and about the nature of their ministry, called as they are to the service of the one Lord (Chapter 9).

In the meantime, the Christian church has been split into many churches. Is the restoration of the one, holy, universal and apostolic church possible, and if so, according to what model? What service can the church of Rome and its bishop perform here? And what is the relationship between the one universal Christian community and the broken society of the world (Chapter 10)?

In each of these chapters I shall try to examine the state of affairs in ecumenical and theological conversations among Christians in such a way as to make clear the connection between the service of humanity and the service of God. Eventually, in an epilogue, this should produce a credible answer to the questions 'What is faith?' and 'Do we still need the church?'

1

Alienation from Church and Religion

'On Sunday morning when the bells ring to call the congregation and minister to church, there is in the air an *expectancy* that something great, crucial, and even momentous is to *happen*. How strong this expectancy is in the people who are interested, or even whether there are any people whatever who consciously cherish it, is not our question now. Expectancy is inherent in the whole situation.'[1]

That is how the theologian Karl Barth described the sphere in which the community comes together. Two generations and two world wars lie between us and his description. The quotation comes from the time of a new self-confidence in the church and in Christianity, a new verve in mission, to which for example John Mott and the 1910 International Missionary Conference in Edinburgh gave classic expression in the slogan, 'The evangelization of the world in our generation'. Between 1800 and 1900 the proportion of Christians in the total population of the world had increased from 23.1% to 34.4%. New ecumenical initiatives were beginning to emerge in a climate of international reconciliation. Theology seemed able to leave behind the rearguard actions with the nineteenth-century criticism of religion, on the one hand as the result of a much more positive evaluation of the phenomenon of 'religion' by a large number of scholars, and on the other hand as a result of the critical exegesis which made it possible for believers to give a better account of their faith. The churches themselves, often deprived of the privileges which had been ensured them by the age-old alliance between church and state, had achieved a new emancipation, as movements with an authority of their own over against the leading ideologies and with a contribution of their own to make in the sphere of the social emancipation of large areas of the population through a far-reaching diaconal network.

However, historical developments seldom turn out as expected.

After seventy years, and in sight of the year 2000, we have to note that the proportion of Christians in the total population of the world is declining – according to some it will fall as low as 16% in the year 2000; that the ecumenical movement has not been able to prevent the emergence of two hundred new Christian churches and groups each year; and that the international concern for reconciliation, diverted by the split betwen socialism and capitalism since 1917, shaken by the catastrophe of two world wars and the holocaust, crushed by forebodings of an apparently inevitable nuclear disaster, is still not enough to make, for example, the United Nations a real instrument of peace; and that all the dedication of Christians to a gospel of liberation and real *diakonia* has not been able to prevent the world from having to struggle with poverty and oppression on an unprecedented scale.

As if all this were not enough to make us modest and careful about associating God's presence too closely with belief and church membership, the state of affairs in Christianity and the church itself, especially in the long-established Western churches, should give us cause for reflection. Whereas at the beginning of the twentieth century the church could still proclaim the gospel loudly from the rooftops, since then many people have been alienated from the church and religion. We may still hear the church bells ringing, but they bring tidings of God to only a few. For most people the tranquillity in our cities on Sunday morning has little to do with the Lord's day; it is all a matter of the 'morning after the night before'.

In his play *Waiting for Godot*, Samuel Beckett introduces two figures on the stage who kill time waiting, waiting for the absent 'Godot', who in fact never comes. They kill time by playing and eating, and ward off boredom with meaningless conversation. Theirs is an existence without future, without a destination. Or is there a vague longing, perhaps the promise that Godot will come? A prayer and a curse for pity, craving for meaning, which may not in fact be satisfied in the play itself, but which nevertheless seems to be the only reason why those who are waiting do not put an end to their lives, why the actors do not bring their play to an end. At last they say, 'Let's go', but then they go on sitting there. The lights just go out. This is a symbol of existence without prospects, alienated from God, dominated by Godot – and at best a doubtful illusion: 'Perhaps tomorrow will be better, but things will never turn out well' (Cornelis Vreeswijk).

The churches have not really flourished anywhere in the last thirty years except in conservative evangelical circles (Billy Graham and other revivalist movements, the Pentecostalist churches and the 'electronic church') and, remarkably enough, after the troubles of decolonization, in the young churches of the Third World. Between 1970 and 1985 the number of Christians in Africa increased at a rate of six million a year, of whom almost one and a half million were converts; in Latin America by about eight million, but exclusively through births; in Asia by about three million, of whom 800,000 were converts. The number of Christians in the Soviet Union increases year by year – both by birth and by conversion – at a greater rate than in Western Europe, where every year two million children born of Christian parents and some one million church members withdraw from the church. In North America the increase in converts is 670,000 a year (as opposed to an increase of two million in births). This means not only that in the year 2000 there will be almost as many Christians in Africa (one in five) as in Western Europe (393 and 431 million respectively), and in Latin America as many as in Europe and North America put together, but also that two-thirds of Christianity will be outside the Western world. A large number of them will be living in the less developed countries (1143 million); 40% of them will be white. So more than 60% of all Christians are now already living in countries without complete political and religious freedom.[2]

In the midst of freedom and prosperity, then, the church and Christian belief seem to be in decline. Sociological investigations in Holland, moreover, seem to confirm the claim that God in Holland will soon be like God in France.

In the light of the facts revealed by a recent survey,[3] only 22% of the population of the large cities still believe in a personal God. As defined by the survey, that is a God who is personally concerned for us, a God who is personally interested in each one of us. Next, 34% still believe in 'a Higher Power'. 24% are uncertain whether there is such a thing, and 21% are certain that there is not.[4] Among those aged below thirty-five, the results are even more striking: only 23% believe in a personal God, as opposed to an average of 34% and 39% for those who are older than thirty-five.[5] This percentage is only half that in 1966.[6] But perhaps the most surprising thing is the pattern among church members themselves. Among Roman Catholics and Reformed Christians in Holland, the number of those who believe in a personal God hardly differs from the overall average, including those who are outside the church, and is little more than a third. The same thing holds, *mutatis mutandis*, for other facets of the church's confession: views of Jesus, and belief in life after death.[7]

Thus all along the line, identification with the church's confession of God, Jesus and eternal life has declined. There is no doubt that agnosticism, unwillingness to say anything, has increased markedly.[8] In most churches ethical attitudes and behaviour differ markedly from the ethics and discipline which are officially commended – the exceptions in Holland are the members of the Reformed churches, but one wonders how long that will last.[9] Religious practice – churchgoing, Bible reading, prayer – is declining further year by year. Since 1965 weekly churchgoing among Catholics has more than halved, from 53.9% in 1965 to 23.9% in 1981; church attendance in the Reformed churches declined from 50% in 1965 to 13% in 1979; only in the Calvinist churches was there less of a decline.[10] Anyone who is so inclined can of course stress that 34% of people still go to church 'regularly' and 63% 'now and then', but the decline is a more certain fact. According to the findings of the 1981 survey of the involvement of young Catholics in the church in Germany, regular church attendance in this group declined between 1952 and 1980 from 50% to 16%, and the number of those who rarely if ever went to church increased from 27% to 60%. Of this group of Catholics, about 60% found worship out of date and irrelevant to their lives.[11]

Thus there seems to be a clear correlation between the extent of belief in God and the extent of involvement in the organized church. Of those who believe in a personal God, more than half (54%) said that they had been in church the previous Sunday, and 70% of them said that they went to church regularly. Among those who believed only in some higher power, the figures were 17% and 23% respectively. That goes against the uncritical attitude which one can often hear expressed, namely that one can believe in God just as easily without being connected to the church in any way. Of course, that does not explain what correlation there is between the two, nor does it demonstrate that religious independence or religious independentism is impossible. Reduced participation and a departure from standardized confessions in a process of 'partial identification' does not directly imply the collapse of all forms of religion or views of life as collective systems for providing meaning. Church, worship, religion and a view of life evidently form a kind of hierarchy of meaning in which people gradually leave behind the systems of meaning which have been handed down to them. Moreover, 91% of Dutch people believe that you can be a believer without going to church, and only 10% say that they do not believe. 81% still regard themselves as having been brought up in a particular faith and therefore as heirs of a religious system of meaning; more than 70% still have their children baptized; 51% still regard themselves as 'definitely believers' and 27% more regard themselves as 'believers in some way'. Many people (from 76% to 31%) think that belief and worship are important for realizing the most important values in life – love, peace, inner harmony and happiness, and to a lesser degree health and prosperity. Even among those who do not go to church, 29% think that faith contributes in some degree towards realizing these most important values in life, and only 4% find that faith has a detrimental effect. Moreover, 15% of them still regard themselves as definitely believers and 22% as believers in some sense.

So in Holland – as indeed throughout Western Europe – we find very different forms and gradations of belief in God, religion and church allegiance side by side; here historical tables indicate a gradual shift from church membership and, at a much more leisurely tempo, a departure from belief in God and religion. This process can only be described as a gradual process of alienation from the church which in a second or third generation results in an almost complete absence of Christian inspiration and tradition.[12] In one group only the personal significance of faith will decline, without much change in the way in which it is conceived; in another group, it is primarily the actual beliefs which come under pressure, although personally people still attach a good deal of importance to faith. The remarkable thing here is that there is not much difference between the way those who belong to the church and those who do not belong to the church look at life, i.e. in 'the complex of convictions and attitudes by means of which people give significance to their existence'. There are much greater differences in social attitudes, above all in terms of moral behaviour and political choice.[13]

In saying this, I am not making any theological value judgments. Such empirical facts like this make it clear that Christianity in the West includes people who are searching and people who have found; people who can still give a lead and others who have nothing but questions; people who still have no doubts and people who hardly have any religious longings at all. Is a symbiosis of such people by definition the beginning of the end of the church and religion? Does a departure from the required forms and formulations of belief automatically mean the loss of personal faith? In what respect are the crisis of the church and the departure from religion 'alienating' for human beings? Or is membership of the Jesus movement and of the people of God itself alienating – although it need not be that?[14]

Here we come to a number of theological interpretations and value judgments.

First of all an interpretation is possible which can only regard a departure from the required and hallowed tradition in forms and formulations of belief in God and discipleship of Jesus as a betrayal of the innermost nucleus of faith, which rests on the acceptance of the God who reveals: *fides ex auditu*. Is not the crisis of the church a consequence of the disappearance from the existence of Western man and women, but most deeply also from the Western view of the church, of the sense of transcendence, the holy and the numinous, that which is worthy of absolute desire? Granted, prayers are said, but they are more programmes of action than cries of anguish and need from the depths. Terms like grace, salvation, the will of God are used, but what is meant by them hardly differs in existential terms from the ideals of non-believers, and often falls short of the latter in radical quality and dedication. Does not the vision of God 'in himself'[15] threaten to disappear behind the visions of salvation that we Christians have developed, especially in the Western world? Is not much Christian proclamation and appeal caught up in the call for self-liberation and the solidarity of the masses, the new humanity of Feuerbach or Marx's new man after the class struggle? How can 'love and justice, grace and liberation'[16] so become the human cause that they also remain God's cause, in the way in which we human beings react to them? How can the fulfilment of a human 'I', which has been enslaved for so long, and the struggle for the world-wide 'we', which has been oppressed so much more strongly, not only purify but integrate our longing for the all-embracing 'you' of God? As far as the Catholic tradition is concerned, the Second Vatican Council has given full expression to the longing for more human freedom, self-fulfilment, acceptance of the 'human potential'. Followed by popes and bishops, it has encouraged commitment to world-wide justice and solidarity, and made it the criterion of the church's involvement.[17] But are we in the Western world successful in retaining within the secularized world a true relationship to God, which is the distinguishing mark of prayer?

Now in a secularized world the superficial references to God fall by the wayside and humanity and the world come to occupy the centre of attention and concern. Faith withers, as it is now unable to put down roots in a longing for God, from which it draws its psychical energy and vitality... As with all other realities, God is done justice to as he really is only when he is worthy of being longed for: there is a reason for him, he exists, and we become aware of that only when our desire for him is aroused. And from our perspective, how else do we come into our own as subjects, how else do we come to life than by feeling touched by a God who fulfils life?[18]

From this perspective, the decline of belief in a personal God, from whom and for whom all human beings live, is the real cause and background of the crisis in the church. Why should people be assembled as the 'church', *kuriake ekklesia, ekklesia tou Theou*, if not for God's sake? The crisis for religious belief in the West is the deepest cause of the decline in commitment to the church. Only when this crisis has been overcome can there be a future for the Western churches. All reforms and improvements in the quality of church forms will get nowhere unless that concern is predominant, regardless of whether they come from the so-called 'progressive' or the so-called 'conservative' side.

A second interpretation seeks the cause of the decline of the church in the West less in a crisis over belief in God than in the abandoning of the true ideals of the Jesus movement. The Christianity of the West has allowed itself to be replaced by the prevailing pattern of middle-class values, by compromise with those holding political power, by the neglect of prophetic criticism of the human, all too human concern for a right to property, the middle-class freedoms, ideas about what is 'normal' and 'fashionable'.[19] It can be pointed out that Christianity began as a movement of the utmost strangeness, which criticized and corrected the forms of society of its time.

The Jesus movement did not fit naturally or obviously into either Roman-Hellenistic or Jewish society. Jesus himself was someone with a special eye and ear for minorities, outcasts, sinners, non-Jews. He adopted a critical position towards the trends of his day: he was neither a political zealot nor a pious Pharisee; he was not a friend of the leaders of the people, the Sadducees who obscured the Jewish identity by collaboration and assimilation with the Romans, nor, however, was he a supporter of the ghetto and a flight from the world, like the group of Essenes in Qumran who gave priority to being a community of the pure in the midst of an accursed and impure world. Although he himself was made an outcast and exterminated as no one's friend, in the name of God he nevertheless set in motion a movement of radical friendship and solidarity. People – his disciples, followers and kindred spirits – joined it who were not afraid to lose their reputations or their lives, but were nevertheless ready to stand up and be counted as a movement – as people of Jesus, people of God in the cities – above all in the cities – of the Roman empire.[20] The earliest Christians stood out by their views and behaviour: they did not go into the army, they did not join in sports and amusements, they did not celebrate any national feast days, they did not charge interest and did not borrow money from the banks. They avoided legal procedures, and did not engage in divorce, but they did not make anyone the prisoner of marriage either. They had no defenders in the senate or the city government, but protected the victims of that government. They preached love for all in need as the supreme commandment, but mutual solidarity and love for their opponents was also part of that command. Thus for some centuries – and often again after that, wherever it was a minority group – the church was an underground church, a catacomb church, a movement of dissidents.

When it became a great church, a majority church, a state church, it took on all the characteristics of ruling powers: the church itself became oppressive, dominating culture, claiming politics for itself, protecting capital and riches.

In recent years this alliance between church and state, church and bourgeois culture, has gradually crumbled in Western society: the French revolution introduced the autonomy of politics; science, technology and culture have since then gone their own way, independently of the church; the social emancipation of Western people has come about through the political struggle and trade unionism rather than by the plea of the church. That was the painful process of secularization. The Western answer to this was first a complete rejection, and after that a new alliance: an agreement with the dominant patterns of culture – except in the spheres of marriage and sexuality; a welcoming of middle-class rights of freedom, but also the retention of a number of social privileges – subsidies, tax concessions, the social status of church leaders, easy access to the media.

Now this second alliance – laid down in concordats, confessional politics, and the formation of confessional societies – is itself on the decline. And, say people who adopt this second approach, that is a good thing. In the long run, the radical deconfessionalizing which marks the end of the alliance between church and society opens up the possibility of a new appeal, a reconfessionalizing. Ultimately a new, confessing and critical church can grow, with active members, involved in an authentic 'community of discipleship' (J.B.Metz). In the future there is room only for such a voluntary church, an eclectic church, an elite church, which can guarantee the authenticity of the programme of Jesus, truly messianic liberation.

The quantitative loss of church members makes possible a qualitative intensification of participation. In the end that is more healthy for everyone: Christians become the leaven in the loaf, the salt of the earth and not the 'marmalade of the people' (Bishop Krusche).

In this view of things, ecclesiology and christology together begin from a new 'theology of Jesus'. Only this last factor can be a guideline for faith and for praxis based on faith. A new approach to Jesus of Nazareth – who he was and what he wanted – is the indispensable condition for the rebuilding of the church and for a new ecclesiological order which is taking form in critical communities and basic communities everywhere, especially in the Third World.

A third interpretation is possible. The church of the West has, it is argued, neglected the Spirit; in other words, it has lost the sense that God shows himself to human beings as the Spirit who inspires their hearts and understanding and leads them to all truth, who is a pioneer in the world through the Jesus movement as the new humanity. In it, human beings need to experience salvation as healing, redemption as security, hope as enthusiasm. But the cumbersome institutions of the church, its massive liturgy, the complicated and far too intellectualized preaching, the lack of warm human contact in city congregations and parishes, all prevent people from being attracted to the church and Christianity. No wonder that the church still flourishes where heart and feeling, body and senses, relations and friendship are still part of the natural pattern of human life, as in Africa or among the kinds of church where such values are cultivated anew, among the Pentecostal churches, the independent churches, the charismatic movement, the Youth Council of the Taizé brothers.[21]

So what is needed is a new pastorate which pays attention to the experience of togetherness; a new liturgy, above all for small groups, house communities, in which ecstatic prayer has a central place and not the exposition of rational truths or moralizing verbalism. It is a good thing that the sick, the handicapped, the enslaved, the lonely, potential suicides should find a warm welcome in such groups. Is that not the working of the Spirit, the Comforter? And from that perspective cannot Jesus' ministry be seen first of all as a 'healing ministry'? The accent must lie on the lame, the blind, the crippled. Why are they constantly left aside or forgotten in interpretations of Luke 4.18-22, both by classical theology, which interpreted Jesus' healings above all as an indication of his divinity, and by the modern stress on liberation and justice, which interprets sickness and handicap above all as a product of social injustice and exploitation, and Jesus' activity and life-style above all as a prophetic call to the struggle? But the sick and the handicapped are seldom the cause of a struggle, and for them the hope for a better tomorrow is an empty consolation – no less empty than the classical tale of compensation after this life. Only when broken people can experience salvation now, already, through the mediation of the church event, is the church truly the body of Christ, in which all members live together and suffer together.

This concern, too, calls for a new order for the church: more freedom from below, less detached dogmatizing from above; more room in the church assembly for 'ordinary people', with their longings and needs. It calls for another kind of church leader: less academic and learned, shaped more by his own experience in dealing with all kinds of human concerns, less concerned with logical explanations of the problem of God and more versed in listening to the whispering of God's Spirit in human hearts.

Unlike the three previous ones, a fourth assessment of the crisis of the church in the West seeks the cause less in the content of the church event – God, Jesus Christ and the Spirit – than in the methods and forms of the pastorate: in the quality of catechesis, building up the church, diaconate and liturgy. A new and powerful lead can and must bring about change: by reorganization, a better use of the means of communication, vigorous evangelization, better training of pastors, an increase in the number of vocations for religious and church ministers. However, opinions differ over the direction of this powerful control, particularly within the Catholic church.

One group attributes the decline in church commitment to the excessive amount of tolerance accorded in recent years, which has made people confused, has diluted the teaching of the church, undermined church authority and set adrift valuable features of the church's tradition. In particular, departure from a central church government – for the Catholic tradition, from the church of Rome – and far too much emphasis on the specific features of different contexts has brought unlimited pluralism. As a result, a wide range of value-systems is on offer in our Western world. Eastern and other religious revivalist movements find an easy market in divided Christianity. In it, belief and the church are there 'for anyone who wants them'. Each individual puts together his or her own package of articles and beliefs and uses his or her own conscience for ethical orientation. That leads to a disintegration of ideas and communication within the community of faith, within which, of course, almost everything is voluntary. Political colour, spending patterns, relationships are all part of the adiaphora, things which are nothing to do with faith and on which the church does not need to pronounce any judgment. Mixed marriages – which have increased enormously in the West since the 1960s – introduce differences of opinion into the home. It is quite possible for a Roman Catholic to take yoga lessons, be a vegetarian and have Hindu friends, demonstrate against nuclear weapons and nuclear energy and go to a Protestant church. You can be a member of a secular society, read a secular newspaper, vote for a Socialist or Communist party and at the same time be a member of the parish council or even study theology. And there will certainly also be people who are faithful to the Roman tradition, love to hear Gregorian chant but listen to Protestant radio broadcasts and vote for a liberal party. This complex situation, in which partial identification with the church's confession goes with privatization of belief and a syncretism of all kinds of religious images, leads to alienation from church and worship.

It is argued that only a powerful central authority, the reinforcement of the ecclesiastical authority of bishops and synods, a return to the sources of the church tradition and much clearer church discipline will put an end to this confusion and alienation. The way to achieve that is to have magisterial pronouncements on the differing views of theologians, a return to a far more closed and controlled training of ministers, a catechesis which is an introduction to official church teaching, a clear condemnation of anything in human behaviour and in the laws of society which does not coincide with traditional practices and norms, and the restoration of the penitential practice of the church, as a guidance for the moral life. Only an advisory capacity can be allowed to all advisory and participatory organizations which have grown up as a result of the emancipation of Western man come of age – here the Catholic church had to make up a great deal of ground after Vatican II. The church is not a democracy but a christocracy, and the rule of Christ is exercised through the church leaders who are his representatives by apostolic succession, in the service of, but often in conflict with, the will of the people. When it comes to the truth of faith you cannot act on the basis of a majority vote. It is given by God himself as a pledge entrusted to the church and its leaders, preserved authoritatively and handed down through those leaders with the support of the Holy Spirit.

The second group recognizes that the description of the situation as given above is broadly accurate, but it wants to counter confusion and fragmentation in another way. The fact is that people themselves want to be responsible for their faith and their action must be looked at in a more positive way. Among other things that is a consequence of better education and training, of better possibilities of communication, of the world-wide exchange of ideas on a scale which Christianity has never experienced before. Moreover, it is no loss that Christianity has begun a dialogue with the great religions of the world, in which, as the church fathers bear witness, the Spirit of God himself is at work to make himself known. In a number of respects the church has a good deal to make up, because for so many centuries it has rejected such dialogue out of prejudice. And as for dialogue with all kinds of dissidents and marginal groups within Christianity, they are the stepchildren of Christianity; they present to the church an unpaid bill for too detached a faith, too little concern for warmth and reassurance. Of course, the ecumenical movement shows that an attitude of tolerance and dialogue does not exclude a new direction for Christianity, and osmosis through mutual influence (convergence) is in the long run the best way of achieving a new consensus.

Therefore an attitude of trust is needed, coupled with a developed programme of training from the grass roots. The faith must be taught, not the teaching believed. Educational centres, adult catechetics, the formation of groups, youth chaplaincies, conversations about baptism and church membership, the creative treatment of prayer and meditation, liturgy and sacraments, a deep concern for ecumenical conversation, and mutual advice among churches about the task of the missionary and ecumenical community – that is the course the church must choose. Authoritative control does not go well with this. We are all mutually responsible for one another. Of course the proclamation of the gospel and the call of the Christ event must come first. It is also a good thing to challenge people to be more aware in their church membership. Those who become members of the church by birth must become more aware through conversion. The pastorate must be directed towards making this growth in faith possible. The church itself must become a church of catechumens, which is concerned to make new disciples. For only if it constantly gains new disciples can it remain a dynamic reality which brings the gospel 'in season': to you and your children and all who are afar off, as many as the Lord our God shall call (Acts 2.38).

As to the forms of ministry: of course the church needs presidents at the eucharist and leaders of local communities. But their leadership must bear witness to deep roots in the faith and experience of others, a profound respect for the convictions of other churches and religions, and readiness to learn from developments in the social sciences and technology, from social and political involvement, from solidarity with all who are searching and all who are in need. It would also be a good thing for the experiences of women in the faith to be made more use of in the service of the church community, through much greater participation in the ministry. And if there are too few presidents as a result of certain obstacles, like the obligation to celibacy, as in the Catholic church, then the possibility should be considered whether it is not better, for the sake of the kingdom of God, to begin to recruit from people who do not opt for celibacy.

The church must be careful not to condemn too quickly. It may not break the bruised reed nor quench the flickering flame. But it must not hesitate to speak prophetically in all the situations in which true humanity is threatened, or when the continued existence of humanity itself is put at risk.

A fifth interpretation of the crisis of the Western church is possible. This holds that the departure of the church from many areas is not just a loss. The church is now the victim of its own catholicity.[22] A church which wants to be a world church and a church for the world, the universal sacrament of salvation for all humanity, as witnessed by Vatican II, must not be surprised if the church has in its midst a great many people who can accept only part of the content of all its traditions. It is equally obvious that people will constantly leave the church for the world. We would have too narrow a view of the gospel were we again to confine it within the temple and set a guard on the temple courts, simply because the gospel sounds much purer there and runs less risk of being misunderstood; were we to regard only the disciples in the synagogue as invited guests in the kingdom of God and not those living in the highways and byways with other needs; were we again to begin to look for a church for the ninety-nine righteous rather than the one lost sheep. Is not the gospel full of alienation, and from the established church at that? Is it not also full of openness to outsiders? Precisely because believers are aware of God's universal offer of salvation they should not be jealous if many kinds of healing and salvation can also be found outside the church.

The fact that people in the West have put basic values like love, peace and justice high on their lists without including on them the names of God, Jesus Christ or the church is at least also a result of the influence of the church and the gospel in previous centuries, which have acted like leaven in the loaf. From this point of view the loss of insight and the loss of membership in the church is perhaps only apparent. The important thing is that people should allow everyone else their rights in God's name; it may follow from that, in God's way and God's time, that God too should have his rights. At all events, God's honour is the salvation of living humanity (Irenaeus). Is not this quest for humanity, for justice to be done, itself an implicit confession of God? 'Only God can begin from God. We can only begin from humanity, and in seeking one another presume and hope that God is seeking us. We need not begin from God. He does that himself. We must seek his creation' (Gregory of Nyssa).

More than anyone else, Karl Rahner and Edward Schillebeeckx have stressed this centrifugal character of the gospel and the church. This is matched by the model of the restricted (Thurlings) or controlled (Goddijn) people's church.[23] By that they mean a church which everyone can go to, though not everyone need go to church; a church supported by much good will, both from those who show an unassuming trust in the church by belonging to existing church organizations – in Holland 250,000 volunteers are involved in all kinds of church work, and church attendance every Sunday is still between one and a half and two million – and from those who have looked for voluntary social involvement as a way of serving God and for whom the church is in fact an ally in the struggle for justice and peace.

Finally, there are those – a sixth group – for whom this picture of the church as a catalyst for justice and centripetal catholicity is still too optimistic and romantic. The fall away from church and religion, they say, is connected with the negative function of religion, which has finally been seen through and unmasked by the people of the West. This fall away is the end-result of a process of emancipation, a welcome end to religion. At any rate, 'religion seems to alienate people from themselves, it causes anguish, it goes against science, it calls for a closed mentality and produces repression. It is characterized by the harshness and fixation of the super-ego; it entangles the individual in a web of heteronomous norms; it is in fact a defence-mechanism against the problems of human existence, including death.'[24]

> Religion and religious faith have become superfluous, for example because the need for them arises either out of anxiety, which we can allay in better ways, or out of curiosity, which we can satisfy in better ways. Religion and religious behaviour have become surrogate satisfactions of a need which we can now satisfy more specifically, for example by developing an independent and courageous attitude towards existence with all its questions about purpose, meaning and direction.[25]

Such notions are the echo of the criticism of religion made by Feuerbach, Freud and Nietzsche, which have been very influential in the West, or rather, which have not yet been influential enough in the world elsewhere. So within the foreseeable future, other people in the world will also be asking the same questions:

> Is not God from the outset a projection of man, opium of the people, resentment of those who have fallen short, illusion of those who have remained infantile?... Why believe in God? Why not simply in man, society, the world? Why in God and not simply in human values: liberty, fraternity, love? Why add trust in God to trust in ourselves, prayer to work, religion to politics, the Bible to reason, the hereafter to the here and now?'[26]

The echo of this modern criticism of religion seems to be particularly strong in the sphere of welfare work, the new civil religion of the welfare state, where many former Christians have found a way to a religionless humanism with social-critical elements or elements contributing towards the fulfilment of human potential.

The religious question of meaning is often said to be 'somewhat impolite'. On that presupposition, perspectives on life, religion, denomination and church membership are simply the last unanswered question on the books of co-ordinating authorities which have to fulfil their statutory obligations. A great many initiatives begun by Christians, in caring for the sick, in teaching, in peace and development work, have also been severely criticized from the perspective of an anti-religious attitude – sometimes verging on rancour in the form of hostility to former domination by the church and religion – by those involved in welfare work outside the sphere of the church and Christianity. This situation has deprived the churches of active, committed members, and reinforced the image of religion as a relic appealing to pious and socially neutral people, without any influence in the sphere of politics and science. Why still plead for it?[27]

Other interpretations could easily be added to the six I have given above. Certainly a number of other factors are involved: the theological developments of the nineteenth and twentieth centuries; the economic progress of the West; the fragmentation of the philosophical foundations of Western Christianity in modern times as a result of the influence of Hegel, Kant, Husserl and Heidegger; the historical 'mistakes' of the churches, who abandoned their opposition to science and emancipation too late, so that both intellectuals and workers in many sectors of industry do not come to church; the rapid social changes and intensive migration which tears people from their roots in a traditional heritage. However, this chapter has been concerned to demonstrate how the situation of the Western churches appears in a global perspective and the context which must be the starting point for a plea for the church. Each of the interpretations I have outlined above has a programme for implementation and a theological view of the church. Is it possible also to accept all of them, for the sake of the future of the church? It seems to me that the following elements from these interpretations form a 'new ecclesiological order'.

1. It seems pointless to respond to the growing distance between faith and the church in their traditional forms – standardized confessions, a socially accepted code of behaviour – mainly by criticism of the church leaders. Those who see the crisis of the church above all as a crisis of belief in God and find in concern for the immanent – humanity, earthly justice – anxiety about the transcendent, are probably not completely wrong.[28] Those who persuasively prophesy the end of all religion confirm this. Despite all the just criticism of churches and their leaders it must be said that even if these had done better than their best – whether in a progressive or a conservative direction – the crisis for religious belief would have remained the same. But by the same token the remedy does not lie in nineteenth-century solutions, in the slogan 'Back to the firm authority of the *magisterium*, back to the positivism of revelation and the fundamentalism which refuses to defend the content of the faith against science and technology!' Nor is a reform of church structures – more freedom and participation for everyone, the exercising of authority in dialogue – enough to make the church attractive again for those who have lost sight of it. What seems necessary is a common search – by all Christians together – for a contemporary belief in God, a contemporary, recognizable inter-

pretation of the Jesus event, a new experience of the church as the community of the disciples of God's Spirit. The leaders must be called on to focus their leadership above all on these key elements.

2. At all events, those who point to the negative connotations of faith and church membership in the past, those who have suffered under compulsion and moralism, anxiety and tabu, and who therefore have parted company from the church for ever, can teach us that religion and a view of life *can* be intrinsically repellent and that it is therefore important to look for patterns which are healthy and which benefit humanity. In its traditional Western form, belief in God has perhaps been too much governed by a sense of sacrality in the objective order which has now almost disappeared. This approach suggests a God who intervenes in the course of world history, and who therefore – as the Almighty – has its guidance permanently in his hands. He is terrifying because he apportions suffering and happiness to humanity apparently at whim, so that a whole theology is needed to justify his action here (it is called theodicy, and is concerned to exonerate God from blame for the negative side of life). Only at certain moments and by certain signs does he give access to grace and salvation to some – the elect – especially in the sacraments of the church. Finally, he has set up – heteronomously – external rules for human behaviour, backed up by the sanctions of heaven and hell, which are applied regardless of context. Those who transgress them are sinners before God and have to ask for his grace. Rejecting this idea of the holy as something that breaks into an otherwise profane existence and is seen as the real sphere of God's action, philosophers, psychologists and social scientists have sought the sacral and the holy in human self-transcendence: human potential (Maslow), ultimate justice (Horkheimer), basic trust (Erikson).

Does this not mean that theology – in the pastorate and the preaching of the church – in dialogue with these sciences, must undertake an investigation of the structure of human longing, to see what humanity finds 'holy' (Vergote)?[29] Not every human desire is desire for God. Not every human experience is a religious experience as such. Those who are satisfied with an 'anonymous Christianity', a 'theology of secularizaton', an agnostic silence about the ultimate goal of humanity and the world, who are satisfied with a largely implicit confession which consists in the practice of human justice, will constantly find that this does not of itself solve the problem of God and the question of the driving force behind human action. These are the questions which are on the church's agenda, not to be answered heteronomously, with reference to a divine mandate and revelation from above, but on the basis of the human experience of longing. That happens where our human, personal and collective striving is expressed in and tested by a vision of a more than personal history, in such a way that a personal biography – like that of Moses and Jesus – becomes a normative ethic, and personal fates – those of prophets and apostles – are 're-experienced' in terms of vocation and guidance: martyrs, confessors, ascetics, guides within a communion of saints in the time and space of the church event as it can be experienced now. Thus God becomes a God of people (Schoonenberg) by human beings becoming 'people of God' in a marvellous exchange.

3. To argue for a 'pastorate of persuasion and invitation' (to use the words of the late Bishop De Vet and Bishop Bluyssen) and to have confidence in what others regard as an aging remnant, to have one's eyes open to all the good that human beings do in society, even if they have left the church, presupposes a great solidarity with specific human destinies and respect for the ongoing human quest. True 'people of God' in search of God – which is what church members are – should serve their neighbours. This calls for neighbourliness and solidarity with those who hunger and thirst for righteousness, with the footloose young who still have no ties, with those who are in distress, in their work or precisely because they have no work. Here it is not just a matter of getting results and winning the battle, much less of maintaining abstract human ideals through verbalism; it is a matter of real encounter with the Creator God and his Spirit in the face of the poor, the imprisoned, the unfortunate and the maltreated. This presupposes a way of thinking which makes it possible for us again to identify ourselves with the instructions given by Moses and Jesus, as they wrestle quite specifically over a way for humanity. It presupposes that there are ritual forms of expression to go with the stream of desire, which non-intellectuals can also understand, ways of expressing birth and death, love and separation, joy and sorrow, vocation and rejection, sending and sin; which can be experienced in witness and in liturgy in such a way that they bring us into contact with the life-style of all the people of God who went before us. The activity of Jesus, the man of God, suggests that God makes himself dependent on this event – the church event in all times and places – as the way to salvation and justice.

4. This programme could be supported only by those who have again become clear why the church is needed. That is impossible

without going to 'school' again, without re-reading the programme of Jesus, without a life-style of discipleship. Here faith is not simply, nor primarily, an interpretation of reality (that is *gnosis*) nor a ritual fulfilling of obligations towards a heteronomous power (that is *cultus*) but a praxis: a way of being which automatically gives us visions and is praise of God even outside the hours of prayer. This praxis is the praxis of the kingdom of God; in other words, it is the will of God, the guidance of God who wants his creation to be good. This presupposes a specific community of disciples, a visible church in which there is room to become a disciple, in which there is a remembrance of the experience of faith down the centuries; where the longing for meaning in the midst of the meaninglessness of suffering is guided by the programme of Jesus: by the right adminis-tration of word and sacrament, by a *disciplina*, a life-style, which is constantly renewed and explained, and by a structure of ministry which keeps the movement faithful to its origin.

The theological view of the church, ecclesiology, is the art of showing the vision of God in humanity within the history of a community of disciples. This book must deal with its structures – faithful remembrance, authentic forms of expressing the holy, guidelines for behaviour and the functions which serve to preserve continuity and identity. It must do so remembering that the church leads a diaspora existence, in the midst of many who search for God, as a community of people of God, always ready to give account of the hope which is in them, with a good conscience.

2

Living under the Rainbow

The church: discovery of a gracious God

Then the woman asked, 'Why are you a Christian?' And I was evasive; I couldn't find the right words to answer her. Did I know myself? Was what I wanted to say to her – for a theologian reacts to such a question like one of Pavlov's dogs – what I really felt? Or was it simply a play on words, a language-game learnt from youth which it was impossible to unlearn, spectacles I needed for reading reality, but which might act as blinkers for others? I was sad, because the question was more authentic than the answers on my lips. Many people who have made their faith their work will feel sympathy with Jeremiah's words as he stammers at the beginning of his prophecies, and will fervently use the ancient prayer which comes before the reading of the gospel in the Roman liturgy: 'O Lord, open thou my lips...' All human words must be weighed carefully if they are to say anything about God and things of God. They can all be used against us. I decided not to say anything without consulting an advocate. And the only one who can stand beside Christians is Jesus himself, who is our best spokesman (I John 2.1). Nothing can be said about being a Christian, or about the church which calls on him, without referring to who he was and what he wanted.

It began with Jesus, though he himself, a son of the ancient Israel, is not the beginning of God's good will towards humanity. With Israel, Jesus bears witness that from the very beginning God's good will is the driving force behind all life, all society, and that the 'people of God' is the artistic result of God's initiative in creation. Among all the things that arose out of primal matter – or nothingness, or chaos – humanity already lay in God's plan. The history of the earth and of mankind, all that happens to us and even what is done through us, is the constant unfolding of God's creative initiative of grace. No human being is beyond the horizon of God's possibilities of growth. Within the horizon of God's own possibilities with his creation lies the disclosure of his grace through humanity itself: it was given us in the womb, as a free gift. This is not the privilege of Israel or the people of Abraham, or even of the Jesus movement. Humanity has discovered God from the time of the earliest peoples, in primitive anxiety and terror, in the torments of pain and distress, in the joys of life and love, in the longing for happiness, life without end, love without limits, peace without desolation, pleasure without shame – God who reveals himself without surrendering himself. Among the many gods, humanity finally discovers its God as the one who makes himself known, who hides behind the power of matter, the groaning of nature, the vicissitudes of history, the longings and prayers of the human heart. Here humanity lets itself be guided by seers and poets, by heroes who lay down their lives for the way that they have chosen, by ancestors who gave peoples their existence, by kings concerned for their people, by grey-haired sages aware of what in life is good and can be trusted.

Humanity learns from evil, though it seldom overcomes it. Humanity accepts its limitations and its suffering, although it never has peace from them. It learns to distinguish what leads to peace and what enhances life and calls that good; it learns to distinguish what leads to misery and what sows corruption and calls that bad. Through ongoing reflection, going to and fro between the golden calf and the tent of the covenant, it learns what it must do 'in all conscience' to keep life on the right lines. And it learns to bring the human conscience into line with God's own programme, God's own will, God's own plan with his creation.

This leads to the development of systems of serving God, human religions. They do not fall from heaven, but come into being on the basis of human experiences and desires, coloured by the naked facts of the struggle for survival. They arise in the rhythm of birth and death, the fortunes of the people, its liberation or its downfall; they arise through interaction with the hostile powers of nature and history; they arise in the deliberations of the tribe, in stories by the fireside, in the delight of harvest, in joy over the safety of cattle, people or city. Songs, sayings, rules of life and parables are remembered, and later, when language and writing enrich communication, they are written in stone, set down on parchment, multiplied on paper, printed in books, recorded on magnetic tape, never to be forgotten.

When we Christians say that 'it began with Jesus', we presuppose all this: the many religions before him, in his time, and for centuries afterwards. The religion of Israel, his people, by which he lived, and the religions of humanity, God's own creation, to which his disciples bring his message and life-style. Jesus does not stand alone, nor does he emerge from nothing, though he is unique, and owes his whole existence to God's grace. And of course it is precisely the same with us.

In this way I have already said a good deal about the nature of the church which we have chosen and why we have chosen it: it constantly brings us back to the man of Nazareth with whom everything began. First of all, it makes little sense for us to think ourselves free from all alien influences, to act as though we were the ones who had discovered the only truth about God. In all periods of its history, the church makes use of ideas from surrounding culture, and much of what we confess is also experienced in other ways of salvation. In that case, what is the origin in church history of the ineradicable need to set limits: limits to God's goodness, limits to his election, limits to church membership and limits to the community? If only we could make it clear why we Christians tend to describe all that is not Christian as paganism, idolatry, evil and deception! Did the Jesus movement make its distinctive progress at the expense of the religion of Israel? Did Christian life flourish – through an abomination of history – over the bodies of Jews?

No, God gathers people to himself as people of God, from the beginning, century after century, in his time and way, and never apart from human faith. He teaches them to discover their God by a process of divine maieutic and so proves to be their redeemer. This discovery alone frees us from religious arrogance and prevents the church from taking over God's throne and itself pronouncing judgment. Perhaps, then, I am a Christian and want to remain one because the God and Father of Jesus Christ is a forgiving and gracious God who in his name forbids human beings to condemn one another, asking them to forgive as he himself forgives.

My plea for the church ends where the church of Jesus Christ has refused to plead for sinners and dissidents. Where it helps people to live under God's rainbow, its case is won.

The church is never perfect: a plea for a provisional ecclesiology

The theology of the church – ecclesiology – has not only suffered from church leaders and theologians, who felt that they should set its limits, but above all from the fact that ecclesiology tends to present 'the church' as something cut and dried, an object to be described, an independent entity or hypostasis. In that case the church is a fossilized entity, overwhelming people, that even speaks to them as an authority.

However, that was not the case from the beginning. The history of the theological tractate *De Ecclesia*[1] shows that a separate 'theology of the church' is quite recent and only got a firm footing after the Reformation. The church fathers – for example, Clement of Rome, Ignatius of Antioch, Irenaeus of Lyons, Cyprian of Carthage and Augustine of Hippo – discuss the church, on the basis of scripture, as a facet of God's history of salvation. Luke's story of the course of the gospel from Jerusalem via Antioch to Greece and Rome is repeated throughout the Mediterranean basin. The story of the church is the story of the mission and the conversion of believers from all over the place, who as a result are called into the story of God's dealings with humanity, which begins with Adam. The plea for the church is in fact, for example in Irenaeus, a long list of witnesses: former disciples, and disciples who now in life and death stand as guarantors of the truth of their confession and service.

That did not change as the proclamation of the gospel reached the frontiers of the Roman empire through Augustine of Canterbury, Boniface and Willibrord in the north and through Ephraim, the Cappadocians and later Cyril and Methodius in the east.

In the Middle Ages, when the church of West and East seemed to be 'established' and the identity of the church's confession and service had been safeguarded by the canon of scripture, the conciliar creeds and canonical definitions, an ordered structure of ministry and a well-regulated liturgy, the great theologians continued to discuss the church in the wider context of their tractates on God's grace (*De gratia*) and faith (*De fide*). Of course the church is a part of faith, a hinge (the literal meaning of *articulus fidei*[2]), as witness Augustine's saying, 'Without the church I would not have received the gospel nor accepted the faith.' But for that very reason the church can be discussed only in the framework of the trinitarian creed: it is an initiative of God in history – the church from Abel – an initiative within creation. The church is God's field, God's building; it is the community of those who are hallowed in Christ – the Lord's body, bride, flock. It is those who are anointed by the Spirit of God, the messianic people, the first harvest of God's kingdom.

The origin of a separate tractate *De Ecclesia* lies, sadly, in the fifteenth-century disputes over the respective competence of popes and councils. The development continued in the discussions with

Febronianists and Gallicanists and came to a climax in the Roman Ultramontanism of the nineteenth century. Vatican I (1870) was the first council to produce a decree *De Ecclesia*. As a result of all kinds of circumstances, only a torso was accepted: this dealt with the competence of the bishop of Rome.[3] The Vatican II constitution *Lumen Gentium* is really the first more or less complete conciliar document about the church that the church has ever accepted. Up to Vatican II, it was very difficult not to begin discussions of the church with its organization and the institution of the church, rather than with the saving event which lies behind the organization.[4]

The Reformation churches, too, have long identified the doctrine of the church with canon law. In all kinds of matters like church membership, the ministry, the edification of the congregation and the sacraments their thinking has been primarily in terms of organization and administration. The link between them and the central saving event of 'God with us' has been lost. With the Reformers, especially with Luther, things were still different. The ecclesiology of the Reformers is an explicit consequence of their view of salvation, justification and reconciliation. In the seventeenth and eighteenth centuries, as a result of the great emphasis on the personal relationship between man and God, in which reconciliation proves to be justification of the individual (*iustificatio impii*), people lost sight of the fact that Jesus' way to salvation is bound up with the church. Reconciliation was really thought to take place between the individual and God, and anything to do with the church was seen as part of a system of laying down conditions, in which only good order was important. The mediating power of the Jesus movement was thus played down and the role played by church order over-stressed.[5] In reaction, the Counter-Reformation so identified the organizational and institutional aspects of the church with the means of salvation that it left no room for the free play of God and the power of the Jesus event, which breaks through structures – Christ present as the living one among his people.

Changes came about in the nineteenth century.[6] On the Catholic side this was the result of the theology of J.M.Sailer and the so-called Tübingen school (Von Drey, Möhler, Kuhn), although they failed to get the better of the opposing forces of Ultramontanism and the Roman school (Perrone, Franzelin). On the Protestant side, changes were hinted at by Jacobi and Schleiermacher, but their theology was overshadowed by the emergence of critical thought and liberal theology. In the twentieth century, a more balanced and dynamic way of thinking about the church gradually came into

being, going back to patristic and New Testament thought. Karl
Barth again described the church as event, the result of the Word
of God;[7] Karl Rahner laid more stress on the church as the sphere
for hearing God's word, though that too is always a living event.[8]
J.B.Metz describes the church as a 'community of discipleship'.[9]
Yves Congar, J.Hamèr, P.C.Bori and J.Tillard[10] have all stressed
the character of the church as communion, which is realized through
tradition, the celebration of the sacraments and mutual solidarity.
Küng, Ratzinger[11] and many others began from the notion of the
'people of God', which was already worked out before the Second
World War by Koster, but at that time had been temporarily
overshadowed by the idea of the Mystical Body. Exegetes – e.g.
Schweizer, Käsemann, Marxsen, Schnackenburg, Hahn and Kert-
elge[12] – have shown how different views of the church stand side by
side in the New Testament, though eventually they do converge.
Renewed interest in Israel led to a demonstration of the Jewish
roots of the church event. And the ecumenical movement reminded
the many churches of their common Christian identity.

For a number of reasons this ecclesiology of our century – the
century of the church (Dibelius) – has a provisional character
(Malmberg).[13] In the first place, there is an awareness of the context
of the church event, both in the New Testament and in our own
time. The church of Jerusalem is different from that of Antioch,
Ephesus, Corinth or Rome. And the church of Western Europe has
different characteristics from that of Latin America or Africa or
Eastern Europe. Of course, everywhere and at all times it is
connected with the kingdom of God and the programme of Jesus.
But because 'people of God' are the subjects who respond to the
words of God by their faith and conduct, the unity of the church is
always a task to be realized, and never a firm certainty. There is
therefore no such thing as an established ecclesiology, even within
the ecumenical movement, where the plurality of historical and
present-day contexts is sensed most strongly.

Moreover, we have become more acutely aware that the church
and the kingdom of God do not coincide (Loisy). The church is also
dependent on existing sociological conditions (Weber, Troeltsch);
and group interests, power struggles and the quest for status also
determine the structure of the church. The criticism of the Frankfurt
School and the Marxist analysis of society demonstrate the way in
which the structures of church power are interwoven with civic and
economic interests. Therefore the church constantly needs to be
reformed and revised: *ecclesia semper purificanda*. Sometimes it

even seems that more of the church is to be found outside the church than inside (Hoekendijk), and that the kingdom of God is understood better within liberation movements than in church circles.

Above all, however, the church is a provisional organization, because it lives on longing. That is implied in the very concept of the *ekklesia*.

Ekklesia tou Theou:
God in search of humanity, humanity in search of God

The word 'church' comes from the New Testament term '*kuriake* ekklesia' (like the Dutch 'kerk' and the German 'Kirche');[14] by contrast, the Romance languages (French 'église' and Spanish 'iglesia') reflect the original Greek term even more clearly. In secular Greek that word means the local assembly of the people which forms the official authority in the polis. Attempts are often made to connect the origin of the term *ekklesia* as applied to the groups of Christians in the cities of Greece and Rome with this secular usage. In large areas of the New Testament we do not in fact find the term at all, and it really occurs only in those parts which come from the sphere influenced by Hellenism, especially in the letters of Paul and the Acts of the Apostles. Such a connection with the secular Greek meaning is not insignificant. It gives the church an institutional colouring: it is the authority which represents human beings to God and God to human beings, which has a specific responsibility for government in the polis of humanity. This significance comes through in the names of some sects (the Assembly of God), as also in views of the church as the representative, viceroy, of God in Christ. Moreover, in the Catholic tradition, the church-*ekklesia* eventually came to be identified with the *clerus*, the pastors of the church. As leaders they could be called the special representatives of God or Christ, and at all events without them there could be no question of a lawful 'assembly of God'. As Cyprian said, the church is where the bishop is (*Ubi episcopus, ibi Ecclesia*).

However, the New Testament use of *ekklesia* was probably connected, rather, with the use of the term in the Greek translation of the Hebrew scriptures, the Septuagint. The term occurs there 96 times, 72 of which are a translation of the Hebrew *qahal (YHWH)*. Almost always it is connected with the assembly of God's people for a special event – a feast, a decision, a prayer and a sacrifice to God. This occurs, for example, in Deut.4.10; 9.10; 18.16; 23.1;

31.30; Ezra 8.1; 13.1; Neh.8.2-17; Ps.21.22,25; 25.12). The translations *kyriake ekklesia* (thus e.g. Num.20.4; Deut.23.1; Ezra 13.1) and *ekklesia tou Theou* are synonymous with it.

Alongside this, the same *qahal (YHWH)* is also translated 35 times by *synagoge*, which on the other hand is also the translation of the Hebrew *edah* (gathering, meeting) or of *k^enesset* in the later Jewish, Rabbinic milieu (cf. the present-day Knesset in Israel). Both *ekklesia* and *synagoge* denote the assembled people of Israel, very often (mostly in connection with the *ecclesia*) in the context of the service of God: obeying the law, singing God's praises, acting in accord with his will, rejecting anything which is contrary to it. Sometimes the term denotes smaller assemblies, at others also the whole people; the latter is more common.

In the New Testament we find the term *ekklesia* 114 times in all. 65 of them are in Paul, 23 in Acts, 20 in Revelation and there are occasional instances in Matthew (16.18; 18.17), James (5.14) and II John (6,9,10). *Synagoge* is now almost always reserved for the Jewish communities (except in James 2.2). *Ekklesia* is mostly used for the Christian community and only once applied to Israel (Acts 7.38, as a quotation of Deut.9.10). The earliest community of Jerusalem is called *the ekklesia* of God. Obviously polemic with Judaism has already done its work. The Christian *ekklesia* of Jerusalem graced itself with the name given to the assembly of the people of Israel.

The *ekklesia tou Theou* in the New Testament regarded itself as a mode of Judaism[15] and continued to do so when the Jesus movement spread into the Graeco-Roman cities of the Jewish diaspora. The church of Christ could not but understand itself as the continuation in the name of Jesus of what God had begun with Abraham and Moses and David, though it broadened the invitation to enter into the covenant with Abraham so that it also included those for whom hitherto only the covenant with Noah had been valid. All who live under the rainbow are from now on called to live within the sphere of the *qahal YHWH = kuriake ekklesia*. From now on, life in accordance with God's directions, singing his praises, worshipping him in spirit and in truth, is no longer confined to the children of Israel, nor to those who have access to the temple of Jerusalem. Through mission and preaching, the church which is in Jerusalem extends to Samaria, Antioch and from there to the whole world (Acts 1.8; Matt.24.14; 28.20). God in search of people allows himself to be found by all who call on him.

However, seeking is not in itself a guarantee of finding. Finding

God depends on God letting himself be found, in free grace. The human longing to belong to those in whom God is well pleased and to whom he shows mercy can only be fulfilled by God himself. It is ultimately God himself who calls men together to the *qahal-ekklesia*, his initiative in human history. Here the children of Abraham – the people of Israel – are the first to be called, as the New Testament also bears witness (Rom.1.1-5). The *ekklesia tou Theou* which comes into being among other peoples is like the branches of a wild olive grafted on to a cultivated olive (Rom.11.13-24): they live from the hallowed Jewish tradition. But along with the Jews, they thus live from God's own creative and gracious presence. Therefore no one can boast, either about being, for example, a Jewish Christian, or about his or her own membership of God's church. Like the Synoptics, Paul makes it clear that the final verdict on who belongs to God is given by God himself. Weeds and tares must grow up with the wheat until the harvest, and everyone must heed the saying, 'Do not judge so that you are not judged'. Like the Jews (Rom.3.9), Christians too can be cut off by God (Rom.11.22). Salvation is not guaranteed by birth or tradition, 'For not all who are descended from Israel belong to Israel, and not all are children of Abraham because they are his descendants' (Rom.9.6f.). This is shown by the story of Isaac and Ishmael, of Jacob and Esau; it is shown by the saying of the Lord to Moses in Ex.33.19: 'I will be gracious to whom I will be gracious, and will show mercy on whom I will show mercy', and by the prophetic sayings about the 'remnant' of Israel (Isa 10.20-23) and God's freedom as to whom he counts as his people and whom he takes as his bride (Hos.1; 2).

Thus to be 'people of God' remains a matter of vocation and grace. Among those who count themselves the *ekklesia tou Theou*, sin and disobedience remain a reality. Therefore no single specific group, church, people or community can regard themselves directly as *the* 'people of God'. And terms like 'elect people', 'covenant people', 'people of God' are dangerous clichés when they are simply identified with 'church' or 'Israel'. They objectivize God's salvation as an event, as something which is at the disposal of the 'church' or 'Israel'. That fails to do justice to the eschatological provisionality of the church of God as God's ongoing work of gathering people together.

The church is an event among men and women,
not an authority which addresses them

Thus in what the New Testament, following the Old, calls the
kuriake ekklesia, the lines of force come together between humanity
in search of God and God in search of humanity. Both are bound
together through mutual longing. The rich vocabulary which the
New Testament uses for this mutual search – again following
statements in the Jewish scriptures about the relationship between
God and his people – is the language of longing. Expressions like
people of God (I Peter 2.9f.), body of Christ (I Cor.12; Col.1;
Eph.1), new covenant (I Cor.11.25), bride of the lamb (Rev.19.7;
21.2; Eph.5), God's flock for which he cares (John 21) are not
descriptions of what the church always is, but summon us to think
and act as seekers of God and as those who are sought by him. The
specifically 'new' element in the New Testament is that the presence
of God is no longer localized in temples and sacred rites, but again,
as of old in the Torah, in the living encounter of people concerned
about God. They come together in the tent of meeting; where two
or three are gathered in the name of the Lord, there he is in
their midst. They are living people who allow themselves to be
incorporated as living stones into God's building, God's temple,
which is not made of stone and silver. What we have now is no
longer *the* holy, but the holy ones; not holy places, things, buildings,
rites, authorities, but what is holy to us, because it is holy to God.
Therefore being the church can be described only in verbs which at
the same time express joy over the chance which is given us to follow
the way of God in the midst of far from friendly surroundings –
amidst those who are without hope and without God in this world,
the *atheoi*. We are the church in the constant company of the one
who is God's right hand, the crucified Messiah, Jesus, who lives as
God's Christ; as branches which abide in him (John 15); as those
who, raised to life with Christ, seek what is above, where Christ is
seated at God's right hand (Col.3.1); as members of a body called
to Christ's peace (Col.3.14), to Christ who is all in all (Col.3.11; I
Cor.15.28).

Although membership of this community is experienced as grace
and gift, it never becomes a possession; it always remains a task,
both for the individual who is called by his name and on whom God
makes his face to shine, and for the community: those who come
together around God's grace and God's calling, wherever they may
be in the world.

Both within the separated traditions and even within the ecumenical movement, we constantly succumb to the temptation to replace being the church, in terms of grace and calling, with '*the* church' as an external authority, which we set up by our actions and words and to which we apply as attributes all the images of the bond with God that I have mentioned as attributes. In that case *the* church *is* the body of Christ, the people of God. It does not make much difference here whether when we say 'the church says' we mean the bishops or the synod or even the whole community. In every instance we are talking about the church as though we stood outside it. Social psychologists call this phenomenon 'alienation'; some theologians speak in this connection of the 'hypostatization' of the church. In part that is a natural and inevitable linguistic phenomenon, just as we talk about the state, society, the media, attributing to them all kinds of views and influences as though they were active subjects. But that does not make it any the less dangerous. Such a way of talking is not biblical, for in the Bible *ekklesia* always means the specific group of people who come together in the face of God, both when it denotes local groups, which it does most obviously, and also when it denotes the universal church everywhere. Being the church becomes an ideology when we begin to detach the phenomenon of the church from the personal and daily history of the people who try to follow God in Jesus Christ. This is of direct consequence for an ecumenical view of the church: the unity of the church of Christ and its truth is not a matter of negotiations between authorities, or of weighing up interests, nor is it a fight among departments over who has the most truth. It is an alliance between people who want to draw consequences from their search for God and their discipleship of Jesus for the way in which they meet, work together and so on. Wherever in the world people find one another in this search for God, the bonds grow between those who over the ages turn in longing to God: 'You and your children and all that are far off, every one whom the Lord our God calls to him' (Acts 2.39).

So the description of the *ekklesia* of Jerusalem remains normative for all later views of the church, written, as it is, in verbs:

'And they devoted themselves to the apostles' teaching and fellowship, to the breaking of bread and the prayers.

　　And fear came upon every soul; and many wonders and signs were done through the apostles. And all who believed were together and had all things in common;

and they sold their possessions and goods and distributed them to all, as any had need.

And day by day, attending the temple together and breaking bread in their homes, they partook of food with glad and generous hearts,

praising God and having favour with all the people. And the Lord added to their number day by day those who were being saved' (Acts 2.42-47).

The church is an ongoing school for the community of disciples

In the description of the early Christian community at Jerusalem in Acts, which I have just quoted, and in many other places in the New Testament, the stress is on the teaching, *didache*. Here 'devoting themselves to the teaching of the apostles' does not mean that the first Christians sat down to study or followed catechism instruction. However, in the Jewish sense of 'learning' (*lāmad*, cf. Talmud) they taught themselves to live by the faith and instruction of the apostles.[16] Moreover, we cannot read Paul's letters to his communities as anything other than letters to encourage young churches to continue the way they had begun, to go on reflecting on the implications of the gospel and not to strike out in other directions, to give an account of the hope by which they lived. Similarly, the Gospels aimed at handing on the story of Jesus to particular communities in Palestine, West Syria or Asia Minor, as he handed on God's story with humanity to the group of his disciples. Being the church is therefore a constant process of learning by people in search of guidelines for life from the gospel of God in Jesus Christ, which is itself inherited from the way of Israel with its God and of God with Israel.

In that learning process, as in the New Testament Gospels, the central issues are: 'Lord, teach us to pray.' 'Are you he who is to come or do we look for another?' 'Did not our hearts burn within us when he spoke to us and opened the scriptures to us?' Once real questions cease to underlie the answers given by the church's tradition, the formulas of prayer, the christological dogmas, liturgical forms of expression, faith loses its tension. That hymn of desire which expresses the depths of faith – God, my God, where can I find you, how shall I love you? – is written in the language of love. The language it uses is very different from that of reference to established practice. The language of reference to established practice – sometimes wrongly purporting to be an expression of the certainty of faith – quenches the real desire for God, just as the question of God in our world has been weakened by our way of treating it like practised users and consumers. Hence my view that a very important task for Christians, especially in the Western churches, is to venture to put the real questions afresh and to listen to what is being asked by their neighbours and friends, by thinkers and poets, scientists and politicians, meeting together over these questions. Of course that does not mean making the church a debating club. Learning to believe presupposes a search for guidelines for thought *and action* which mark us out as disciples of Jesus from other citizens of the world.

First of all this affects the question of God. Why and how should we believe in the God who seeks us and wants us to seek him, now that both science and the holocaust have discredited him as the omnipotent cause of all things? How do we pray if we no longer believe in miracles, and there are no longer apostles to perform their many wonders, apart from the miracles of technology? How are we to live if there are no longer any values and norms which we know to be generally accepted as values and norms given by God?

Because of these burning questions, those in the sphere of the church have therefore gradually come to write a new score for the hymn of desire that lies at the heart of faith, and to learn again to join in the old song of the *communio sanctorum* from the heart. Those who believe are in no hurry. And those who still do not believe or can scarcely believe should be able to find the church a place of openness and hospitality. The church as a whole should begin to think of itself as the catechumenate, as the community of those who want to learn to believe, as the community of the disciples of Jesus.

Moreover, the experience in faith of other disciples also contributes to that learning process. One of the most important elements in the building up of the church, the driving force for coming together, must be a readiness to learn from others: through the recollection of the faith of Israel, the recollection of Jesus and his disciples, the recollection of the wrestling of the church in faith down the ages and influence from the confessions of other churches throughout the world.

In this connection, ecumenical commitment from the churches is not just an attractive feature, but an essential quality of the 'communion of saints'. Anyone who wants to learn what faith is has ultimately no other course of finding out than examining all those who in their own ways look to God and follow Jesus. The community of faith can only bear fruit by learning from the cumulative experiences of many people, from generations down the centuries, from Christians in different contexts and many different circumstances. *So an aging church, with no new members in its midst, is as good as dead.* Only by adding to the community of faith constant new disciples, dressed in their white clothes, does God hand on his gospel over the ages. Thus a real community of disciples must be not only ecumenical, but also missionary.

A third important factor is the role that this community of disciples plays in what we call history. How can we combine that ecumenical learning process by which we discover together what it means for us to be the church with the service of others? Looking for God and following Jesus is neither a quest for personal happiness nor a collective therapy. As Christians we are not followers of a succesful guru, but of a crucified rabbi without authority to teach (Matt.7.29), who has told us clearly enough not to seek our own lives. Anyone who means to follow him and to help in building up the church must therefore embody the quest for the kingdom of God. That means a life in accordance with God's criteria: a society in which God comes into his own because human beings act justly; where one person no longer makes others his victims; where peace prevails, not through a balance of terror but through a balance of justice of which Paul already speaks in II Cor.8; where there is enough to eat for all, freedom of thought for all, human rights for the oppressed, education, care of the sick and universal freedom of movement. Vatican II called the church the 'sacrament of universal salvation' and the 'sacrament of the unity of mankind': 'All those, who in faith look towards Jesus, the author of salvation and the principle of unity and peace, God has gathered together and established as the Church, that it may be for each and everyone the visible sacrament of this saving unity.'[17]

That quality, too, is not something that the church has automatically. It is given by virtue of its calling. Here Christians join others in making history, but contribute their own ideas about the direction of history – tentatively expressed in the sphere of the church.

In this way, through the quest for God, learning from others and inspired by the programme of Jesus, i.e the kingdom of God in human history, the church comes into being time and again in human faith.

There is no lack of joy here. Plumbing the mystery of God, gathering together with others to listen to what the Spirit has to say to the church, joining other citizens of the world to shape history in accordance with the criteria of the kingdom of God, is no business for narrow zealots and activists, but a liberating praxis, which also gives the glorious freedom of the children of God to those who join in it (Rom.8).

It will be clear that such a process of learning requires mechanisms for counsel, dialogue and conversation. Any group which calls itself the church must be a listening post more than a platform, a receiver more than a transmitter. A learning process does not tolerate any 'trials' for false doctrine; a hospitable church does not tolerate excommunications; a church which seeks to serve God in history by standing up for human rights cannot at the same time tolerate in its midst the violation of conscience, the prevention of people from utilizing their talents, a refusal to allow women their own role in giving guidance to the community.

Finally, in all searching and questioning, listening and teaching, counsel and liberating joy, *one way* must be marked out for the group as a whole to follow. John the Baptist and his followers had to do that when it became clear that the activity of Jesus was blessed by God (Matt.11); the disciples had to do that in Gethsemane (Matt.26.31-35) and in Jerusalem after the passover (Acts 1.6); Christians from the Jewish and Gentile world had to do that when both were incorporated into the same Christian community (Acts 15); disciples have constantly had to do that when the nature of their task and the character of their allegiance was at stake. In our day there are important questions about riches and poverty, the exploitation of the earth, the nuclear threat, the infringement of human rights. We cannot remain neutral here. We have to choose. That is also part of the church as a constant learning process.

The one church of the future

What can such a view of the church as the 'people of God' mean for the future unity of the church and its place in the world?

In the 1970s it was said with varying degrees of emphasis that the ecumenical movement was not primarily concerned with the unity of the church but with the wholeness of the world. Within the organized ecumenical movement, for example within the World Council of Churches, that leads to tension between those who are active and those who are reflective, between diakonia and liturgy, between those who are zealous for social needs and propagandists for spiritual revival, between champions of the greater 'ecumene' and those of the lesser.[18]

All that seems to me to be an unnecessary and barren contrast.

The biblical word *oikoumene* is not concerned with the world or the church as such, but with the kingdom of God which is meant for the world (Matt.24.14), the kingdom through which this world will be changed, by a process of the conversion of those of whom, by definition, the church consists. Ecumene is the desire of all those who seek the kingdom of God. This has the following implications for our view of the church of the future – the church of the ecumene:

1. The ecumene, that is to say, the kingdom of God in the human world, is impossible if church people cut themselves off from those outside the church. The church is often compared with Noah's ark: the ship that protects a few faithful against the 'flood of sin'. Rome and the Reformation suffered from that image of the church as a ship, with people arguing over who was to steer it. The Western tradition as a whole constantly risks forgetting that both clean and unclean animals were included in Noah's ark. Moreover, after the flood God did not opt for a new earth without problems, but for the same earth, with the firm resolve that afterwards, too, he would make the rain fall on just and unjust alike, on weeds and tares, which will grow up with the wheat until the harvest. It is not for human beings to keep other human beings from God's face, for God himself acts in the witness of Israel and of Jesus by removing barriers. Therefore the ecumenical church of the future can never be a church of the pure, the *katharoi*, escapists who herd themselves together in the face of the evil world and the evils of the mainstream churches. It could well be that we have not yet spoken out enough about this ecumene of God's care for all human beings – Christians, Jews, Moslems, Hindus and unbelievers – that cannot tolerate the exclusion of one human being by another which degrades him or her into becoming second-class citizens of God's kingdom.

2. The ecumene, that is to say the kingdom of God in the human world, is impossible without personal encounter in faith, the tangible mutual solidarity of men and women. Dogma, liturgy, buildings, ministry and church organizations are not ends in themselves, existing in their own right quite apart from men and women concerned to serve the kingdom of God. The paper ecumene of reports, agreements and statutes must be connected with what Vatican II called the spiritual ecumene.[19] That is the association of people of flesh and blood – in marriage and friendship, in working groups and as colleagues, in welfare groups and prayer groups, in politics and education – who know and nurture one another's undivided longing for God, who together hand on to one another the ideals of Israel and Jesus, who live together and form their

society on the basis of the same inspiration of the Spirit. The ecumenical movement owes its greatest success to this sort of group work and this sort of living relationship of students, soldiers, partners in mixed marriages, religious, activists, discussion groups. Churches who have a future will consist of a combination of such groups. This is the secret behind the growth of the churches in the Third World and of the Evangelicals.

3. The ecumene, that is to say the kingdom of God in the human world, is impossible without some choices. Tolerance and dialogue, respect for, and encounter with others who live and think differently does not justify any colourless indifference. Freud said that indifference is the ash of hate. Real tolerance bears with others without hate and excommunication, but at the same time it issues a real call. The choices with which we are confronted – and that is what stamps us as a critical community, not our criticism of the 'official church' – are those which go with the search for God's own criteria: living according to God's kingdom, i.e. God's plan, God's guidance, God's will. To establish them often requires a good deal of stamina, communicating the faith widely to contemporaries and those older and younger than ourselves; historical criticism and an ongoing critical interpretation of our practices; clear thinking and steadfastness within the community, which goes by the compass of the scriptures and bears witness to its trustworthiness. These are no moralistic recipes, no legalistic rules of conduct, no new rules for purity. But they are part of true discipleship, *disciplina*, which is the hallmark of our being the church.

4. The ecumene, that is to say the kingdom of God in the human world, is impossible without humility and longing, without looking to God. Power struggles and claims to be right do not fit in with God's ecumene. The divisions which sadly we continue to see in church and society are the deepest consequence of the usurpation of God's truth, usually with a view to power. The conflicts between East and West in 1054, between the Latin world and the German world in 1517, between Communism and capitalism in 1917, between North and South in our day, are part of one and the same drama. Who knows the way to salvation? Who has God on their side? There are heroes and victims, but most are victims; the masses, the people, the grass roots, are figures in a conflict between princes, bishops, financiers, scholars. Therefore God-with-us and the ecumene of the kingdom of God are always to be found among ordinary people; immigrant workers in Egypt, captives in Mesopotamia, shepherds in Bethlehem, pilgrims in Jerusalem, port workers in Corinth, male

and female slaves in Rome. And while theologians make agreements and bishops consider whether they are practicable, ordinary villagers in the Dutch countryside break bread in the meal of the kingdom of God which they celebrate together; while princes and party leaders put forward proposals for disarmament and reject them again, women stand up for peace and young men of eighteen refuse to go into the army. While Rome and Geneva and Constantinople argue over the true faith, partners in mixed marriages, and their children all over the world, look for an answer to their deepest questions about God, about Jesus, about a church in the spirit of God. That is how ecumene comes about, sometimes, and becomes the church of the future.

Of course this is not meant to be an argument against the organized ecumene or a criticism of ecumenical theology, a rejection of bilateral and multilateral conversations, or a condemnation of an over-cautious church government. But it profoundly legitimates what happens here and elsewhere, and is all too often branded as illegal or, perhaps even worse, as experiment. The new ecumenical church which we seek will probably emerge, as Darwin believed that humanity itself emerged, not suddenly, by itself, not made by God in a day, but slowly, in a constant process of selection from the pattern of experiences in small groups, after infinitely many failures. Above all it will emerge from a constant urge to survive (M.Bourke), or rather, from constant service to all life: a worldwide process of learning under God's rainbow, the ecumene.

3

Knowing God: A Way of Being

Certainly in Western theology as it is at present, it has become impossible to talk about the church as the 'people of God' without giving a central place to the question of God. That is not just the speculative question 'Does God exist?' – though that cannot be ignored – but also the question, 'Can we assent to God as he is and can we experience and know God in that way as a living God?'[1]

Believing in God always takes on meaningful content only when it is coupled with 'experiencing God', i.e. when real-life human history, a people's weal and woe, are recognizably bound up with and focussed on 'God'. Here 'experience' does not just mean 'perceive', in the empirical sense of the word – God in himself cannot be experienced – but also meet with, encounter. In all the religions that we know, the tradition of faith demonstrates that belief in God is something that can be experienced in this last way (as a result of which, of course, it is also accessible to empirical perception through the scholarly study of religion); sacrificial rituals, a calendar of feasts, a tradition of prayers, commandments and prohibitions to guide conduct, a narrative tradition about earlier experiences of God, make it clear that anyone who has encountered God or gods experiences and orders life differently. Conversely, we have already seen that where the whole idea of God is put in question by more modern developments, so that many people do not even raise the question of God, the traditional forms of expressing experience of God in a church context – the sacraments, listening to the scriptures, church discipline and penitential practice – cease to have any object and therefore cease to have any purpose. Church reforms, liturgical renewal, a healthier concern for men and women as subjects responsible for their own history, a relativizing of the church's claims as a result of the process of secularization – all this is clearly inadequate as a remedy if the crisis is over belief in God itself.

Who is God?

The question 'Who is God?' is prior to the question 'Does God exist?' That is not only because the history of belief and unbelief seems to show that demonstrations of the existence of God depend very much on the image of God that we may have formed – all kinds of traditional images have made people stop believing in God – but above all because the existence of God is only worth demonstrating if he is our living God, whom we can serve in our own lives and experience in that service.

The old catechism gave far too simple an answer to the question 'Who is God?' Indeed, it can hardly be called an answer: 'God is our Father who lives in Heaven.' Feminists have attacked that image of God as Father,[2] but so too have many teachers and catechists, since fathers are in a bad way in our 'fatherless society' (Mitscherlich). Heaven as God's dwelling place is under attack from the theological criticism of theism, that form of religious belief which understands the existence of God as the existence of absolute being resting in itself, from which only incidental relationships, inessential to God himself, find a way down to humanity below. Theism presented a picture of God in himself, without any real relationship to all that we experience as existing, characterized above all as *prima causa* and *causa sui*: the first cause of all being which unfolds itself in a series of secondary causes; itself not further created, since it is uncreated outside time and space; omnipotent, since it is infinitely independent of all that is created, seen and unseen.

In the end, runs the theological criticism of the death-of-God theologians,[3] this picture of God is no different from that of the deists of the Enlightenment. God becomes an unmoved mover; more something than someone, an ultimate hypothesis for thinking people, a metaphysical gap-filler. In one scheme of natural laws, in which causality is the all-determining perspective on reality – one thing leads to the other; everything is the result of something else – reason calls a halt to thought at the frontier of infinite causality in time and space. That 'halt' in time is called creation at the beginning and consummation at the end. We call that 'halt' God, and what happens between the two limits is safely open to human knowledge and experience, without belief in God really making any difference. For convenience, we continue to call the 'halt' in space heaven, though to begin with in the age of space travel that seemed to cause some problems: the first Russian cosmonauts solemnly declared that they had not come across God, and the first Americans who followed them soon afterwards found it necessary to say the Lord's Prayer solemnly in the midst of the harmony of the spheres. Thus the myth of the storming of heaven lives on in the age of Aquarius.

God: a reflection of human longing?

In recent years much has been said and written about God in the awareness that we must get beyond this picture of God, that people must be freed from the oppressive bonds of fossilized tradition and false images of God: God as judge, bogey-man, despot or accountant, or as the unmoved, almighty architect who set the universe in motion, who looks down from above on all our secret sins beneath. We have taken to heart the criticisms of religion made by Feuerbach, Marx, Freud and Nietzsche and seen how much their rejection of religion was based on an image of God which they inherited from the Enlightenment and which was also beginning to distort the biblical tradition and the tradition of the church. Feuerbach was right: our images of God are the reflections of our human desires and needs. Nomads have a shepherd god, hunters an archer god, farmers a god of the harvest, city-dwellers a judge god, tradespeople a book-keeper god, captives a liberator God. Such reflections are not just the hall-mark of primitive peoples, but find their way into highly developed and established religions. The Jewish-Christian tradition has not escaped this fate, and in the course of time has also come to reflect the desires and needs of the people of God who confess the tradition. The God of Abraham, Isaac and Jacob has different features from those of the God of Moses or of David. Although he remains the God of Israel, the God of rabbi Jesus, the true God whom we worship and serve as members of his church, was from Jesus' time on found essentially to be the God who overcomes suffering and death. But then Augustine and Thomas Aquinas, Luther and Karl Barth depict him in quite different ways again. The emperors of Byzantium liked to see God as almighty; for the Middle Ages he is the *prima veritas*; for the philosophers of the Enlightenment he is a mathematician; for Kant he is a super-moralist; for Hegel a super-German. Feminists want *her* to be like Aletta Jacobs; Marxist Christians portray him with the beard of Karl Marx; liberation theologians encounter him in the form of the poor, the oppressed, the destitute.

And yet Feuerbach was wrong. For the fact that people form a picture of God in accordance with their own needs and desires does not in itself mean that this God who forms men and women in his own image, as the scriptures of Old and New Testament bear witness, is superfluous. The fact that I long for something and dream dreams to still my longing is not in itself proof that the dream and the longing are hopeless. The fact that religion arises from longing is no proof that it is an illusion. And even the experience of illusion does not put an end to the experience of longing, just as the experience of the way in which many human desires turn out badly does not in itself lead to fatalism. Simply as human beings, living between cradle and grave, towards the end of our life we come up against the absolute of death. We want to survive, not just to hibernate in death but to conquer it, to live on, to have new experiences, to be able to make new history. Thus our humanity transcends itself: we know that we are borne up, in a kind of oceanic consciousness, by all being before us and around us.[4] The living person is at one and the same moment both creative freedom and the result of history and environment. And we press on with plans for a better tomorrow, even in the bitterest distress, because we have experienced trust and expectation, because we fervently look for definitive justice and truth.

Within the experience of human self-transcendence the experience of the transcendence of God is at least possible – I do not say necessary, as it cannot be compelled or proved. Any expression of Christian belief in God must therefore be in the context of the same experience. Of course, in it we do not 'discover' God – we move towards him, as the God of Israel and of Jesus – but we find him in the very experiences of the people of God: in the wise men and prophets of Israel and ultimately in Jesus' unique experience of God as Abba. Even if we answer the question 'Who is God?' like Pascal – he is the God of Abraham, Isaac and Jacob, the God and Father of Jesus Christ – we must be able to express ourselves to all those for whom this answer does not contain, or no longer contains, any living experience of God.

Belief and knowledge, responsible belief in God?

That does not seem to have become any easier for the theology of the West. We have the legacy of a number of ways of thinking of God which sought to solve the age-old problem of belief and knowledge. Which of them are usable?

There is one approach, alive above all within the Reformation tradition, which rejects any arguments for belief. Believing is a gift of grace. Except as a question in a catechism, it is illegitimate to ask

'Who is God?' or 'Does God exist?' Believing means assenting to and confessing God's existence, making it the starting point for all thought. You cannot raise any niggling questions about it. I remember the first lecture about God as Creator that I ever heard, by Edmund Schlink, the Lutheran theologian at Heidelberg, in 1968. In the hey-day of the death-of-God theology he began his lecture like this: 'That God exists is evident from the Psalms of Israel. There God is called by his name. Anyone who thinks that God cannot have a name, or who is uncertain whether he can call on God, does not belong among the circle of believers and stands outside the Jewish-Christian tradition. These lectures on creation are not meant for him.' That was a good Reformation introduction along the lines of the dialectical theology of Karl Barth; like him, Schlink was one of the main figures in the 'Confessing Church' who opposed the Nazi regime, precisely because the Nazi regime had distorted the true face of Israel's God by painting it over with Aryan religion. But dialectical theology here is a direct heir of a way of thinking which goes back to Augustine. It is characterized by the saying of the mediaeval thinker Anselm of Canterbury: *Credo ut intelligam*: first believe, and then understand reality with new eyes. We do not learn to know God, but God makes himself known by revealing himself and making himself knowable by us. Anyone who is not called by God himself through grace to come to know God will never find God by himself. All our religious needs – our longing for hope, certainty, security, power – intrinsically lead to idolatry and surrogate worship rather than to the true confession of the one true God of Israel, the Father of our Lord Jesus Christ. The attraction of this way of thinking for the church – the people of God – is that its first duty then becomes the making of a powerful confession. Only the quality of faith can convince outsiders. Only committed church membership centred on word and sacrament can keep belief in God pure.

The disadvantage is that believers in dialogue with their contemporaries – atheists, members of other religions – are really excluded. As a result the church finds itself in the ghetto. So a second approach is needed, which also has good historical credentials.[5] This approach recognizes that the most important element of faith in fact lies in assenting to the existence of God in prayer and action, and that this is also the most eloquent witness to the *authenticity* of faith. But theology calls for more. It cannot avoid the question of *truth*. In its capacity as the art and science of the vision of God, theology claims that the story of human desire for God is at the same time the story of a divine initiative in history: that what we experience as human beings is always experience of a reality directed by God. Therefore we cannot refuse to defend this claim over against the other human explanations of reality, especially in the sciences: natural sciences, behavioural sciences and philosophy. Each of the sciences approaches reality with a language, method, search pattern of its own. Of course, theology, too, has its own search pattern, but its distinctive feature is that it seeks to give a total picture of reality, looking for the basic foundation, the basic support, the basic purpose of all reality. Without conversation and dialogue with the many partial search patterns of the sciences, theology all too quickly becomes an abstract way of whiling away the time, more akin to the realm of aesthetics or the erotic; it is something for amateurs, irrelevant to the real problems of humanity and the world. Moreover, *Christian* theology has to justify itself in the face of other forms of belief in God, atheism and unbelief, which are almost the natural starting point for most contemporaries of the people of God in the West. So the saying *Intellige ut credas* (Thomas Aquinas) is a much better place to begin from if we want to maintain the attraction of the Jesus movement. Here we can continue to build on the thinking of the fathers of the early church, who were in a similar situation. The Reformation chose the other approach because of the circumstances of the time: it inherited the situation of the late Middle Ages, in which the Christian church also occupied a superior position over against Judaism and Islam and hardly had to engage in any real conversation. Only the great voyages of discovery and colonialism brought large-scale acquaintance with Asiatic religions. Moreover, comparative religion is a fairly new conversation partner for theology, as too is an atheism which people have chosen for themselves.

Various possibilities are open to people who want to give an explanation of religious belief.

One approach looks for 'openings' in reality which at least do not exclude the existence of God; another looks for faults or shortcomings in human life which cry out to be made good by God; finally there is a third way which seeks to see all of existence, both its ups and downs, as focussed on God.

As Bonhoeffer showed very acutely, the first approach (which takes up Descartes, Leibniz and Hegel) makes God a God of the physical or metaphysical gaps. In the end he becomes an *x* factor which fills in still-unexplained 'openings' in our view of reality, like the still-unexplained beginning of matter or life, the still-unexplained leaps in evolution, the phenomenon of the creation and annihilation (death) of the cell, the question whether or not we should expect the total end of matter (entropy). It is not far from that to the God of deism – the clockmaker and architect of the universe, who is perpetually at rest until the end. Every new scientific hypothesis makes the hypothesis of God more superfluous.

A number of American Christian Science films are instances of the dangers of this way of thinking about belief in God. They follow the lines of the classical cosmological argument for the existence of God, though the advantage of that was that it did not just look only for openings in reality but also for the deeper dimensions of reality. Things are no better when, on a higher level of abstraction, as in Hegel, God becomes a cipher for a closed process of rise and decline. God, who is still the primal ground and goal of an autonomous reality, plays the part of metaphysical God of the gaps in a system of tautologies. Hegel's attempts follow the lines of Anselm's famous *ontological* argument for the existence of God: because the ideal Idea must also be reality if it is to be the ideal Idea of being, this Idea must also have existence. There are also the necessary theological variants in our day: Paul Tillich's Ground of Being, Whitehead's process God, Teilhard's Omega Point, Han Fortmann's 'Invisible'. Feuerbach's criticism of religion, which is still valid today, applies to all these structures: why assume and accept as a hypothesis something else behind the reality that we perceive if this reality can also be explained and accepted sufficiently in itself? There is also the criticism of Nietzsche, Camus and many others 'after Auschwitz', who say, 'What does such a supportive ground and ultimate Being of beings do to help us to accept the quite unacceptable shadow sides of reality – misery, pain, sickness and death?' This justification for the existence of God cannot explain the negative and absurd side of reality nor make it acceptable without turning human beings into slaves and prisoners.

Does the other way of thinking to which I referred – the one dearer to the Reformation – offer better perspectives? It begins from the 'blemishes' in the human perspective of happiness. It begins from the search for grace, morally just and conscientious action, and takes note of evil, sin, and unprincipled injustice. But the fact that we *can* take note of all this indicates a perspective of truth and goodness, of grace and mercy. In this perspective God challenges us as the end-point of the human struggle for goodness, as All-good, as Ultimate Justice (Horkheimer), the one who gives eternal rest, the Comforter, the Saviour, the Reconciler, the Future.

In fact it is the more Augustinian thinkers who have found this approach a means of expressing their belief.

Of course Pascal is the prime example here, but many people have followed in his footsteps: first Kierkegaard, then Moltmann in our days. Roman Catholic theologians, like Metz, and also (in my view) liberation theologians think along the same lines. The experiences of suffering and contrast in humanity provide them with a springboard towards the existence of God; God as a God of hope and liberation for suffering humanity, the poor and the oppressed.

Their thinking follows the lines of what Kant called the 'moral argument' for God; though what for Kant was simply a postulate of practical reason was not really a proof of God. With Bloch and Horkheimer they reverse the idea that religion is opium: soothing misery, assuaging poverty, maintaining illusions.

Just as the first approach easily leads to concordism, to all too hasty arguments from scientific lacunae in the interpretation of reality, so the second approach can easily lead to a dualism that puts good on God's side and evil on man's. Finally, neither the first nor the second approach is very effective as a response of faith. They have both led to more misunderstandings than conversions. Does it not follow from them that it is better to give up such approaches, such elements in a natural theology altogether, and simply abandon ourselves to the 'God of Abraham, Isaac and Jacob', leaving the God of the philosophers to the philosophers?

I want to argue for a third way. Not because of the statements of the First Vatican Council which solemnly declared that there is a natural knowledge of God nor because of the solemn oaths against modernism which Pius X made Catholic ministers swear on their ordination – to the effect that God can be known by nature and not simply on the basis of the biblical revelation. It is purely and simply because of the insight that biblical faith is itself in the long run the product of human interpretations and choices about reality. Biblical faith, too, is born out of a longing for green pastures, of a fear of death, of the mysterious experience of love and fertility, of the need for security in a camp surrounded by enemies, of despair at the inexplicable fate of those who die early, of the feeling that people live for the life of their children (but why do they?), and of wonderment at the terrifying but also delightful reality of nature.

Biblical faith, too, must respond to the criticism of the 'church fathers of atheism', Feuerbach, Marx, Freud and Nietzsche, that in the end, however regretful it may seem, God proves to be the product of human projection, inhuman conditions which call for correction, infantile illusions which come up against the harshness of life, a repudiation of the basic experience of the nothingness and absurdity of existence, as a result of which people dare not accept chance, so that they could be really free.

Such a response of faith has three tasks which are not performed by the two other approaches: the purging of false images of God which have been produced by the theological tradition itself and by misunderstandings among outsiders; the initiation of a conversation about the acceptance of the existence of God which has the character of a case for God (like any case, its main feature will be depriving all counter-arguments of their force); and a demonstration of how the human longing for security, meaning and purpose itself contains a way of life and mode of being, an experience of totality and purpose, that is evidently parallel to the deepest intention of the Jewish-Christian tradition. This third way is less concerned with response to the fact 'that (a) God exists' than with the fact that God makes us live in a particular way. It is a response of faith which takes the form of being rather than talking. It does not seek to make a particular interpretative practice credible. It does not speak about God without indicating the implications of the kingdom of God. Given the perspective of the Bible, the significance of the name of God in Exodus 3 and the term 'Abba' which Jesus handed on to his disciples, Jewish-Christian belief in God is not primarily concerned with acceptance of the existence of God but with the experience of our own existence as being supported by God. Belief in God is surrender to a mode of being which weaves God's care, God's initiative, God's guidelines, God's way and God's kingdom into the web of our existence. Only faith lived out in this way can give an explanation, by making outsiders say, 'See how they love one another, see how they serve justice, see how their views fit in with the way they behave, see how they hope against all hope, see how they overcome death!'

All these questions and doubts can find a place in responsible belief in God. But we should be all too aware of the inadequacy of our images and pointers and take seriously to heart the criticism of outsiders. As Gregory of Nyssa put it; 'The true vision of God consists in looking for him, not ceasing to desire him.' Or as Eckhardt says, 'Many people want to see God with the eyes with which they see a cow; they want to love God as they love their cow. From a cow you get cheese and other useful products. That is the behaviour of all those people who love God for the sake of outward riches and inward trust: they do not really love God, but are concerned for themselves.' As soon as God is made a pretext for human desires, Feuerbach is right and serving God vitiates serving man. But as long as God is the object of desires, the one to whom we look, all our hope is already a way to God. 'No one possesses God in such a way that he no longer needs to look to him and no one can look to God without sensing that God has already been looking to us for a long time' (D.Bonhoeffer). 'But sometimes, when I think that You are truly alive, I think that You are love and lonely and that You seek me with the despair with which I seek You' (G.K.van het Reve).

The God and Father of Jesus Christ

If we can only know God through being, then for Christians as 'people of God', knowledge of God calls for a distinctive way of being. The church stands or falls by this way of being. It is the church.

The distinctive character of Christian belief in God is determined by the figure of Jesus of Nazareth. Christians are those who seek to embody his style of belief in God and service of God (vision and praxis) in their lives. There are two aspects to this: Jesus gives a quite distinctive colouring to Jewish belief in YHWH by his unique 'Abba' experience; and Jesus himself enters the reality of God. In other words, from now on belief in God is indissolubly bound up with the fate of Jesus of Nazareth.

Both aspects call for clarification, because there are countless misunderstandings among Christians, misunderstandings which can even lead to incredibility, for example if Jesus is identified too easily with God (the ambivalence of 'Lord') if he begins to replace God (God is dead, long live Jesus!), or if God the Father is understood above all in ontological and genetic terms, so that all the emphasis lies on a kind of family bond between God and Jesus.

Anyone who reads the New Testament account of the message and ministry of Jesus cannot fail to note that both are supported by a strong and living belief in God. Jesus lives by Jewish spirituality and its experience of YHWH: the God of Israel, of the patriarchs, of Moses and the prophets. But within this spirituality he produces two correctives which Old Testament belief in God needs in the light of late Jewish distortions.

1. The omnipotence of God, seen by the Jews above all in terms of the covenant, the election of Israel, crisis (judgment, disaster) for the nations, is now extended to 'the many', that is, to all men: non-Israelites, Israelites who stand outside the law (Torah), the

unclean, apostates, collaborators. That is clear above all from the miracle-stories and the parables about the kingdom of God (the prodigal son, the wheat and the tares, the heavenly banquet). Thus the tribal God (Elohim, YHWH) becomes a God for all people; the God of judgment and election becomes a God who calls and saves all. Of course this element was already present in part of the prophetic tradition (Deutero-Isaiah). Jesus radicalized it.

2. Jesus uses the form of address 'Abba', an intimate name for an earthly father, in Mark 14.36f.; Gal.4.6; Rom.8.15, taken into the Greek text without being translated from the Aramaic, which is a sign of historical authenticity, and elsewhere translated *patēr* (Matt.11.25f.; 26.39, 42; Luke 10,21; 11.2; 22.42; 23.34-36 and, alongside 'Abba', in Mark 14.36); in a number of places it is said that Jesus addresses 'the Father' in prayer (in the passages mentioned, and also in John 17, the 'high-priestly' prayer). The use of the address 'Abba' does not denote primarily the Father/Son relationship between Jesus and the Father (for the early Christian community took this divine name over directly and also prays, 'Our Father'), but the nature of God's dealings with humanity and ours with God.

For Jews, 'Abba' as an ordinary, 'secular' term for father above all denotes paternal authority: the father is the authoritative figure, the one who has *exousia*, authority, and whom his children have to obey and treat with piety. The father is also the one who is there to care for his own, his family, and to protect them; he comes to everyone's rescue; he gives advice. He is the focal point of the whole family (or paternal house); everything revolves around him and forms a community through him. The father's authority was undisputed in Judaism. Children had to please their father (Prov.15.20; 23.22, 25). 'To sum up, one can say that in Jesus' time what the *abba* signified for his son was authority and instruction; the father is the authority and the teacher. Being a son means 'belonging to'; and one demonstrated this sonship by carrying out father's instructions.'[6]

Moreover, it is very striking that Jesus never reflects on the intrinsic nature of God,[7] but always about his relationship towards people and how people must behave towards him. The 'will of God', the 'way of God' and the 'kingdom of God' are an essential part of Jesus' belief in God and thus also of the distinctive character of Christian belief in God.[8]

Thus 'Abba' does not denote primarily a kind God. It follows from it that God is good and merciful, but equally that he is the criterion, the arbiter and the judge. It is dangerous and one-sided to attempt, as others do, to infer 'intimate converse with God' from the term; we may not blot out from his experience – and ours – Jesus' wrestling with God (at the end of the Gospel of Mark). Even less does the name 'Abba' provide the basis for a naive pietism: God will look after us. Nor may 'Abba' lend support to a sexist image of God. Of course Jesus uses the term in its Jewish/patriarchal sense, but that does not in itself make God male. The divine name is not used anywhere in the Old Testament with a masculine pronoun. Feminist theology rightly points this out.

In the New Testament, too, the term 'God' (*ho theos*) also denotes the one who transcends and supports all that is earthly and human, the 'shepherd of being' (Heidegger) who is worthy of worship, the one who may not be identified with any human reality or any reality within the world. Jesus is almost never called God directly – certainly never in Paul, and when he is, it is in a later, more Hellenistic phase, and certainly not in the Jewish sense of YHWH or in Jesus' own sense of 'Abba'. The exceptions are John 20.28 (Thomas's 'My Lord and my God'); John 1.1 ('And the Word was God'); cf. also Heb.1.8; II Thess.1.12; Titus 2.13; II Peter 1.1. Jesus does not use of himself the 'messianic titles' which are given to him in early Christian preaching (Son of man, Lord, Christ, Son of God; perhaps 'Son of man' is an exception?). The titles all stress God's action in and through him: they are functional, not ontological designations, although they seek to say 'who Jesus is' and not just 'what he does'. This also applies to the title Son of God. Exegesis has discovered the Old Testament roots of all these titles.

But in that case what of the 'incarnation'? What of the pronouncements of Nicaea and Chalcedon which have been incorporated into our creed? It is worth while bearing in mind here the development of the language of faith. Its starting point is the preaching of Jesus' resurrection. God raised him from the dead. That is the earliest form of the proclamation. Despite his apparent failure, this man with this programme and this life-style, who was executed by the Jews and Romans, henceforth lives at the right hand of God, as the Son of Man who is coming on the clouds (Dan.7.14; Matt.28.18-20), as the 'Son of God' who definitively occupies the place of the kings of Israel (Pss.72; 110). Through his resurrection Jesus is appointed 'Son of God'. Secondly, the evangelists bring this appointment forward: to the beginning of his appearance in Capernaum or his baptism through John (Mark, Luke, Matthew); to the beginning of his life (Matthew and Luke); or finally, to the beginning of God's own being (John; cf. Colossians; Ephesians). Only in the centuries afterwards did a conflict of authorities arise under the influence of Greek trends (Gnosticism). The question here was whether Jesus could ultimately be left out of Christian belief (as Socrates can be left out of Socratic belief, Buddha out of Buddhism and Mohammed out of Islam). The church firmly rejects all views which detract from the divine mission which Jesus permanently fulfils. That means the rejection of any attempt to remove the tension in the relationship between Jesus and God. Both those who declare Jesus to be only a man and those who see him as only God are condemned (cf. I Cor.1.1f.; 4.2f.). Here belief in the resurrection also becomes a distinctive feature of Christian belief in God. This is not just a belief in immortality; Christians share that with many religions. Many religions, including primitive religions, have expressed the view that the end of human life is not the ultimate reality of each personal human life, in all kinds of forms (reincarnation, eternal hunting fields, paradise myths). Resurrection belief is the belief that a life according to the criteria of Jesus enters into the reality of God. As he is raised by God, and sits at God's right hand as a standard for all generations (living and dead), so too those who follow his way enter into God's own life, the Father's house, as sons of God, reborn to new life and incorruptibility. The Christian God, the Father of Jesus, is a God of the living, not the dead. Death no longer characterizes life as the ultimate end; it is 'a beginning begun for good'. The dying day of the saints of God is therefore rightly called their birthday (*dies natalis*).

Belief in the resurrection is impossible apart from Christian belief in God; Christian belief in God is impossible without belief in the resurrection: then is your faith vain (Paul in I Cor.15). Of course this does not mean accepting all the mythical conceptions about eternal life or historically conditioned rational hypotheses about the existence of soul and body which can subsequently be separated. Nor does it make death less difficult and painful as an experience of absurdity and negativity. The experience of discontinuity cannot be wiped out by belief in the essential continuity of the person. Of course life can be coloured by this: the praxis of rebellion and liberation has its roots in the belief that God will lengthen our days and that our names are written in the book of life, on the palm of his hand.

The distinctive relationship between God and Jesus has also led to Christian belief in the Trinity. As 'people of God' we share in the life of Father, Son and Spirit (I John 1.3,6; I Cor.1.9; II Cor.13.1;

Phil.2.1). Here, too, many misunderstandings constantly threaten to arise. Some 'rules of language' can help here:

1. It must be stressed that YHWH-Abba-God is one and only one. Christians do not practise any Hindu-style tritheism.

2. Within the Old and New Testaments, 'Father', 'Son' and 'Spirit' (*pneuma*) are primarily indications of God's activity among us. The Son and the Spirit are called the Father's witnesses and instruments (God's two hands, Irenaeus) precisely in order to indicate how much God is both transcendent and immanent.

3. Both the Son and the Spirit work through human history. That is true most of all of Jesus, who is 'anointed' (sent) by God's Spirit; it is also true of the *christianoi*, the anointed, who receive his Spirit.

4. The Son and the Spirit make possible the presence of God in our history. We human beings share in God's own divine life, share in creating God's kingdom and God's history, not by our human longings but by the divine initiative of grace.

5. Either a christological or a pneumatological basis of the church – the people of God, the Jesus movement, those anointed with the Spirit – is concerned with putting in the light of God's initiative what happens through human beings and among human beings: the building up of the body of Christ, the renewal of the creation according to the law of the Spirit of life (Rom.8). 'For all who are led by the Spirit of God are sons of God. For you did not receive the spirit of slavery to fall back into fear, but you have received the spirit of sonship. When we cry "Abba! Father!" it is the Spirit himself bearing witness with our spirit that we are children of God' (Rom.8.14-16).

This reference to Jesus of Nazareth protects the church from an 'ecclesiological monophysitism', as though the church of God were conceivable without the specific community of the disciples of Jesus. The reference to the Spirit of God prevents the church from regarding itself as a purely human association for religious matters and a club or association with specific aims; i.e. it protects it from an 'ecclesiologial Nestorianism'. Just as the Spirit of the Lord rests on Jesus and makes him the Christ, the anointed of God, so too the Spirit of the Lord rests on the people of God, as the event of Pentecost bears witness.

6. References to Jesus and references to the Spirit may therefore never be played off against each other in ecclesiology. Just as it is as logical to say that the Spirit proceeds from the Father and the Son as it is to say that the Son proceeds from the Spirit and the Father, so it can also be said that the church is moved by the Father

and the Son in the Spirit, or that the movement is from the Son and the Spirit who leads people to the Father. These are all expressions of the divine and human mystery of God in search of humanity and humanity in search of God.

7. By way of correction to views of the church from the past which reduce the event of the church to the visible and the institutional, to a movement and an organization, on the basis of a historical mandate of Jesus – the church as 'instituted' by Jesus – it would be healthy for us to put more stress on the contribution of the Spirit to the formation of the church, setting aside the phobia of spiritualism and enthusiasm which has characterized church history. More than ever, people of God need the 'inspiration' of God's direct breath of life which ensouls them.

> Perceptible and yet not perceptible, invisible and yet powerful, real like the energy-charged air, the wind, the storm, as important for life as the air we breathe: this is how people in ancient times frequently imagined the 'Spirit' and God's invisible working. According to the beginning of the creation account 'Spirit' (Hebrew *ruah*, Greek *pneuma*) is the 'roaring', the 'tempest' of God over the waters. 'Spirit' as understood in the Bible – as opposed to 'flesh', to perishable reality – means the *force* or *power proceeding from God*: that invisible force of God and power of God that is effective, creatively or destructively, for life or judgment, in creation and history, in Israel and later in the Church. It comes upon man powerfully or gently, stirring up individuals or groups to ecstasy, often producing extraordinary phenomena, active in great men and women, in Moses and the 'judges' of Israel, in warriors and singers, kings, prophets and prophetesses...
>
> The Spirit is *no other than God himself*. He is God himself close to man and the world, as the comprehending but not comprehensible, the bestowing but not controllable, the life-creating but also judging, power and force.
>
> This is important. The Holy Spirit is not a third party, not a thing between God and men, but God's personal closeness to men... The Spirit is of one nature with the Father and the Son.[9]

Thus knowing God within the sphere of the church becomes that way of being which is mentioned in II Peter: sharing in the real nature (*physis*) of God (II Peter 1.4), becoming 'people of God'.

4

Through Jesus Christ Our Lord

People are fond of describing the church as the Jesus movement. 'Movement' here, as I indicated in the previous chapter, does not stand for an action-group or club of people who are pursuing a particular aim. And 'Jesus' is more than the name of the group. It means being moved now by Jesus, the one who lives in our midst. This being 'moved' is more than an inner disturbance or spur to action. It is a matter of being moved in a particular direction. The church of Jesus is concerned with salvation from God for those who want to be 'of God'. As Vatican II says, it is the universal sacrament of salvation.

Therefore it is impossible to leave out of account what 'salvation from God' means in a Christian sense when we are talking about the church. That would devalue ecclesiology once more and make it a glorified organizational theory. Nor, however - if our plea for the church is to remain a plea – is it enough simply to presuppose that salvation from God is a known quantity and to make it a postulate for the church, saying 'Outside the church there is no salvation', as though 'church' could be defined in terms of salvation and 'salvation' in terms of 'church'. That happens where the starting point is all too obviously 'the mystery of the church' or where what is celebrated in the church – the sacraments, the memory of Christ – is itself celebrated as 'salvation'. However much all this may be said to be a gift of Christ, it does not coincide with God's salvation, but leads towards it, just as the church, too, does not coincide with God's salvation, but is a sacrament, an instrument, an effective sign of it.

What Christian salvation does mean is discussed in theology under the heading of soteriology, the interpretation of the saving significance of Jesus' life and death, what he has done for us, his saving (*soteria* = salvation) action for human beings. That is what the church lives by: according to the church fathers it stems from the wound of Christ, out of which blood and water flowed after the spear-thrust from the soldier by his cross (John 19.34). Therefore ecclesiology cannot be done without soteriology.

First, some misunderstandings must be removed. For a long time theologians made a sharp distinction between christology and soteriology, as if who Jesus *is* – his person and nature – could be described independently of what he wanted and brought about – his programme and mission. Now that we have found new access to Jesus of Nazareth, like the disciples gathered around him to whom the scriptures bear witness, through what he says and does among men and women looking towards God, who he is and what he does run into one another.

Moreover, this avoids the misunderstanding that what he means for humanity – in the name of God – depends exclusively on what he means for God – in the name of humanity. It is not as though his historical appearance in the midst of humanity only became gospel once he had given his life, and then not on the basis of that life but on the basis of his death, or rather, on the basis of his existence with God, before and after this life. Such a christology – once mockingly described by someone as 'Jesus appears... and disappears' – is matched by a timeless soteriology: a doctrine of redemption which extracts the death of Jesus from the specific course of his life leading up to his death, and in which the fact of his death – the death of the second person of the Trinity – is 'redemptive' quite apart from the reason for it, so that the way in which it came about is now irrelevant. Here it seems that redemption would have been achieved even if Jesus had not died by an execution, but by accident.

In recent years there has fortunately been very profound reflection on the real reason for Jesus' death in the light of his ministry. In my view this is also crucial for ecclesiology.

Towards an ecumenical soteriology

In all the theological works of more recent years a good deal of attention has been paid to the theme of redemption and liberation. Schillebeeckx wrote a book of nine hundred pages on it. In one way this is the main theme of the Latin-American liberation theologians. Pope John Paul II devoted an encyclical to it (*Redemptor hominis*). In recent political theology, both Protestant and Catholic, the central questions have been: For what did Jesus die? What does his death mean for us? Exegetes have written many detailed studies, especially of the letters of Paul and the Synoptic Gospels, in an attempt to discover how Jesus himself and his disciples understood and came to terms with his cruel execution, which seemed to run so counter to what he had proclaimed to them.

For a long time theology was crippled at this point by the sixteenth-century controversy over justification and reconciliation, of which the Heidelberg Catechism and the Council of Trent are an echo. That blocked discussions, because it prevented an unprejudiced approach to the biblical language about salvation: everything was read from the perspective of justification by faith alone *versus* sanctification through good works, and reconciliation on the basis of God's grace alone *versus* sanctification on the basis of merit (of the man Jesus Christ and those who are sanctified in him).

This controversial theological problem of grace and works, of God's justification and human righteousness, of the unique place of Jesus' sacrifice and the need for discipleship on our part, seems gradually to have been tackled and resolved. Furthermore, we see how many traditions have discovered the richness of New Testament language about Jesus' activity, death and resurrection. Perhaps these two things are connected with a changed view of sin and sinfulness, the traditional background to the Western doctrine of redemption. Finally, there are different contemporary interpretations of Jesus' death as a consequence of his activity. While as yet there is no synthesis between them, perhaps they match the present need for redemption even more closely. Views of the church, the way in which faith and salvation are experienced and celebrated within it, could be influenced by this development.

The rediscovery of a consensus over the justification of the sinner and the unique sacrifice of Christ

The essence of the classical Reformation criticism of the Roman Catholic doctrine of grace and redemption, justification and sanctification, was that this doctrine made man autonomous, that it obscured the freedom of God's initiative, that it anticipated God's judgment and consummation which were still to come, and that it legalized, secularized and objectivized salvation, grace and revelation. The church was said to be talking of a kind of repetition and continuation of the *opus Dei*, which had already been realized once for all in Christ. Hence the opposition to a eucharistic doctrine which explained the Lord's Supper as the church's sacrifice, and to a view of ministry which saw the church's ministers of word and sacrament above all as priests offering this sacrifice.

In fact, some Catholic theology, in a very specific interpretation of Trent, made the church, its sacraments and ministries a kind of continuation of the incarnation. This approach spoke of the many sacrifices of the mass which count in the saving work of Christ and said that pastors appear *in persona Christi*. Since Vatican II, as a result of a theological return to the sources, a good deal of misunderstanding on this point has been removed. In 1957 Hans Küng wrote his book on Karl Barth's doctrine of justification, in which he gave a new interpretation of Trent which countered many of the objections from the Reformed churches. Protestant authors – and church writings – showed up those quietistic distortions of the doctrine of justification which suggested that in the light of God's grace human beings could only rest on their laurels. Catholic theology – especially Rahner and Schoonenberg – again began to stress that God's grace is needed for any act of love, hope or faith, for liberation from sin, for forgiveness and encouragement, in order to live according to God's will and law. However, there can be no rivalry between God and man here. Oppositions of God to man, grace to works, pose false alternatives. So does an opposition of salvation from God to discipleship of Jesus.

Although by no means all Reformation theologians would subscribe to such thinking, the great churches of the Reformation do seem gradually to be dropping their mistrust of it. In the pastoral letter of the General Synod of the Dutch Reformed Church about the Roman Catholic Church in 1950, differences over grace and works, the sacrifice of Jesus and the sacrifice of the mass are still fairly broad. Its verdict is that the Roman Catholic church makes human beings autonomous, obscures the freedom of grace, anticipates God's final judgment, which is still to come, and legalizes and secularizes salvation, grace and revelation. The *Guidelines* of 1961 ('The Reformation Attitude to the Roman Catholic Church and Its Past') are still dominated by mistrust. In *Our Attitude to the Roman Catholic Church. Reorientation and Appeal* (1969), the roles are almost reversed: in the light of the *New Catechism*, which is strongly coloured by the thinking of Schoonenberg, there is praise for the developments in the idea of sacrifice in the eucharistic doctrine of the Catholic Church, and Answer 80 of the Heidelberg Catechism is said no longer to apply. There is not a word about differences over the doctrines of grace and reconciliation. That is even more the case with the most recent writings from the Reformed side ('Between Recognition and Acceptance', 1980) and the combined synod of the Dutch Reformed and Calvinist Churches ('Our Task for the 1980s').

On the Catholic side, too, the old controversies over this point are no longer brought out. At Vatican II they are hardly ever mentioned explicitly, except in the Constitution on the Liturgy, where in the discussion of the eucharist and its relation to Jesus' death we find a subtle term: the eucharist perpetuates (*perpetuaret*, no.47) the sacrifice of Christ 'until he comes'. Here Jesus Christ is the mediator whose once-for-all sacrifice of his life (Rom.8.3; I Cor.5.7; Heb.10.12) 'for us' (I Cor.11.24b; Eph.5.2), 'for our sins' (I Cor.15.3b) and for all (Mark 14.24b par.), brings about redemption. Here human beings remain free to accept this by faith and to live by it. There is no such thing as determined predestination. God hands himself over to human faith. Despite what might sometimes seem appearances to the contrary, the role of the man Jesus, his obedient service to his Father, is not misunderstood docetically or monophysitically. Just as God and Jesus encounter each other in the obedience of the kingdom of God, the will of God, so too God and humanity encounter one another by virtue of reconciliation in Christ within the sphere of the church.

In international ecumenical conversations, too, this has become the dominant line of thought. In this connection I must mention the discussions about justification and reconciliation in the German churches round about 1968. These led, for example, to a declaration by the United Protestant Church (*On the Understanding of the Death of Jesus*, 1968). This still talks of satisfaction as the real saving work of God who does 'what is sufficient' (*das Genügende*, cf. Karl Barth) before himself and for us and thus wipes out our guilt from sheer grace. Very recently, however, the 'Alliance of Protestant Churches in the German Democratic Republic' has noted and – albeit with some hesitations – accepted a new declaration which permits the gradual replacement of the term 'justification', understood in terms of satisfaction and the obliteration of sins, by the term 'acceptance' of the sinner, understood as forgiveness and a new start. Here there comes to be considerable stress on the connection between a doctrine of justification and reconciliation understood in this way, and mutual human forgiveness and reconciliation: people who accept one another as God accepts them. Moreover, this change within Lutheran and Reformed thought has found its way into a wider ecumenical context. In 1972 the World Mission Conference in Bangkok on the theme 'Salvation Today' caused storms of protest because of the shift of accent which it called for in soteriology from 'redemption' (in the sense of a ransom paid by Christ) to 'liberation' (in the sense of freedom from the powers of evil which is still outstanding and still to come). While Bangkok could still build a bridge between the parties – the traditional Western theologians and the rising generation of Third-World theologians – by means of the rather more neutral term 'salvation', in subsequent years the theme of liberation gained the upper hand. This is evident in texts from the World Council of Churches, supported by the political theology of Europe and North America (Moltmann, Metz, Winter, Cone, Shaull) and through the liberation theology in Latin America. In the bilateral dialogues between Lutherans and Catholics, Reformed and Catholics, Anglicans and Catholics seem to have overcome the old controversies on this point. That has consequences for ecclesiology, because in all the traditions the starting point is a church of saints *and* sinners as a 'mixed reality' in which God's reconciliation is achieved now, within the reconciling action of human beings.

In 1966, H. Kuitert already expressed the consensus in these terms: 'Reconciliation – which happened once for all in the past – is realized among us in the "remembrance" of this representative act of Christ, i.e. by the constantly repeated receiving and – in our case – giving of forgiveness, as practised in ordinary life in the form of mutual solidarity (pro-existence) and as celebrated in the Sunday eucharist.'[1] Thus reconciliation in Christ, faith in the gracious God and mutual service are linked with one another in the sphere of the church.

The 'relative' place of 'justification' and 'reconciliation' in the soteriology of the New Testament and the history of theology

'Justification of the sinner', 'redemption' (in the sense of liberation by ransom as in Mark 10.45) and 'reconciliation' (*katallage* as in Rom.3.24f.) occupy only a small place within the totality of the riches of the New Testament stories, images and concepts used to explain the significance of Jesus' message and life-style for and through the disciples.[2]

Jesus himself talks of God's 'salvation' (which is itself already a metaphor: wholeness = being made whole) in terms of the coming or the proximity of the kingdom of God (Mark 1.15), the beginning of the year of grace (Luke 4.18-22) and rebirth (John 3.3-8), eternal life (John 3.15f., 36; 4.14; 5.24; 6.27, 40, 47, 51-58). All this was implemented not just by his death but already by his earthly ministry and was experienced by the disciples in faith, healing, liberation from possessions, forgiveness and rehabilitation, a new interpretation of the law, the revelation of God's power and glory or simply in 'leaving everything and following him'. They experienced liberation in becoming a new community of disciples, which meant table fellowship with sinners, the impure, the outcast and even traitors. To begin with, Jesus' death – not on a death-bed but on the cross, and therefore murder or execution (Acts 5.30; 10.39) – was simply experienced as a disaster, despair, failure (Luke 24: the disciples on the Emmaus road), abandonment, a curse (Mark 15.28: This was to fulfil the saying, 'He was numbered among the transgressors', Isa.53.12), betrayal (Judas), denial (Peter), flight (Mark). There is much evidence to support the view that Jesus himself experienced his death in this way, as witness what must be an authentic saying, 'My God, why have you forsaken me?' (Mark 15.34), which is not to be interpreted simply as a later theological allusion to Ps.22. Commentators see different levels in believers' interpretations of this murder or martyrdom for conscience's sake, which in itself is 'the most certain fact in the whole history of Jesus' (W.Trilling). The earliest stratum is concerned with those who brought it about: Pilate, the Romans, Judas, the Jewish leaders. Their line is that it did not have to happen, and should not have happened. Therefore God punished those who perpetrated the deed. Israel lost its privileges (Mark 14.58; 15.29; 15.38: the Temple loses its function, is destroyed, desecrated); Judas commits suicide. A second stratum looks for explanations in the ministry of Jesus: his death inevitably followed from it. Thus the growing conflict with the Jews becomes a scarlet thread running through the Gospels, marked by announcements of the passion (for example Mark 8.31; 9.12, 30f.; 10.32-34; 11.18; 12.8; 14.7f.; 14.21; 14.24f.). A third phase is the interpretation 'it had to happen', namely in accordance with the divine plan 'according to the scriptures' (Mark 8.31). People found scriptural texts in the Psalms (Ps.22) and in the prophets (especially Isa.49-53, the 'servant of YHWH' texts) and in Zechariah (the apocalyptic phenomena surrounding the death of Jesus), and began to interweave the story of the passion with references to these texts (e.g. Mark 14.21; Luke 24.26).

On a fourth level – much more the level of acquired belief than that of more or less rational explanation – Jesus' death was contrasted with his resurrection. This is the structure of the earliest preaching (for example in Acts) and the earliest confessions (e.g. I Cor.15.3-8; Phil. 2.1-11): You Jews killed Jesus, as was prophesied by the scriptures, but God raised him from the dead, as is said in the Psalms. The resurrection is the event which rehabilitates Jesus, the one who was crucified and accursed. The disaster was transformed into a saving event by God himself, but only in the resurrection.

Finally, the crucifixion itself – as interpreted in faith – was made a saving event. This has happened in Mark 10.45: The Son of Man has come to serve and to give his life as a ransom for many; I Cor.15.3: Christ dies for our sins according to the scriptures. In the eucharistic tradition – itself already the echo of the beginning of the acts of remembrance by the early church, though based on an initiative of Jesus – this is confessed explicitly (Mark 14.24: This is my blood of the covenant, which was shed for many; Matt.26.28: ...for the forgiveness of sins; Luke 22.19f.: ...My body which was given for you...; my blood which was shed for you). Paul himself takes up this tradition (Rom.3.24f.; 4.25; also I John 4.10). Many other images – with the Old Testament associations that go with them – can be added. Already in the eucharistic tradition we find covenant (Ex.24) and new covenant (Jer.31), and the day of YHWH (Luke 22.16,30). After this, in Paul and the Synoptics and the later letters, there is some Jewish and Hellenistic conceptuality: salvation (Acts 2), liberation for freedom (Gal.5.1; Rom.8), ministry of the new covenant (II Cor.3), being children of God (Rom.8; John 1.12), peace (John 21; letters of Paul, passim), incorporation into Christ (all the texts which relate to *koinonia*; Rom.6), being changed and reconciled with God (Eph.2), being heirs of God (II Cor.5.18-21; Rom.5.10; Eph.2; Col.1.22), sitting at the right hand of God (Eph.2), becoming heirs of God (I Peter 1.4), sharing in Christ's suffering and glorification (Rom. 8.17) as the first-fruits of the Spirit (Acts 2; Rom.8.23), being destined to have the same form as the Son (Rom.8.29), indeed even sharing in God's own being (II Peter 1.4).

Why was all this remembered in such great detail? Because it also encouraged later generations of Christians who knew how to choose from the many metaphors of their time those which were most appropriate for expressing belief in the saving value of this disastrous event.

So we can explain Paul's stress in Romans and Galatians on 'justification', 'reconciliation' and 'redemption' in terms of his dispute with the Jews over the question of the continuity and discontinuity with the Jewish law which dominated his mission. And Luther's preference for precisely this image of salvation according to Paul can be understood against the background of the domination of the gospel by the law in the Christianity of his time. This happens in the same way as Latin-American theologians quite justifiably prefer 'liberation' as a metaphor of salvation.

The consensus on the significance of Jesus' life, death and resurrection for the life of those who believe in him and follow him – his disciples – is based on the recognition of the pluriformity of such 'images of salvation' in the New Testament.

Moreover, in most modern theological discussions of christology and soteriology, we find a summary of the different 'paradigms' of the saving character of Jesus' life and death. Schillebeeckx mentions sixteen key concepts (interpretations) of the source and destiny of redemption through Jesus Christ.[3] Gerd Theissen analyses six different 'symbolic fields' in Paul's doctrine of redemption (liberation, justification, reconciliation, transformation, new life, participation – *koinonia*).[4] In addition to the main Pauline type of 'reconciliation' Schnackenburg[5] distinguishes two further 'types' of soteriology in the New Testament: the Lucan pattern of the way which must be followed in the Jesus movement and the Johannine pattern of the gradual revelation of the 'life' that comes to us in Christ. The last two soteriological frameworks are concerned, much more strongly than in Paul, with the whole of Jesus' life, from cradle to grave. Here Luke attributes hardly any saving significance to Jesus' death, which for him is merely a transitional phase: John weaves death and resurrection together to such a degree, in the typology of the lamb of God, that for him too the saving significance of the cross as such is overshadowed by the eternal service of this lamb (John 1.29-36; 19.14; Rev. 5.6ff.; 6.1; 7.14-17; 12.11; 13.8; 14.1,10; 15.3f.; 17.14; 19.9; 21.9-14, 22, 27; 22.1-9).

This exegetical broadening of the perspective – which fortunately is safeguarded in the liturgical traditions of East and West – is matched by a similar broadening of consciousness in the history of theology.

If we compare the confessions of faith in the early church with those of the Reformation it is at once striking that the explicit stress on the saving significance of Jesus' death as expiation for our sins is a specific characteristic of the latter. The Apostles' Creed mentions only the fact of Jesus' death – as do also a number of ancient confessions in the New Testament – to ward off any form of docetism. The so-called Nicene creed adds that he was born for us and suffered for us – an echo of the New Testament 'for us' in e.g. Gal.3.13; II Cor.5.21; 8.9; Gal.2.20; 8.32 and in the Lucan tradition of the eucharist. Thus incarnation and the passion narrative are bound up together in one soteriological conception without much stress on redemption from sin. Only in 675, at a council in Toledo, was there more explicit mention of Jesus being made sin for us, taking up II Cor.5.21, or as becoming a sacrifice for our sins, who suffered for our misdeeds (DS 539). The Reformation confessions of faith (NGB 20-24, Canonical Rules of Dort, chs.II,III-IV; Geneva Catechism, questions 43,57,59,66,71; Heidelberg Catechism, Sundays 5 and 6, 11-13, and also in the discussion of the sacraments, questions 66-74, [baptism] and 75-85 [eucharist]) put strong emphasis on the saving significance of the death of Jesus as reconciliation and satisfaction aimed at the justification of sinners. The Heidelberg Catechism makes this almost the only hermeneutical key for the interpretation of the Apostles' Creed in a real revision of it. All the titles of Christ are derived from the event of redemption, understood as liberation from sin. The incarnation also takes on this tone: it is a covering of sin before the face of God. There is almost no answer which is not governed by the tension between sin, judgment and grace.

That makes the almost complete absence of this thinking in terms of reconciliation and justification all the more surprising in the more modern confessions of faith in our time.[6] Because most of them come from the Reformed tradition, this absence is particularly striking.

It is eloquent proof of the phenomenon that every age makes its own 'soteriology', as we also know from the history of theology. As early as 1838, F.C.Baur distinguished three periods in the doctrine of redemption: the mystical (up to Anselm), the juridical (up to Kant) and the moral or subjective (from 1800). A century later G. Aulén outlined its history in terms of three main types, those of Christ the victor, Christ the victim and Christ the model. In a recent study Greshake[7] draws a distinction between redemption, understood as *paideia* (nurture by the divine Logos, the divinization of humanity and the consummation of creation), as a restoration of the true relationship between God and humanity (in the form of the restored order or contract between feudal lord and vassal: Anselm), and finally as an intrinsic element in history (since Hegel and modern times). Pannenberg[8] sums up seven soteriological themes, attributed respectively to Irenaeus, Origen, Anselm, Luther, Schleiermacher, Kant/Ritschl and Gogarten/Ebeling.

The conclusion of this overall survey can only be that while we may welcome the ecumenical consensus between Rome and the Reformed churches over God's redemptive work in Christ and man's share in it as expressed in terms of reconciliation in Christ and justification of the sinner, the marks of historical conditioning are very obvious. The paradigm of reconciliation and justification is in itself only one choice from a large number of Jewish and Greek metaphors for salvation. If the paradigm is made binding as *articulus stantis et cadentis ecclesiae* (as something by which the church stands or falls – as it was at the time of the Reformation), or as the 'centre of scripture' (as a canon in the canon, the norm for expounding the rest of scripture, though in my view that place is occupied by Jesus himself, his life, his death and resurrection), or as 'the only hope and comfort in life and death' (Heidelberg Catechism, Sunday 1, question 1, though ultimately that can only be the role of the love of God itself which bears witness in many ways to the needs of humanity), Rome and the Reformed churches run the risk of distorting the kerygma of the New Testament. Throughout the ecumenical movement this paradigm, which is typically Western, is more of a blind spot than an aid to understanding the signs of God's grace. It does not seem to work in conversations with the Orthodox churches of the East and the young churches of the south; it does not provide any understanding of God's mighty acts. The historical misunderstandings over it between Rome and the Reformation need to be removed as quickly as possible for the sake of this broad ecumene of East and West, North and South, in order to make room for us to see the wider content of 'through Christ our Lord'. That should help us at the same time to bring to a much speedier conclusion the other points under discussion between Rome and the Reformed churches (especially over the sacraments and the ministry). In fact there are other articles of faith which are more open to discussion than this, after Anselm's all-prevailing theme of reconciliation.

Redemption: from what and for what?

One reason why 'reconciliation' and 'the justification of the sinner' have fallen into the background as key concepts for salvation in Christ – and therefore for a sense of the church – could be that conceptions of human sin and sinfulness have changed and that there has been a shift in humanity's 'need for redemption'. What we call salvation continually changes with the problems of our existence that we would like to see healed.

A sense of sin, guilt-feelings, a tormented conscience, anxiety about failure and impotence towards ruling powers form the specific background experience to the mediaeval preference for redemption as reconciliation. The historical explanation of Luther's passionate search for a 'gracious God' lies in his Augustinian spirituality, the mediaeval anxiety about hell and divine judgment to which the church of his day had responded with an obscure system of obliterating sin before God, and his opposition to the strait-jacket of the monastic struggle for perfection. As a child of his time, Luther shared these experiences with his opponents. The doctrine of Trent on sin and original sin, the doctrine of sin which was worked out in detail after Trent, the propaganda for private confession as a sacrament to maintain the 'state of grace', the penitential manuals, the examinations of conscience, the catalogues of sins, the Puritan morality of the seventeenth century and the Victorian morality of the nineteenth, the narrowing of sexuality to a mechanism for procreation in the twentieth century and the denial of the intrinsic human goodness of all experiences of pleasure – all this forms the social background to a sense of sin, and of the church – which is anything but biblical. Both Rome and the Reformation have contributed to it, and in both traditions it has led to the hypertrophy of the doctrine of reconciliation-through-satisfaction and the justification of the sinner.

In addition to this there is the association of the dogma of redemption with the theology of original sin. Paul's typology of Jesus as the new Adam in Rom.5 and I Cor.15, re-read in the light of Augustine's doctrine of original sin and of Anselm's doctrine of satisfaction, led to an almost mythological conception of redemption as liberation from the doom of original sin. Sometimes this was even filled out with the conception of paying a ransom to Satan or of redemption as a divine stratagem which led Satan to kill God's own Son, the ultimate consequence of which was for him to lose his grip on mankind. Not only does the New Testament show in numerous places how Jesus himself and his disciples challenge such a belief in Satan and demons, but it is certain that Paul never uses such a mythological conception as an inherited doom of sin. He does, however, talk of 'disobedience', of the consequences of the actions of Adam – the original man – which led to sin and death, and he does talk of righteousness in Christ: 'So that, as sin reigned in death, grace also might reign through righteousness to eternal life through Jesus Christ our Lord' (Rom.5.21). Any idea of a kind of inherited sinfulness and inherited guilt is alien to the New Testament, as is indicated, for example, by Jesus' criticism of particular late-Jewish conceptions of the transmission of guilt 'from father to son' (John 9.2: the story of the man born blind). According to the New

Testament, sin is specifically a misuse of freedom, a rejection of one's calling, living in conflict with the new life of the Spirit. Sin is missing the mark (*hamartia*) by those who want to know God's will. That was already true of the Old Testament and the law (thus Paul in Rom.1-3), but now God's righteousness has in fact become manifest in Christ, in whom the law – which is now the law of faith (Rom.3.27) – has come into its own (Rom.3.31). Since it is a matter of falling short in one's calling, sin is not handed on or inherited. As Berkhof well put it: 'Anyone who stresses "sin" must play down the "original", and vice versa.'[9]

Even if, like Schoonenberg,[10] we interpret original sin as the sinful situation of humanity and the world into which we were all born (thus too the *New Catechism*), the dogma of redemption is very difficult to reconcile with it. Whatever the cross of Jesus may mean for believers, it is itself the painful proof of our sinful situation, the direct consequence of sin as 'the beast in man',[11] which did not disappear even after Jesus' execution, either in the world or in the church. Here we come upon the essence of the non-Christian criticism of the traditional dogma of redemption, the fact that the experience of salvation leaves so little mark: 'Why do not Christians look more redeemed?' (Nietzsche).

From what, then, are we redeemed if even after Christ, humanity and the world still continue to show signs of the old Adam and his world? Is it from the feeling of guilt, so that, being finally free in Christ, we can mobilize all our human potential towards our own fulfilment, selfhood, growth in self-acceptance? That is the way in which redemption is currently interpreted by the latest descendants of Freud who, citing Maslow, Rogers, Schutz and many others, among them a number of gurus like Baghwan Sri Raneesh, interpret 'salvation' as encounter, sensitivity, self-fulfilment, being made whole through feeling good, liberation from the strait-jacket of norms and fashions, heteronomous morality, I'm OK, you're OK.

Although all this is understandable against the background of a sense of sin and moralism, of the glorification of asceticism and a mysticism of suffering, it is a tendency that is hard to reconcile with Christian conceptions of salvation. Especially things like self-surrender, self-denial, service, giving one's life for others and finally Jesus' own ministry of service to the kingdom of God and his martyrdom are here left completely out of account.

Are we then perhaps liberated from 'the powers', in the sense that we have the strength to carry on the battle against the powers of this world? That is an interpretation of salvation in Christ which perhaps has rather better biblical credentials. We find vigorous advocates of this model of salvation in a good deal of Western political theology – especially on the Reformation side, as for example in a Dutch contribution to the Conference on World Mission held at Melbourne in 1980 (*The Power of the Cross*). In this conception exorcism becomes the paradigm of salvation. It is a question of challenging the powers of this world, calling for a change of structures, breaking through the vicious circle of possessions, violence and the abuse of power. It seems to me that the drawback of this exorcism theology is that it almost personifies the structures of injustice; that the New Testament criticism of belief in powers and demons cannot be heard strongly enough in it; but above all that nowhere in Jesus' career up to and including his execution is there a call to challenge unjust structures without personal conversion and repentance. Also according to the evidence of the New Testament, his death is an unmistakable instance of 'the murder of the prophets' (cf. Acts 7.52; Matt.23.29-37). However, Jesus' preaching of the kingdom of God is directed against any identification of the kingdom of God and the state of salvation and any interpretation of *metanoia* as being identical with social revolution. However right and necessary revolutions of this kind may be, Jesus' disciples choose – not as neutrals but as participants – another way, the way of discipleship and the call to join the community of disciples (Luke 9.53). That implies renunciation of power, non-violence, persecution and the cross day by day. Where they are required of disciples, the ways and means which lead to the coming of the kingdom of God match the character of God's guidance: God's peace cannot be established with violence; it calls for love of the enemy and not for his annihilation, calls on the rich and powerful to repent, but says nothing about anathema or excommunication, except in the case of those who are converted and are already disciples (Ananias and Sapphira, Acts 5).

So if it is not original sin from which Jesus, the crucified Messiah, frees us, if it is not guilt feelings and the structures of evil, and if the pattern of the wrath of God which must be stilled, or a violation of God's honour which calls for satisfaction, are approaches which cannot stand up to the criticism of exegetes, from what does God free us in Jesus Christ, and for what? What salvation can be found in the church of Christ?

Before we turn to some contemporary answers it is worth pointing to a comprehensive answer which is often given and seems to put an end to all problems. This answer runs as follows: redemption has been achieved in principle, objectively: death is overcome, peace has been made with God, the new covenant has taken effect. God has prepared a dwelling place for those who love him. But all this must still be achieved subjectively and in actuality, in all human life and in mutual human relations and finally also in the consummation of all things: God all in all, a new heaven and a new earth. The difficulty of this answer is that it does not become clear why this is only so in Christ and not already in Israel. Moreover, does not the Old Testament in particular teach us that people only speak about liberation and redemption specifically on the basis of their personal need for redemption? Is not prayer, the cry of distress before God's face, more honest and original than any song about the exodus, experienced as God's great act of liberation? Even the etymology of words like redemption and liberation make it clear that this is primarily a matter of personal liberation and redemption, of suffering people, of women made widows (the institution of the *go'el* or 'redeemer'), exploited slaves, innocents who die prematurely. Of course there is also mention of the liberation of Israel, of the people of Israel, and so on. But like 'corporate personality', that is not the abstract idea of a nation (as we might talk of an independent Zimbabwe or Nicaragua); 'Israel' denotes the specific people, the generations, the tribes, the families in villages and cities. That is the way in which Jesus also talks about the liberation of humanity. He goes through cities and looks for people with their personal need for salvation. And if all kinds of supra-personal and inter-personal issues come up here – as we are constantly beginning to see more clearly from our knowledge of human behaviour and our insight into social structures – this fact should not mislead us into beginning to interpret 'redemption' in ideological terms by objectifying it as an event apart from those who cry for redemption and liberation. The liturgical 'through Jesus Christ our Lord' and the paraliturgical 'for Jesus' sake' with which we end prayers has thus been an objective confession down the ages of the need for subjective redemption and hope for a concrete redeemer, helper or liberator.

Contemporary interpretations of Jesus' death

The fact that there are many models for redemption and many interpretations of Jesus' death in the New Testament and the history of theology does not excuse us from the task of developing contemporary interpretations and models. We have to, if only for our preaching and pastoral work, and also for mission and for 'giving account of the hope that is in us'.

I can see three types of interpretative models in contemporary theology.

1. Jesus' death: representative suffering – one for us all

Some theologians, dissatisfied with Anselm's doctrine of reconciliation, in which Jesus' suffering for us and for our sins is seen as satisfaction to God in place of us – and thus as vicariously substituting for something which we human beings could never have achieved – have tried to use the concept of representation and to adapt this to the doctrine of redemption. They prefer to take up Rom.5 (the Adam-Christ typology) rather than Rom.3 (Jesus' death as reconciliation). Elements from the doctrine of incarnation in the early church and especially in Irenaeus play a part here, as do ideas from Teilhard de Chardin and Karl Rahner, for whom Jesus is the supreme fulfilment of human possibilities and as such is the firstborn of a new generation of children of God. Here Jesus represents human beings to God without replacing people around him and after him. And he represents God to men, by achieving God's will – thus he is without sin – though he does not replace God: there remains the interplay of the personal relationship between God and man in him. Precisely by being firstborn from the dead by virtue of his resurrection, Jesus redeems people from the hopelessness of sin which leads to death. The one who stands for God's cause and represents God to humanity is rehabilitated by God though he is cursed by men, so that subsequently he can also represent human beings to God and be their agent: he speaks for us best because he has been able to serve God's cause to the point of martyrdom. Other martyrs will follow in his footsteps, who have served God's kingdom 'in him' and sealed the new covenant with their blood, thus standing as witnesses before God's throne, concerned with the fate of those who come after them.

In her book *Christ the Representative*, Dorothee Sölle[12] has developed these ideas further (although – and this is somewhat confusing) from the perspective of a post-theistic theology: the danger then is that Jesus takes the place of God in the actual experience of faith. Karl Rahner,[13] Joseph Ratzinger[14] and Alois Grillmeier[15] use these ideas as a basis. Ratzinger says: 'In Christ he (God) wanted to become the Omega – the last letter – of the alphabet of creation.'[16] We also find this thought in W. Kasper (*Jesus the Christ*), as in H. Küng (*On Being a Christian*) and W. Pannenberg

(*Jesus – God and Man*). Its advantage is that the death of Jesus is not isolated from his life 'for the kingdom of God' and that christology (who is he?) and soteriology (what did he want?) are closely connected. Jesus' pre-existence and his pro-existence (solidarity with humanity) have an organic connection. In this kind of soteriology it seems possible, above all, to arrive at a consensus with the Orthodox traditions.

The drawback is that the tragedy of the cross, the culmination of human criminality which is constantly repeated in the history of the martyrs, is somewhat played down. It is difficult enough to see death as a human fulfilment, which is what Heidegger tried to do, and which Rahner in particular further develops as a theme. It is even more difficult to transcend through philosophy the fate of the executed Jesus and the whole history of human suffering. The saying about the grain of wheat which falls into the ground and dies in order to bring forth an abundant crop is first an announcement of Jesus' death and only after that of life.

2. Jesus' death: God's solidarity with suffering humanity

More or less in reaction to rather too superficial a theory of the 'firstborn' and to some degree in protest against an image of God which by definition makes God emotionless and unchangeable because from his side he cannot enter into any real relation with creation (as Scholastic theology supposed), Jürgen Moltmann, particularly in his book *The Crucified God* (1972),[17] has described the suffering and execution of Jesus as suffering which God himself overcomes in an 'active passion' of Jesus which at the same time signifies a divine abandonment within the Trinity.

On the one hand Moltmann paints a realistic picture of the tragedy of Jesus: he is condemned and executed in the name of the law and in God's name as a common political troublemaker and heretical blasphemer. He died a bitter death, abandoned by God. Rejection by men (Mark 8.31) and abandonment by God (Mark 15.34) combine to make up Jesus' suffering for God: this is the cup which he hopes and prays to escape, but which he nevertheless drinks in the 'darkness of God' (Buber) and in judgment (it is still the cup of God's wrath). So Christ is not the supremely perfect man who offers his life to God in utmost faith but the poorest of all the doomed of the earth. This affects not only his 'human nature' but at the same time his divine personhood (cf. Heb.5.7f.). Far from God, without God, he has tasted death for all of us (Heb.2.9). He becomes a curse for us (Gal.3.13).

From this point Moltmann can develop further both his political theology and his doctrine of the Trinity.[18] God becomes himself in the history of his salvation, in the history of the kingdom of God. But that does not come about without suffering. Only in suffering is the true human need for redemption revealed. God reveals himself in those who suffer, the poor, those without rights. Saving history is quite specifically the history of God's love for those who suffer, which does not will the suffering that overcame even him and seeks to challenge it in a history of liberation.

We cannot say that Moltmann's view takes the fate of Jesus too lightly or that by speaking of God's suffering he describes God too much in human terms. Moreover, this soteriology bears fruit in a real liberation theology, so that there is a response to the real need for the redemption of present-day men and women in slums and prisons all over the world. The interest of the World Council of Churches in Moltmann's theology which is evident, for example, in texts from the Nairobi Assembly, is a sure indication of its contemporary significance.

But questions do arise. The most important is whether the experience of being abandoned by God on Golgotha does not go directly against the whole of Jesus' attitude to life: his life in relation to Abba, his father, that so permeates his ministry, above all to the outcast. And is the fate of Jesus on the cross so unique – in comparison to other prophets and witnesses who are and will be tortured and killed – because he was crucified as the Son? Is it acceptable to say that God himself suffers and dies in Jesus? And above all, how can God, who hates suffering and wants to remove it from the world, choose this means of execution for his Son? This is an age-old question which was also raised against the classical doctrine of redemption.

Moreover, Dorothee Sölle accuses Moltmann of having a sadistic concept of God. Must one attribute to God what in the end can be more than adequately explained from the history of human injustice: that the righteous are always crucified, as Plato said four hundred years before Christ? Does Moltmann's view not remain all too much within the framework of a theodicy? We cannot explain the crucifixion of the righteous one, so we look for the justification for the crucifixion in a transcendent purpose of God. Formally speaking, it does not make much difference whether this purpose is then expressed in terms of the wrath of God or of his share in suffering. In both cases, it seems to me, Jesus' humanity and his obedience to the death are not taken seriously enough. Moltmann's soteriology is the legacy of part of the Reformation – especially that of Luther – which all too quickly declares the work of Jesus to be the *opus Dei*. His paradigm seems especially easy to accept within the ecumenical movement, although elements of it can clearly be used by liberation theologians like Jon Sobrino and some Asian theology (Kitamori) is also sympathetic to the same point.

3. Jesus' death: martyrdom for God's good cause

The interpretations I have mentioned so far seek to explain the execution of Jesus in supra-historical, metaphysical or ontological terms. There is an approach which seeks to take its historical significance more seriously as a starting point, in accord with our new 'historical access to Jesus of Nazareth' (Schillebeeckx). In fact christology and soteriology are connected very closely indeed.

Schillebeeckx must be mentioned first of all here, though he can refer to a large number of exegetical positions (most of which are not purely exegetical) and though other elements, especially from the first interpretation, can be found in his work. In his *Jesus*,[19] Schillebeeckx establishes that the earliest level in the New Testament interpretation of Jesus' death by the disciples sees him as the eschatological prophet, who is tortured and executed on the charge of being a false prophet. However, Jesus is the true emissary, the true agent of God's cause, the kingdom of God which is concerned for humanity (cf. Acts 7.51-53). This explains Paul's remarks about the law; Jesus, the teacher and prophet of the new law – the real law – is rejected by Israel on legal grounds. The other disciples are also faced with the choice of following him in his dealings with and interpretation of the law – with the authority (*exousia*) of God (Matt.7.29) – or of rejecting him and remaining true to 'Moses'. Jesus' martyrdom as prophet and innocent sufferer is the supreme moment of choice, for the disciples as well: is this suffering and death a sign of God's election (because the pious and righteous have to suffer) or is it rejection and curse? Here Jesus' death is not heroic, nor is there mention of any metaphysical significance to it. The early church came to terms with Jesus' death through prayer and meditation, seeing it as a prophetic sign for the sake of their own perseverance in the 'way' of God.

Of course it is not just his death that makes Jesus 'the reject'. Even during his ministry he and his disciples faced rejection and repudiation. But Jesus' unconditional trust which risked death emerges precisely in that fact: 'Whoever shall lose his life shall save it' (Mark 8.35). Jesus was 'forced by circumstances to give a place to approaching death in his radical confidence in God'.[20] 'Jesus felt his death to be (in some way or other) part and parcel of the salvation-offered-by-God, as a historical consequence of his caring and loving service of and solidarity with people',[21] which becomes tangible in his earthly table-fellowship with sinners and the outcast and in his farewell meal with his disciples, a communion which is stronger than death (as witness its continuation after Passover). Thus Jesus himself understood his death as supreme service to God's cause as the cause of humanity.[22]

It is a historical and theological misunderstanding to suppose that soteriology needs only to begin at Jesus' death or that the offer of God's salvation is shifted after the incarnation. Over against this Schillebeeckx asserts that salvation, i.e. the rule of God, is realized through Jesus and during his life and that this is an event which happens in and among men and women, namely as a relationship with God that is not bound up with the law. Reconciliation with God – outside the law – as outlined by Paul in his soteriology – is not a consequence of a sacrificial death of Jesus, however that might be explained. Rather, Jesus' death itself is the consequence of the reconciliation with God proclaimed and experienced by Jesus, which can only be based on confidence in the righteousness of God who allows men to have their due. We are not called by the New Testament to believe in the saving significance of Jesus' death as an execution but in the saving significance of Jesus life, which, despite curse and execution, is consummated in obedience till death and therefore means salvation from God.

We find comparable interpretations in the Latin-American liberation theologians.[23] There, too, we find great emphasis on the reality of the salvation brought about by Jesus even during his historical ministry: Luke 4.18-22 becomes the key text of soteriology, along with Matt.25.31-45. The preaching of the kingdom of God and the mission in the service of this kingdom replace the classic doctrine of reconciliation (although with Sobrino we find a good deal of sympathy for Moltmann, to whom Miguez Bonino on the other hand is strongly opposed).

Raymund Schwager's view is a very specific form of this third type of interpretation of the death of Jesus as a martyr death for God's good cause.[24] Using the theory of the French literary critic René Girard[25] as a basis, he sees Jesus' death as the culmination of the violent and homicidal element in the human heart and in human history. According to Girard, this emerges from rivalry: one person seeks the life of another because the other nullifies his will, stands in the way of his own desire for fulfilment. At the same time that means that power and violence are glorified – only success and conquest count. Action of this kind always produces victims. The weakest become the scapegoats; they suffer as a result of rivalry between the strong: one must die for all. This is the mechanism of the ritual of sacrifice in primitive religions. At the same time it is the drama of human history. However, as long as there are such representative sacrificial rituals, peace can prevail in a group or society. Now anyone who, like Schwager, reads the Old and New Testaments in terms of the themes of violence, rivalry, the scapegoat mechanism and peace, reconciliation, the gathering together of the scattered and dispersed, has at least hit on a very important aspect of the present need for redemption. The event of revelation itself is identical with the overcoming of violence in humanity by God himself (cf. the many prophetic texts about the re-gathering of Israel, which the New Testament *ecclesia* also takes up).

Rituals like that of the scapegoat in Leviticus or other sacrificial rituals do not ultimately bring peace. That is only achieved through the real conquest of rivalry in consistent service and surrender, which brings about the conversion of hearts. This renunciation of violence already begins with Abraham (Gen.13.5-13) and is provided with permanent models for Israel by Jonathan's renunciation of the throne (I Sam.23.16) and Solomon's judgment on the two women who argue over their child (I Kings 3.16-28); it is a central feature above all in the prophets and especially in Deutero-Isaiah (the Servant of Yahweh cycle). The starting point for a re-reading of the New Testament is Mark 12.10, the parable of the wicked husbandmen, which ends with a quotation from Ps.118 about the stone rejected by the builders that becomes the headstone of the corner (Mark 12.12 par.), which also appears in Peter's preaching (Acts 4.9-12; I Peter 2.4-8). Whether people reject Jesus or believe in him – and a choice must be made – depends on reactions to Jesus' message and praxis of the kingdom of God, namely on whether or not the way of God for Israel, the way of God's *ecclesia*, can be seen in his message and ministry of reconciliation, which from then on sets up dividing lines and leads to disputes. There is much to show that real redemption and liberation coincide with a 'renunciation of power': the Sermon on the Mount, Jesus' table-fellowship and requirement not to judge, not to take vengeance but to forgive and to create new opportunities, the demand for discipleship which he puts to his disciples (no rivalry, no higher desire than the will of God, the kingdom of God, which is not a hierarchy, Matt.23.8).

Once again the scapegoat mechanism crops up; it is better for him to die for the people. The whole narrative structure of the Gospels is built on that. The most important task for Paul and the Jewish-Christian community, as they grow together with Gentile communities, is to achieve clarity over this.

The deepest cause of Jesus' death, however, is his claim to speak in the name of God precisely in this summons to reconciliation and the renunciation of rivalry, indeed to be the Son of God, God's own ambassador, who does the will of the Father and is one with him.

The redemption that we have in Christ is liberation from the spiral of power and authority, from the inbuilt scapegoat mechanism. That is evident from Luke 1.5 (the Magnificat) and from Luke 22.25, the immediate sequel to the pericope about the eucharist, where Jesus once again sums up his teaching by reminding the disciples of the need to avoid rivalry.

Thus in this view soteriology itself becomes the ecumene; the church; Christian brotherhood and unity; boundless, non-violent love and service, which must relate to table-fellowship with Jesus (cf. I Cor.10-11).

Towards an ecumenical soteriology?

The closing sentence of the previous paragraph does not come either from Raymond Schwager or from René Girard, but leads into the last question we have to discuss. Can the consensus of which I have been speaking, which rests on better listening to one another's traditions and better reading of the Bible and the theological tradition together, also be realized in the life of the church? Must not the peace which Jesus himself brought to Jews and Gentiles, the dividing wall between whom is broken down (Eph.2), be matched by peace in his *ekklesia* – God's assembly for peace, specifically around and in the cause of the meaning of the saving work of Christ, so that 'through Christ our Lord' is in fact the hymn of praise for the lamb of God in which all living creatures join?

My view is that the various contemporary interpretations of the death of Jesus which I summarized in the previous section are not exclusive. The cosmic role of Jesus as the firstborn, the boundless compassion of God in the Son as the one who is abandoned and outcast, the martyr death of Jesus in the service of God's good cause, peace, liberation, the end of death, the end of hatred – all this is witnessed to in the riches of scripture and tradition and safeguarded in the liturgy of the church.

In East and West, North and South, however, there are different priorities for salvation as a result of different cultural and economic and political circumstances: nihilism and unbridled rivalry, threats to life, exploitation, oppression, hostility to God. Within the one ecumenical movement these contexts may lead to the choice of the paradigms for salvation. There is no atemporal, metaphysical concept of or recipe for salvation, except the love of God which transcends all concepts and from which nothing and no one can part us.

However, in the world-wide ecumenical context, church and theology, poets and composers, activists and church leaders are faced with a number of requests which I would like to present in the form of theses. It should not be hard to see the connection with what I have been saying.

1. Belief in the saving action of God in Jesus Christ does not simply mean the acceptance – however deep the conviction – of the fact that God has acted for our salvation in Jesus Christ. It essentially implies *metanoia*, which is the hallmark of *katallage*. Without human reconciliation and partnership, any confession of God's reconciliation and partnership becomes an abstract ideology.

2. Salvation from God's side, achieved for us in Jesus Christ, is not just promise or imputation, but God's direct action towards people, experienced sacramentally in the sphere of the church, 'the universal sacrament of salvation' (Vatican II), expressing itself in active discipleship of Jesus.

3. Here it is deistic (that it to say it rules out God as a present and active God) to suppose that in principle God has brought about salvation for us in Christ without our being able to see it in any form, just as it is deistic to suppose that God still has definite salvation 'in store' for us. Both a conception of salvation which falls back on the memory of what has happened and a view which directs all its attention to the expectation of God's creating a state of salvation in the eschaton are in danger of forgetting the actual love of God for people in need as revealed in the risen and crucified one, Jesus Christ. These two dangers are not completely avoided in some versions of the message of the kingdom of God which are current in contemporary theology. The connection between eschatology and the Christian doctrine of redemption must be the subject of more ecumenical theological discussion.

4. Every age has its specific need of redemption. For our time this is the anxious concern for peace and an end to the spiral of violence. Re-reading the Old and New Testaments in the perspective of this

quest for peace and the overcoming of all war and violence is something that not only the Christian churches but also the children of Israel desperately need. Only when that has happened will there also be real dialogue between the church and Israel about the nature of God's messianic action and the role of his servant Jesus in it.

5. Moreover, reconciliation in Christ implies that the 'vicious circle of revenge' (Moltmann) should also be broken through at an inter-personal level, just as God himself did not and will not take vengeance for the death of Jesus. No one is ever completely written off by God, and no one can ever be finally banned from the circle of salvation. This must have consequences for the dealings of Christians with one another in human relationships and marriage ('God has called us to peace', I Cor.7.15), in political parties and associations, between nations and races, among churches and between churches and their dissidents.

6. Any form of belief in election – however well meant, as an indication of God's freedom and the seriousness of the vocation of humanity – must be disputed on the basis of reconciliation in Christ. This has consequences for our thinking which go beyond the limits of the community and consequences for dialogue between the religions. Here the churches of the West have to learn from those of the East, where a sense of God's compassion and *economia* provides a necessary correction to any mistaken limitations to God's offer of grace.

7. Just as who Jesus was can only be confessed by saying who he is – the one who lives at God's right hand, the Lord in our midst – so too what he wanted can only be confessed in what he brings about: *ekklesia, koinonia*. Belief in salvation comes about only in believing prayer and believing service – by doing what he has done (John 13). Where this longing is quenched and one person leaves another in the lurch; where someone can no longer lament his distress to God from the heart; where there are no longer complaints to God about so much suffering among so many; where people do not cry out in distress and accuse God, the church becomes a discussion group, and liturgy mere convention. Soteriology itself becomes a Gnostic ideology and Jesus, our Lord, is buried in the pantheon of demiurges.

8. Finally, past discussions between the churches of the West about grace and merit, grace and works, satisfaction and vicarious sacrifices, the unique sacrifice of Christ and its representation, repetition or extension, as documented in the Roman Catechism and the Heidelberg Catechism, can be definitively written off as

dead ends in the history of theology. The ecumenical dialogue over God's salvation in Jesus the Christ must be understood in the light of the content and the experience of the liturgical and doxological 'through Jesus Christ our Lord'.

5

'Hear, O Israel...': The Function of the Church's Confession

The people of God, dispersed over six continents, divided into thousands of denominations, living in a broken world, are nevertheless called to unity, for the sake of God's grace which is all-embracing; for the sake of Jesus' gift of his life which is unique and permanent; and for the sake of the Spirit, which seeks to bring all to wholeness. This feeling of being called to unity and togetherness did not just come about in the twentieth-century ecumenical movement; for years there has been a constant search for the essential characteristics and instruments in the unity of the church.[1] I would like to call such marks the structures of Christian communion (*koinonia, communio*). Within the ecumenical movement there is constant concern about four such structures:

1. The confession of the same apostolic faith according to the scriptures;
2. Participation in the same sacraments of baptism and the eucharist;
3. A common Christian life-style or discipline;
4. Mutual recognition of ministerial oversight (*episcope*).

Unity both within the church and between the churches is determined and served by these structures. They also determine the individual's church membership in the theological sense of *membrum ecclesiae*: those who reject those structures put themselves outside the community. All these points belong together like the pillars of a bridge: no true confession is conceivable without conduct to match; there are no true sacraments without true ministry, trust in the apostolic heritage and the maintenance of Christian discipline in turn depend on sacramental praxis and ministerial oversight.

When we consider the structures of the church community – and that is what the following chapters are about – we are not primarily concerned with forms and institutions – we shall see that there is a large degree of pluralism in them – but with the content and functions of the church's confession, the church's sacraments, the church's discipline and the church's ministry. This seems to me of fundamental importance for an ecumenical view of the church.

Over past decades consensus and agreement has been growing on all these four points. Great advances have been made, especially over the sacramental structure of the Christian *koinonia* (baptism, eucharist) and its episcopal structure (the ministry interpreted as *episcope* in very different forms). These have been expressed through a number of bilateral and multilateral agreed texts.[2] In addition, a common Christian ethic or discipline is maturing, relating both to questions of world justice and to the quality of individual life in relationship to others.[3] However, all this calls for a fundamental consideration of the problem of a common confession, on which recently an explicit beginning has been made.

Perhaps the reason why confession and discipline has so far received less attention in ecumenical reflection than the questions of ministry and the sacraments is that consciously or unconsciously people felt they could begin from a common 'deposit of faith': the scriptures, the confessions of the early church, the statements of the great councils of the first four centuries.[4] There is evidence of this, for example, in the famous *Lambeth Quadrilateral* of 1888, four principles or characteristics of the visible and organic unity of the churches, which were formulated by the Anglican Communion, and for a long time were regarded by many people as the corner-stone and starting point of the ecumenical movement. As long as churches were prepared – consciously or unconsciously – to go back to the common heritage of the first four centuries, the so-called undivided church, by their own acknowledgment they were not fundamentally divided in matters of faith and ethics, they were not at loggerheads.

In the meantime, as a result of all kinds of developments in church and theology – not least those which I described in chapters 1-4 – many questions have arisen over this common heritage which was once so strong. First of all there is the discovery of the historical development of this heritage and the questions of exposition or interpretation which that raises.[5] All formulations of belief, even the most sacred and solemn of them, are the product of historical circumstances, and as a result of the shift in language over the ages they have to be constantly retranslated and revised, in an ongoing hermeneutical process. The simple recitation of the old words and the simple reiteration of the old code of behaviour no longer guarantees that the original intentions of these expressions of belief are being faithfully observed. Thus contemporary confession and action call for exposition, interpretation and sometimes other formulas, images and codes of behaviour. We need action and confession in a living context.

A second discovery relates to the pluriformity of the confession of the early church. The scriptures give us a multicoloured patchwork of homologies, as these grew up in the first generations. The tradition of the first four centuries is a process of development in which local churches exchanged their formulas and codes of behaviour with one another. Only gradually did a more or less uniform orthodoxy and orthopraxis come into being, and this gradual harmonization was never aimed at producing ultimately unchangeable formulas. The harmonization (*symphonia*) was directed at mutual recognition and the possiblity of common praise of God. Far less was this harmonization meant to be a convenient legal criterion, by which the true faith could be measured. Swearing weighty oaths in confessional formulations is quite a late development within the church, and does not accord with the gospel. All this really points to the conclusion that the fixation of a contemporary confession in a number of normative confessional formulas has often hindered the church in presenting the gospel to the people of the day, though this fixation has never been a complete one.

As a result, many young churches and many of the younger members in the old churches of the West (W.Bühlmann groups them together as the 'third church'[6]) argue that new confessions and new ethical codes must be developed for our time. New creeds have therefore been composed in a number of places and on a number of occasions.[7] Typically these are contextual confessions, addressed to a contemporary situation, and neither meant for eternity, nor claiming to be comprehensive (though confessions of faith have never been that). Such new attempts to articulate the faith often reflect the situation of young churches experiencing missionary growth, in search of a close and wide church fellowship. In that case this quest for new creeds is a sign of their desire for Catholicity – in context.

In addition, over recent decades a number of confessional explanations and declarations have been produced by leading church authorities: in particular situations churches saw and still see themselves compelled to make a pronouncement *in statu confessionis* on a contemporary aspect of faith and action. The model which is cited most often here is the Barmen Declaration (1934), in which the

Confessing Church spoke out against the collaboration of church and state in the time of Nazism in Germany. However, many other examples could be added from the years after the Second World War. Especially in the Third World, synods and assemblies of bishops have tried to take up positions in declarations on issues in society and politics which call for them. It is a typical Western notion, based on the idea of the *Corpus Christianum*, that the *status confessionis* arises only rarely. Church leaders in Korea, Zaire, southern Africa and Latin America, as also in countries in the Eastern bloc, know better (although the last are usually too muzzled to be allowed to speak). However, examples of credal statements can also be found in the churches of Western Europe and in North America: the declaration 'Our Hope' by the German synod of bishops (Wurzburg 1975), the document *Christian Believing* from the Church of England, the confession of faith by the French national assembly of bishops, the declaration of the Dutch Reformed Church on nuclear weapons, the declaration by the North American bishops on racism, and so on. Finally, a number of theologians have translated their theological reflections and systematic theologies into summary new confessions of faith (Pannenberg, Schillebeeckx and Schoonenberg, etc.).

In the midst of this multiplicity of personal and collective reformulations of 'the kernel of belief' there is also the question of an 'ecumenical confession of faith',[8] a confession of faith with practical and ethical implications which all the divided churches could accept and hand on until the time when a universal council could restore unity to as many Christian churches as possible. Although such a council still seems to be a long way away, we should make what start we can towards a confession of this kind.

The World Council of Churches has recently set up and carried out some interesting projects in this direction. The first, 'Giving Account of the Hope That Is Within Us', set up in Louvain in 1971 and completed in Bangalore in 1978,[9] was not aimed directly at producing a confession of faith but at formulating a common Christian account of our hope. To this end, stock was taken of all possible testimonies of hope and faith from all over the world, some written specially for this occasion, by groups differing widely in nature and composition.

The second is the study project 'Common Witness', set up by the Joint Working Group of the World Council of Churches and the Roman Catholic church.[10] This project is aimed at taking stock of forms of common witness which could serve as models for the churches, to be used in the church's contemporary mission and evangelization. Pastoral missions would then have to be developed from the theological consensus and the experience of the Christian communities.

Since 1978, carrying forward both studies, the Faith and Order Movement – in collaboration with the Joint Working Group – has set up a new study theme, 'Towards the Common Expression of the Apostolic Faith Today'.[11]

Whence do these enterprises derive? Why strive for a common confession? And what is the relationship between early confessions – the creeds of the early church – and contemporary confessions?

Homology, pedagogy, apology: the functions of the church's creeds

'Hear, O Israel. The Lord our God is one Lord; and you shall love the Lord your God with all your heart, and with all your soul, and with all your might. And these words which I command you this day shall be upon your heart; and you shall teach them diligently to your children, and shall talk of them when you sit in your house, and when you walk by the way, and when you lie down, and when you rise. And you shall bind them as a sign upon your hand, and they shall be as frontlets between your eyes. And you shall write them on the doorposts of your house and on your gates' (Deut.6.4-9).

Nowhere is there a clearer definition of the real function of the confession in the Jewish-Christian tradition than in this text from Deuteronomy, referred to by its opening word in Hebrew as the Shema.

Confessing is first of all an attitude of life directed to God, a life that observes God's guidelines and sees the love of God embodied in that life in accordance with the guidelines of God, a life bound hand and foot, soul and body, heart and head to the commandments, i.e. to the God-given criteria for living. These are to apply not only at home but also in the city, not only in private life but also in society, at home and on journeys, from generation to generation, from parents to children.

This tradition of experience which relates to thought and action is the echo of an oral and written tradition – the scriptures – in turn the resonance of a tradition of experience. What is written – set down on parchment, engraved in stone, multiplied in books, recorded on tape – serves as a reminder, as a guideline for thought and action and as instructions for children, young people, disciples.

The sequel to the text I have just quoted – 'You shall serve no other gods' – shows that it also serves to protect belief in the face of other deviant religions.

We find the same confessional functions in many of the psalms - remaining faithful to God in the midst of despair, injustice, unbelief, for the sake of 'righteousness'. The New Testament texts which are a summons to 'confess' are just the same. When Jesus asks people to confess him he calls on them to follow him, to join him in his way, not to deny him as the anointed one, the messenger, the one sent by God, who deserves to be listened to and obeyed: 'Lord, to whom else should we go – you have the words of eternal life' (John 6.68; cf. Mark 8.34-38).

The earliest confessions in the New Testament[12] (e.g. I Thess.1.10; I Cor.15.3; Rom.1.4; 10.9f.; I Cor.8.6; Acts 2.36; Rom.4.25; Gal.4.4; I Tim.3.16; Phil.2.6-11) do not require assent to formulas, expressions or dogmas about God or Jesus, but call for 'assent' to God's acts: that God has raised this crucified and excommunicated one, that he is sitting at the right hand of God and that he delivers us from the wrath to come.

Nowhere has a formula to be sworn – not even in I John 4.1-4, which is concerned with the difference between truth and falsehood; different formulas can say the same thing, as is clear from the multiplicity of them. What we find are always doxological homologies,[13] that is, common, public thanksgivings to God for his saving actions (e.g. Matt.10.32; Luke 12.8; Phil.2.11; Rom.10.9f.; II Cor.9.13; I John 2.23; 4.2,3,15; II John 7; John 9.22; 12.42; Heb.13.15). *Homologein*[14] is a technical term for such public speaking and thanksgiving aloud. It involves *marturia* – risky witnessing. Jesus himself is the first martyr and confessor: according to I Tim.6.12f. he bears witness before Pilate with a magnificent homology (cf. Luke 21.13; Matt.10.18; Mark 13.19).

Thus confession as lived-out faith and communal assent to the acts of God precedes the formulated confession and is its first function. The church is constantly aware of this because the old credal texts are incorporated into the praise of the liturgy and rightly also use the vocabulary of hymns. Moreover, they are a part of the scripture-readings which will eventually become 'the New Testament' of which they are later regarded as a summary.

However, the confession also has a second function. If we are to accord with God's saving acts, we cannot avoid having to 'actualize' this salvation in our situation. Therefore the tradition of hearing is closely matched by a tradition of teaching: the story of God's action with Jesus becomes present through recollection and tradition. We learn to believe by being taught by others (*kataggelein* = report, as e.g. I Cor.11.26), but not without involvement; they call us to conversion (*parakalein* = appeal, e.g. Phil.2.1; II Cor.8.4). This leads to *didache*[15] as the instrument of *metanoia*: 'learning' as the pedagogy of faith. That is the pedagogical function of the confession. To begin with, this *didache* still seems to be associated with the way in which those who join the *ekklesia* of God from Judaism and the Gentile world 'learn to believe'. It is therefore connected with baptism and the eucharist, as the signs of entry into the new messianic covenant community of the people of God.

The earliest symbols or creeds that we have are baptismal creeds: that of the church of Rome (which developed into our Apostles' Creed, the twelve articles of the apostles) and that of Jerusalem (which was the basis from which the so-called Nicene Creed emerged in Nicaea in 325 and Constantinople in 381, the creed which was accepted at the Council of Chalcedon as the universal creed for the church of East and West).

At present the Apostles' Creed functions in the church of the West mostly at baptism, and the Nicene Creed in the celebration of the eucharist, but that is a later development. Not until the sixth century was the Nicene Creed taken into the liturgy of the Eastern churches and this custom came to the rest of Europe through Spain and Ireland. The Carolingians encouraged the usage in court liturgy, especially in Aachen. It was only in 1014 that Pope Benedict VIII introduced the Nicene Creed into the Latin liturgy, at the request of the emperor Henry II, initially only on feast days. In the East, too, the practice was not the rule always and everywhere.[16]

In the West the Apostles' Creed became the real *regula fidei* for catechesis and the liturgy: a summary of the confession as a guideline for true faith with an explicit 'pedagogical function': the articles of faith contained in it are literally the joints, the hinges of faith, and in the Middle Ages the theological tractates and catechetical methods were arranged on the basis of the creed. The developed catechisms of the Reformation and the Counter-Reformation follow the pattern of the Apostles' Creed. For this reason, so that believers could experience catechetics and liturgy as a unity, Calvin and Zwingli encouraged the use of the Apostles' Creed as the creed for the Sunday liturgy. But in order to see its pedagogical function we do well to continue to remember the original character of these creeds of the church as baptismal symbols.

However, they are not the only guidelines or forms of expression for the homology or the pedagogy of the church. Scripture, the Old and New Testaments, remains the encyclopaedic source with all-embracing authority. It continually forms the basic material for confessions. A number of other valuable formulations have the same function: prayers like the Lord's Prayer, canticles like the *Te Deum*, the eucharist prayers of thanksgiving, the key sacramental texts and gestures, the feasts of the liturgical year with their fixed hymns and readings. Over the course of centuries catechisms also grew up around the lectionaries (e.g. from sixth-century Rome we have the liturgical catechisms for Lent) or around liturgical customs (above all in the Middle Ages: Amalarius of Metz) and in the East around the icons. Along with other instruments, the 'symbola' are nevertheless normative texts which over the ages have been the church's watchword and distinguishing password and have preserved the 'most important truths'.

Sometimes the creeds have also had an apologetic function, as a test of heresies and a hallmark of orthodoxy, when questions had arisen over particular formulations and conceptions of faith. Heretics who wanted to return to the community of faith had to accept the creeds again solemnly and under oath, sometimes with formulations in which they foreswore their heresy. One example of this is the confession of faith of Reccared, king of the Eastern Goths, made on the conversion of his people from Arianism in Spain about 600. A number of the later confessions from the time of the Reformation also had a similar apologetic function, but now over against the Church of Rome. And in our days there are contemporary texts which witness against particular ideologies that challenge Christian convictions, like Nazism, rejected in the Barmen Confession of 1934, or 'Mobutism', formally abjured in Zaire in 1975 with a reference to the most important Christian articles of faith.

Only in the situation of the church in our time will the need for a response of faith in a contemporary confession again begin to be felt more strongly. Hence in recent years a number of new creeds have come into being, in order to say publicly again in the face of all kinds of ideologies who Jesus Christ is for us, why we believe in God and respond to him, and why we bind ourselves to the church. The transmission of faith from one generation to another is no longer something we can take for granted, at least in the churches of the West. And where it proves possible, we are concerned to overcome the divisions of the church in a new unanimity. So apology, pedagogy and homology are extremely topical functions of the contemporary confession of the church, just as they were in the early Christian confessions.

A common creed?

However, the struggle to arrive at a common contemporary confession is not an easy one. A great variety of confessions has come into being, and formulations of belief have come to be evaluated in very different ways. Within the ecumenical movement the common acceptance of the authority of scripture is a priority, but the precise content of scripture and confession is still a matter of discussion. The function of formulated dogma also tends to vary from church to church, as witness the large number of people who can accept only parts of the official confessional formulations. In many contexts this detachment from the language and conceptuality of the classical creeds of the church is proving to be alienating. Can people of God in India, Africa or Latin America be compelled to accept and to learn the language and the concepts of Byzantium in the fourth and fifth centuries or of Geneva and Augsburg in the sixteenth? And why is a common credal text so important, at the stage when we are beginning to understand the plurality of expressions of faith within the ecumenical movement as a gift of the Spirit of God? The discussion seems to be going in three rather different directions.

The first and oldest approach[17] seeks a return to and a revaluation of the creeds of the ancient church. Most churches have accepted these creeds, especially that of Nicaea; the Council of Chalcedon solemnly declared that from then on this creed was to be held by all the church; over the centuries it has proved to be a good weapon against confusion and heresy; it has come to have a central place in the liturgical gatherings of many churches in East and West; the later confessional writings of the Reformation also begin with an acceptance of the creeds of the early church; it would be extremely difficult, given the theological pluralism within the divided churches of our day to arrive at any similar generally accepted text; and moreover that could only be established at a universal Council of all Christians, which for the moment is not envisaged. So, it is argued, the creed of Nicaea in its original form – without later additions like the so-called *Filioque*,[18] the clause which says that the Spirit proceeds from the Father and the Son, should again be accepted as the ecumenical creed *par excellence*. And we should try to agree as far as possible on the interpretation of this creed. In the long run it could then replace the basic formula of the World Council of Churches, which is a kind of mini-creed for all member churches.[19]

This standpoint is defended above all by the theologians of the Orthodox churches, but also by a large number of Western theologians from the Catholic, Anglican and Lutheran churches. In their view the creed of the ancient church, especially that of Nicaea, is part of the well-tried church tradition and at present is also an indispensable *regula fidei*. Acceptance of it is a condition for membership of the true church; the teaching authority of the church is based on the acceptance of this tradition. Moreover, when theologians stray from the creed of the early church they need to be corrected by the leaders of the church – bishops, synods or the pope.

A second group of theologians and church leaders thinks more in terms of a process by which the churches gradually accept one another's confessions and begin to recognize and value them as legitimate elements of the tradition – though they are sometimes rather one-sided and polemical and never exhaustive. The way to a common confession leads through exchange, accumulation and mutual consultation. Of course the creed of the early church also plays an essential part in this, but it was never meant to be exhaustive. In reality the formulation of new confessions has never stopped. It is a myth to suppose that the Nicene Creed could never be reformulated. For example, the confessional writings of the Reformation are meant to be a revision of the creeds of the early church in the light of the new situation. Especially in the Calvinist tradition there has always been a custom of testing one another's creeds. Formulas of concord were often composed on the reunion of churches after a conflict, in which the confessions of both parties were combined. That also happened within Lutheranism, where in fact confessions of faith from different periods have been combined to form a Book of Concord. In Holland the Reformed and Calvinist churches also combined confessions as the hallmark of their orthodoxy. Within ecumenical discussions in recent years attempts have been made, for example, to bring the Lutheran and Catholic churches closer together by recognizing the Augsburg Confession[20] as an authoritative ecumenical writing. Some people think that something of that kind should also be conceivable in respect of the Calvinist confessional writings.

The ecumenical movement needs to be the setting for this process of exchanging expressions of faith, old and new. In the long run it would then emerge which articles or key points should be universally accepted as normative. The result could then be established and subscribed to solemnly at an ecumenical council.

A third trend is formed by theologians from the young churches of the Third World and a number of theologians from the Western churches. For several reasons they would prefer to envisage a completely new and contemporary formulation of faith, an ecumenical creed to be achieved by laying it before a truly universal council of Christianity. That council must be held anyway, as a response to the needs of the world, to deal with the new schisms which threaten and to contribute towards making good the divisions between the churches. A contemporary and common confession must be one of the first points on the agenda of such a council. This point on the agenda must be prepared for by a search for a common contemporary expression of the Christian faith.

The first argument in favour of this position is the fact that belief relates to God, Jesus and the Spirit, not to formulas by which this faith is put into words: its advocates repeat the words of the Scholastic theologians, *fides non est ad enuntiabilia, sed ad rem*. That has become almost a basic rule of ecumenical discussion. In that case why cling on to formulations from the fourth century which have become completely incomprehensible for so many people? Terms like being, hypostasis, person, substance, omnipotence, body and soul are quite unusable in many cultures. Therefore other concepts are needed in every context in order to put into words the same truth about God.

The second argument concerns the actual content of the classical creeds and the relationship of this conceptual material to the pluriform confessions of the scriptures. The Apostles' Creed and the Nicene Creed are too limited in *two* respects: by their authority they force out the many other New Testament confessions which may express some aspects of salvation more clearly, e.g. Eph.1.1-23 on belief in God's creative spirit; and, secondly, a number of emphases in the New Testament preaching which are quite indispensable in the present situation of the church and the world are completely absent from the Nicene Creed: recollection of the actual ministry of Jesus and his message of the kingdom of God. Moreover, in these creeds of the early church hardly anything is to be found about the central significance of the church and the sacraments. If the creeds are to be a kind of summary and criterion (*regula fidei*) of the scriptures, they must not distort the perspective of the total content of scripture.

The creeds of the early church are quite inadequate to serve as an ecumenical creed not because of what is in them but because of what is not in them. Moreover, they are not in a position to respond to and go beyond the important controversies which arose in the West during the sixteenth century and afterwards over the relationship between God's grace and human free will. And above all, what was so important in the Shema, the unity of faith and action, is utterly neglected in these ancient creeds.

In fact all these reasons have led the churches in many parts of the world, individual theologians, and groups of believers, to try to make new confessions. Why cannot attempts be made within the ecumenical movement – for example in the framework of the World Council of Churches – following the confession of the early church, to arrive at a common confession on all the questions which did not appear in that classical confession because at that time they did not threaten faith or the unity of the church, but now do?[21]

Probably in this case a multiple strategy is the best solution. It would be good for the churches which recognize themselves, for example, in the Nicene Creed and want to express their confidence in it to do so more emphatically and draw the consequences for theology and catechesis. What the creeds of the early church sought to establish as the *regula fidei* remains important for all the people of God.

This is:

1. That God in himself and God who works in history are essentially the same, so that there are no demigods, demiurges and idols;

2. That Jesus, who was born of Mary and died under Pontius Pilate, shared our manhood in all things from cradle to grave, though this does not for a moment deny his origin from God or that in every feature of his existence he was constantly concerned to be God's right hand as the living Lord among his people;

3. That the Spirit of God sanctifies and inspires people, calls them together and heals them in newness of life as a community of saints, bound up with one another in space and time, led into all truth by the guidance of apostles and prophets;

4. That the people of God are also themselves called to be children of God, children at home with God, recreated to live with God beyond the limits of death.

However, all this can be implemented and realized only through the mutual 'communication of faith' between leaders and church members, within the separated churches and between them, in ongoing conversation with witnesses to faith down the centuries.

Therefore the Calvinist tradition of mutual recognition and exchange of confessional writings is also worth considering. It would be good if that could also be practised in liturgy and catechesis.

Finally, the formulation of a *new* common confession cannot be excluded, but on the contrary must be deliberately sought after. The basis of the World Council of Churches is a small beginning towards such an ecumenical creed. The fact of its composition shows that it is not impossible to arrive at contemporary common formulations on a world level, and striking examples can be found of current common confessions on both a national and a regional level. What was absent from the Nicene creed – the activity of Jesus, the message and life-style of the kingdom of God, the sacramental life of the church – is too important for the identity of 'people of God' to be omitted from our common confessions for the twenty-first century. Were we to omit these features we should not be giving an account of the hope that is in us, nor would we be doing justice to the confession of the apostolic faith 'according to the scriptures', which is what an ecumenical creed must express.

6

Baptism in the Name of Jesus

Believers who stand in the Jewish-Christian tradition say that human children are born in the image of God. That evidently applies to all human children, regardless of whether or not they belong to the Jewish Christian tradition. In that case why, in the midst of all these human children, decide on a special 'marking' for those who want to belong to the *qahal YHWH* or the *ekklesia tou Theou*, the 'people of God'?

In fact both the Jewish and the Christian tradition have a practice of 'marking' and 'incorporating' those who make up the people of God. For Jews it is the circumcision of boy children (or of men if they become Jews at a later stage and have not yet been circumcised); for Christians it is baptism with water. However, neither circumcision nor baptism of themselves bring about incorporation into the *ekklesia tou Theou*. Almost all the peoples of the ancient Near East were familiar with the custom of circumcision, as are many people down to the present day; and many cultures have all kinds of forms of inauguration and initiation, including baptism with water. Down to the present day we 'baptize' one another when we pass all kinds of milestones in our lives.

Thus we can argue solely from the fact of circumcision and baptism as pure signs of initiation that the religion of Jews and Christians clearly calls for some token or other of community, for a social 'brand' that is stamped on people of God. This is not, as in the classic slave trade, in order to brand on the mark of a cruel owner or to give people a number to identify them, as happens with cattle, but in order to give them a new identity, as people who belong to the free children of God, who want to spend their lives becoming what they are.

Therefore the content of the marking, whether by circumcision or by baptism, and the difference between the two, over which such a great conflict arose in New Testament times (see Acts 15; Paul's letters to the Romans and the Galatians) is not to be derived from the sign itself. The significance lies in the intention of the community of faith which imposes the sign. Simply by investigating the intentions with which baptism or circumcision is performed we can trace their significance and the various differences between Jewish and Christian initiation rites. And perhaps that might be one way of overcoming the reluctance of Western men and women to accept this kind of marking, which is evident in the decline in the practice of baptism.

As far as Christian baptism is concerned, there is a further specifically ecumenical problem: baptism seems to confirm the division of the churches from one another. That is not simply because there are differences over the time when baptism is performed – whether it is the baptism of infants, of children who are beginning to share in the life of the community, or of adults who can deliberately choose to become members of the community of Jesus – but also because we are beginning to attach denominational significance to the event of baptism: we talk of Catholic, Reformed, Orthodox baptism. Finally, Christians differ from one another over the meaning of baptism, the form it should take and the conditions that should go with it. Reflection on the question why we baptize people at all[1] is therefore an urgent necessity as part of a plea for the church. When we have looked at that question we may perhaps be able to draw some conclusions about ecumenical issues and the pastoral practice of baptism.

The baptism of Jesus and our baptism in Jesus' name[2]

The baptism of Christians goes back to Jesus himself. Not because he himself baptized; in the light of John 3.22; 4.2 that is extremely uncertain. Nor is it that Jesus commanded his disciples to baptize: with the exception of Matt.28.18-20; Mark 16.15-18, the different accounts of their mission which describe their future tasks do not have a command to baptize (cf. Mark 6.7-13; Matt.10.1,5-15; Luke 10.1-16). The so-called baptismal command in Matt. 28 and in the conclusion of Mark, which was written much later, does not connect this command with the historical ministry of Jesus and Luke 24.22-49, the parallel passage to Matt.28.18-20, does not mention baptism at all. Moreover the missionary charge as Luke formulates it in Acts 1.7f. does not give any 'command to baptize'. So it is not surprising that in I Cor.1.17 Paul can say: 'For Christ did not send me to baptize; he sent me to preach the gospel.'

However, the group of disciples began to baptize almost immediately. That is clear from Acts 2.38-41; 8.12-13,16,36-38; 9.18 (cf.22.16); 10.47; 16.15; 16.33; 18.8; 19.5. It is also clear from the missionary charge as formulated both by Matthew and by Mark 16.15-18 after him, and from John 3.5. Evidently people began to understand the practice of baptism which had grown up in connection with the mission and charge given by Jesus. That goes much deeper than a formal command of Jesus to perform a particular rite; it also protects the performance of this rite from ritualism.

Why did the church baptize right from the start? Not because Jesus wanted it so much, but because Jesus himself was baptized, as were the disciples (Acts 1.5), by the baptism of John, and in addition to that with baptism by the Holy Spirit. From the beginning, baptism has the character of an event of grace, a divine initiative in which people may allow themselves to be baptized. It is interesting to see how distinct the baptism of John is from the baptismal practices of surrounding cultures.[3] What marks out the baptism of John from the wide range of baptismal practices current in the ancient Near East of his day is that it was performed once for all and was associated with repentance: it was not just one more rite of purification, like for example that of Qumran, where frequent baptismal baths were the order of the day. On the eve of the great feasts the high priest of the Qumran community had to bathe as many as forty times. A number of baptismal basins have been discovered in the ruins of the Essene monastery in Qumran. They show how much the community of the pure which lived here made purity in all things, in accordance with Jewish models, the nucleus of their religious practices. Here baptism was essentially a matter of self-purification, a rite of purification, often repeated, which makes people pure and ready for the encounter with the Holy One, the one who is to come: 'Be ready, since the day of the Coming One may be dawning.' By contrast, John preached a baptism of repentance for the forgiveness of sins (Mark 1.4). His baptism is more in the prophetic tradition of repentance towards righteousness than in the levitical tradition of cultic purity. It is concerned with the renewal of life which is given as grace. The Synoptic Gospels apply the prophetic sayings Mal.1; Isa.40.3 to his appearance: he is the messenger of salvation, the one who prepares God's way. His message has a prophetic content; it is a call to a new life-style, to stand apart from any summons towards a righteousness of one's own: 'Do not say, We have Abraham for our father' (Luke 3.8). John does not just baptize the impure; he baptizes the pure as well. Jesus, the disciples in his footsteps, and then the church took up this prophetic tradition. They had themselves immersed in the bath of renewal and rebirth which leads to the way of God. The coming of God actually takes place in it; they are anointed with God's Spirit. The Synoptic Gospels regard the baptism of Jesus in the Jordan, which he allowed John to perform, as the beginning of his mission. It was the setting for the epiphany of the Son of God, the well-beloved servant, who is the one after God's heart (Mark 1.11 par.). This is the beginning of the messianic programme of salvation, as it is described in more detail, for example, in Luke 4.18f., taking up the words of Isa.61.1f.: 'The Spirit of the Lord is upon me, because he has anointed me to preach good news to the poor. He has sent me to proclaim release to the captives and recovering of sight to the blind, to set at liberty those who are oppressed, to proclaim the acceptable year of the Lord.'

What Jesus accepts for himself, entering the service of the Spirit of God – which is more than the prophet John could promise – also happens subsequently to all those who follow him and who, as his disciples, accept the name 'the anointed ones', *christianoi* (Acts 11.26; I Peter 4.16). Jesus will baptize them 'with Holy Spirit and with fire' (Luke 3.16). 'John baptized with water, but you shall be baptized with the Holy Spirit not many days hence' (Acts 1.5) – an event which takes place at Pentecost (Acts 2). The church comes into being when people submit to the hand of God which is laid upon them. This is how Peter puts it in the speech which Luke attributes to him on the day of Pentecost: 'Repent, and be baptized every one of you in the name of Jesus Christ for the forgiveness of your sins, and you shall receive the gift of the Holy Spirit. For the promise is to you and to your children and to all that are far off, every one whom the Lord our God calls to him' (Acts 2.38f.). That happens on the basis of Jesus' resurrection.

In fact this view also breaks through the framework of the covenant with Abraham: circumcision alone is no longer an adequate sign of the covenant of God's grace. Everyone may be baptized, Jews and Gentiles. Moreover, in the event of Pentecost – the fulfilment of the prophecy of Joel – God breaks through the limits of the Jewish *qahal YHWH*; or rather, the limits of the *ekklesia tou Theou* explicitly become ecumenical: the gospel exists for the whole earth and for the whole of history. However, the qualifications are not solely on grounds of birth, membership of a particular people or involvement in a particular culture – not that they ever were. Circumcision, as the sign that incorporates men into the people and culture of Israel, is not rejected, done away with or despised – as was to happen, sadly, in later generations; it is relativized. From now on, by virtue of their baptism, even those who are not circumcised – those who are 'afar' – receive the sign of the covenant of God's grace. They are anointed with God's Spirit, and participate in eternal life through rebirth.

This is the hard, messianic core of the meaning of baptism. What follows from it for our understanding of baptism?

First of all, the form and content of baptism cannot be derived from existing Jewish or non-Jewish rites connected with the use of water. Baptism, as a once-for-all entry into the community, relativizes all existing regulations about purity in the Torah. I have already mentioned the cult of purification at Qumran. Reference has often been made to the model of Jewish proselyte baptism: non-Jews who entered the community of Abraham in the Diaspora were not only circumcised; in the presence of witnesses (baptismal sponsors) they were immersed in a form of ritual purification. At first sight the similarity is striking, but it is only superficial: circumcision was the really important element in initiation into the covenant with Abraham, and it was followed by baptism as a first expression of the will to live in accordance with the precepts for purity expressed in the Torah, which from then on had to be obeyed. Here people baptize themselves, rather than being baptized. It is even harder to suppose that the Christian community took over its baptismal practice from Greek mystery religions or temple customs in the ancient Near East, of the kind that we can still find even today, for example in India. In principle, these too can be repeated. But that is not baptism.

All this has far-reaching consequences. Although there is some justification in calling baptism a 'sacrament of initiation', the stress does not primarily lie on initiation, understood as entry into a particular group, becoming a member of an association, being initiated into the life-style of a particular tribe. The external similarity to such 'rites of passage' should not be misunderstood, though the catechetical value of such a comparison should not be underestimated. Many contemporary baptismal catechisms gladly make use of the comparison. However, we would miss the essential meaning of baptism were we to put all the emphasis here.

At the same time this means that the significance of entry into a specific community of the church, membership of the community of faith, obligation to this community's rules of life, follows only indirectly from a first, basic confession which in the New Testament itself is directly connected with solidarity with Jesus Christ and his solidarity with the will of God. Anyone who is baptized enters the fellowship of the suffering, crucified and risen Messiah, Jesus. There is probably no clearer expression of this in the New Testament than Mark 10.38: 'Are you able to drink the cup that I drink, or to be baptized with the baptism with which I am baptized?'

Many other images are used elsewhere in the New Testament to bring out this central significance of baptism. Paul's text from Rom.6 takes it up directly: 'Do you not know that all of you who have been baptized into Christ Jesus were baptized into his death? We were buried therefore with him by baptism into death, so that as Christ was raised from the dead by the glory of the Father, we too might walk in newness of life.' That amounts to a new birth: 'Truly, I say to you, unless one is born anew, he cannot see the kingdom of God' (John 3.5). Thus baptism is a way into the kingdom of God, though not as human beings would like to imagine it (the sons of Zebedee in Mark 10.35-45), but in God's way: by dying, by the death of the old man, by rebirth to a new way of living, which is characterized by service and by justice. In the Letter to Titus we read: 'For we ourselves were once foolish, disobedient, led astray, slaves to various passions and pleasures, passing our days in malice and envy, hated by men and hating one another; but when the goodness and loving kindness of God our Saviour appeared, he saved us, not because of deeds done by us in righteousness, but in virtue of his own mercy, *by the washing of regeneration and renewal in the Holy Spirit*' (Titus 3.3-5). In Col.2.12f. we read: 'In him also you were circumcised with a circumcision made without hands, by putting off the body of flesh in the circumcision of Christ; and you were buried with him in baptism, in which you were also raised with him through faith in the working of God, who raised him from the dead.' And Col.3.9-11 adds: 'You have put off the old nature with its practices and have put on the new nature, which is being renewed in knowledge after the image of its creator. Here there cannot be Greek and Jew, circumcised and uncircumcised, barbarian, Scythian, slave, free man, but Christ is all, and in all.'

Unlike the current Jewish practice of purification, and therefore unlike the tradition of proselyte baptism in the Diaspora, and more radically than in John's baptism, Christian baptism was seen as the real event of the Spirit which constitutes the church, albeit through personal conversion. Baptism is about becoming the church and being commissioned to Christian action as members of the church; it is about rebirth in grace and a decisive choice of life which constantly needs to be consolidated. The new opportunity must be matched by a new life-style. The New Testament has a whole series of images for this life-style, which illustrate it and make it clear what baptism is about. There is mention of purification and cleansing (Mark 3.11f.; Luke 3.16f.: baptism through fire), and also of a new and radical way, without a trace of ritualism. This emerges in many parables and above all in John 13: 'If I do not wash you, you have no part in me' (John 13.8). Allowing oneself to be purified by Jesus means following in his service: 'If I then, your Lord and Teacher, have washed your feet, you also ought to wash one another's feet.' Elsewhere the stress is on renewal and illumination (Titus 3.5; Heb.10.22.32), on anointing (I John 2.20-27) and sealing (II Cor.1.22; Eph. 1.13; 4.30). Thus baptism takes place 'in the name of Jesus' (e.g. Acts 8.16; 19.5), i.e. in the service of his mission, as a share in his messianic commission (e.g. Rom.6.3; Gal.3.27) to life and resurrection. When later, from the second century onwards, the baptismal formula takes on its present trinitarian structure – in the name of the Father, the Son and the Holy Spirit – this original foundation of baptism in christology must not be forgotten. That is also very important for the view of the church which must be presented to divided churches in a secularized world.

The baptism of Jesus himself as the prophetic starting point of the church's practice of baptism, together with baptism in the name of Jesus as the ancient baptismal formula, stamps the church's baptism as a supremely earthly and historical sign, though nevertheless God's Spirit is experienced as being effectively present in it. So in the Christian church, too, we have an earthly and historical movement of people in whom God's Spirit is nevertheless at work as they form the body of the Lord. Baptism is not an initiation into esoteric mysteries or supernatural realities. Heaven does not come down to earth, any more than it does in the church. The church is worth no more than the reality of its members. It is nothing apart from the living faith of the disciples. So there is no sense at all in seeing any church as having quasi-mystical features, regarding it as a self-contained mystery, a hypostasis to which people can refer and which they can even make an active subject, detached from the belief of its members, detached from the earthly, historical movement of Jesus. The church is essentially the communion of saints rather than the community of the Holy; it is more an event than an institution; it is essentially directed by disciples who are also still unfaithful and sinful, though at the same time they are supported by God, who is faithful and holy. That is why it is dangerous to talk about 'the church' unless one means specific communities of believers which call themselves churches. Therefore divided churches (in the plural) are the only specific form of the Jesus movement, and none of them, not even a possibly new community which might claim to be ecumenical, can call itself *the* church of Christ. So on the other hand baptism is the permanent sign that there is a need to strive for a permanent church unity, as willed by Jesus, on the basis of the prophetic programme to which baptism calls us and into which it initiates us, on the basis of God's own initiative, which is aimed at salvation, redemption and justice for all. The ecumenical report on baptism produced by the Dutch Council of Churches says: 'Baptized in one baptism, those who are baptized come to share in the life of specific, local or otherwise well-defined communities which are not in communion with one another, although they all believe that they are a visible sign of the one universal church. Thus reflection on the nature of baptism irrevocably forces us to the need to overcome the division in the churches.'[4] 'For by one Spirit we were all baptized into one body – Jews and Greeks, slaves and free – and all were made to drink of one Spirit' (I Cor.12.13). 'Eager to maintain the unity of the Spirit in the bond of peace. There is one body and one Spirit, just as you were called to the one hope that belongs to you all, one Lord, one faith, one baptism, one God and Father of us all, who is above all and through all and in all' (Eph.4.3-6).

The one baptism and the divided churches

All these testimonies and summons in the New Testament, which together form the Christian echo to Israel's basic law of faith – belief in the one Lord (cf. Deut.6) – stand in sharp contrast to the practice of the divided churches.

Of course the one Lord, the one faith and the one baptism are confessed verbally: the text from Ephesians is a favourite theme on ecumenical Sundays. But in the daily life of the church behaviour follows laws of apartheid. Even baptism, the sign of incorporation into the one movement of Jesus, is felt by many people to have become a sign of conflict. Although as early as the third century a vigorous controversy arose in the church over the question whether baptism is still valid if it is administered in a separate community, this same baptism has nevertheless continued to be administered as the indivisible foundation of the 'link between all those who are honoured by the name of Christian' (Vatican II, Dogmatic Constitution on the Church, 15). Simply on the basis of baptism and the longing for the one new life in Christ expressed in it, to which the grace of the Spirit corresponds, churches are not divided from top to bottom and Christians are not completely at a loss. 'In the sight of God' we are one as 'people of God'. Who shall separate us from the love of God in Christ? The Vatican II Decree on Ecumenism confirms that in various places, with reference to Eph.4.4f.; Gal.3.27f.: 'For as many of you as were baptized into Christ have put on Christ... for you are all one in Christ.' This does not simply denote a vague mystical unity, but also a church community: 'For men who believe in Christ and have been properly baptized are put in some, though imperfect, communion with the Catholic Church... All who have been justified by faith in baptism are incorporated into Christ; they therefore have a right to be called Christians, and with good reason are accepted as brothers by the children of the Catholic church' (*Unitatis redintegratio*, no.3). 'Baptism, therefore, constitutes the sacramental bond of unity existing among all who through it are reborn' (ibid., no.22).

However, the question is whether this declaration on the one baptism in principle is still carried out in practice by church members and church leaders. Many people have begun to think that it is baptism which makes Christians members of divided churches, that the life-giving immersion has become the seedbed of division. We have imperceptibly come to speak of a Roman Catholic, a Reformed, a Lutheran baptism.

Grandparents are already becoming involved in various kinds of tug-of-war as to the denominational allegiance of their grandchildren when it comes to baptism. And there are an increasing number of grandchildren whose grandparents belong to different churches. The grandparents find this tug-of-war difficult to take. They have always learnt from their superiors – theologians or priests – that you become a member of the one church through baptism. In some churches it was even a condition that parents had to be confessing members of the church in which their child was baptized. Nor does it seem to be all that long since some churches did not take baptism in another church particularly seriously.

Granted, over the last ten years there have been many welcome developments in Holland and outside. There have been mutual recognitions of baptism between the Roman Catholic Church and the Dutch Reformed Church (1967), the Calvinist Churches (1968), the Evangelical Lutheran Church (1968) and the Remonstrant Brotherhood (1974). The Division on Faith in the Dutch Council of Churches published an ecumenical report on baptism in 1977 which attempted to give a common account of the meaning of baptism. In many other countries churches express mutual trust in one another's baptismal practices. And the Faith and Order movement now offers the churches a summary consensus on baptism which takes up the central significance of baptism mentioned above and the many different church emphases on it.[5]

More important than such agreements on paper are the living convergences which we can trace in catechesis and the baptismal liturgy: the richness of biblical imagery has been rediscovered and many valuable features have been taken over from the liturgical practice of the early church. Thus the form of the sacrament too, restored to its essentials, is again mutually recognizable. However, perhaps most important of all is the increasing call by many Christians for a recognizable ecumenical form of baptism which demonstrates what in principle is the ecumenical and undivided Christian character of baptism. The question arises in the context of mixed marriages, perhaps for fear of a tug-of-war, sometimes in honest awareness of the call which goes out from the one gospel itself, and often from an instinctive antipathy to traditional denominationalism. The question also comes up in new housing areas, in student communities, wherever Christians live and work with no other link with the churches than the connection with the particular church in which they are involved: where there is only one font, it makes little sense to keep separate baptismal registers. Where an ecumenical community is growing, there is little longing for strictly separate baptismal card-indexes – the fleshpots of ancient Egypt.

However, this could led to the formation of a separate group, the church of those who call themselves 'Christians', the 'ecumenically baptized'. That seems to be what Paul had to cope with in Corinth: 'Each one of you says, "I belong to Paul", or "I belong to Apollos", or "I belong to Cephas", or "I belong to Christ"' (I Cor.1.12). Such a false trend must be rejected. Even an ecumenical denomination – and history knows many examples of this – remains a denomination, a separate group which already sings with a voice of its own in the choir of the divided churches. Any denominational narrowing of baptism must be challenged on the basis of the intrinsic significance of baptism. It is part of the heritage of the Christian tradition, despite its brokenness, to confess that the one baptism brings about communion with *all* the baptized on the basis of the communion of grace with God in Jesus Christ, in the power of the Spirit. It is Christ who baptizes (Augustine), not Peter, nor Apollos, nor Paul (I Cor.1.13,15). Thus we are all baptized *christianoi*, that is, anointed, called, sent on the way of the Christ, the Messiah Jesus. As a result of thinking through this inner significance of baptism, perhaps ways are opening up towards the understanding of this essentially ecumenical character of baptism.

However, that does not mean that there should be no differences of emphasis in the church over the significance of baptism. In the course of the centuries the form of the commission to *matheteuein*, to make disciples, has been emphasized in different ways in the different traditions. These differences have been echoed in theology, liturgy and catechetics. The emphases do not just differ by confession, but also by periods of church history. So the stress on baptism as 'liberation from original sin' from the fourth and fifth centuries gave quite a specific colouring to the New Testament *metanoia*, which for centuries determined a particular conception and praxis of baptism. The stress which Dutch Reformed theology put on baptism from the nineteenth century onwards, seeing it as a confirmation of the covenant, has also stamped the experience of baptism among Dutch Protestants. Recent developments in Catholic theology and catechesis have often interpreted infant baptism as 'a celebration of birth'. That too is an option which has all kinds of consequences; in particular it leads to a marked degree of privatization. Anyone who compares the official 'baptism formulas' which are in use in various churches will find in them accents from particular periods: usually a rather one-sided choice is made from the available biblical imagery.

So it is not surprising that as a liturgist and a catechist the pastor finds great differences in conceptions and expectations among both godparents and candidates, and that his own theological insights about baptism do not always correspond with the expectations of believers. For example, a recent investigation shows that in baptismal preparation and catechesis Roman Catholic pastors put particular stress on reception into the community of the church, the call to follow Jesus and the beginning of a Christian upbringing. But the godparents *expect* a much greater accent on sharing in the Christian tradition and liberation from original sin. Something like 'discipleship of Jesus' is evidently the echo of a more modern christology which has not yet worked its way through to the experience of church members. Of course such a 'discrepancy' in baptismal motives becomes even stronger in the encounter of two confessions, for example in a mixed marriage.[6] Therefore common reflection on the basic baptismal confession in catechesis and proclamation is all the more neccesary to clarify the motives for baptism and to prevent differences from again turning into divisions.

Adult baptism and infant baptism[7]

What I have said so far really applies only to the baptism of adults, who are aware of what is happening. The New Testament texts are addressed to people who can make a conscious choice: choice, conversion, change, renewal of life are key words in the theology of baptism in the New Testament and the early church. When infant baptism does appear in the well-known texts in which there is mention of the baptism of whole families (the so-called 'house texts', e.g. I Cor.1.16 [Stephen]; Acts 10.47 [Cornelius]; 16.15 [Lydia]; 16.33 [the prison warder]; 18.8 [Crispus]), those involved are slaves and children and not specifically infants. Acts 2.39 (you and your children), often adduced as evidence for the need for infant baptism (*inter alia* in current Reformation baptismal formulae), is also about adults of subsequent generations rather than children at the time of writing. It is certainly not specifically about infants.

Does this mean that the practice of infant baptism, which became current in the churches of East and West from the second or third centuries onwards among Christians of the second and third generations, and which originally stood alongside the much more missionary practice of the admission of adults, really conflicts with the intention of Jesus and the apostles? Is the fact that from the sixth century onwards the churches of East and West began primarily to baptize children and from the eighth and ninth centuries primarily to baptize infants a radical aberration on their part? Are those churches right which, like the Baptists and similar groups in all ages, regard only adult baptism as legitimate in the light of the Bible and therefore call for the 'rebaptism' of those who have already been baptized as children? Are those Christians of our day, including famous theologians like Karl Barth, right who have argued for a return to the practice of adult baptism?

The important question is how these positions came to be adopted. Anyone who defends the baptism of children or infant baptism as the real form of the sacrament of baptism is blind to essential aspects of the event of baptism as I have described them above. All those churches which practise infant baptism surround it with structures of belief which make it possible to learn to believe. Infant baptism clearly calls for new milestones at a later stage of life: confirmation, a public confession of faith. Elements of a regular recollection of baptism can be found in the liturgical tradition of many churches: renewal of baptismal vows on Easter Eve, commemoration of baptism at the Sunday assembly (sprinkling with water at the beginning of the eucharist, the lighting of the Paschal candle = baptismal candle), forms of penance and forgiveness which were rightly described by the church fathers as a second baptism (including, very typically, the solemn promises made by religious in the Western Latin church). It is important to show the connection between these landmarks in catechetics and preaching, and also in the shaping of the liturgy.

On the other hand, the practice of the consistent baptism of adults similarly raises the question what we are to make of the New Testament evidence that children, too, could belong to the community of Jesus and even had a place of honour. Excluding Mark 9.33-37; 10.13-16 as direct evidence for infant baptism – that is certainly false exegesis – it must nevertheless be said that an echo can be found here of a tradition going back to Jesus itself which assigns a place of honour in the community of disciples to the child as one of the 'little ones (i.e. in the kingdom of God) to whom this is revealed'. Now if children are not thought worthy to share fully in the life of redemption, salvation and righteousness to which baptism calls us and into which it initiates us, are we in accord with the New Testament? And that is without mentioning the anomaly that children are sometimes admitted to the Lord's Supper and not to baptism.

Both in the case of the baptism of the (very) young and of those of riper years (when is someone adult?) it must be remembered that baptism does not stand on its own. It does not do so as a sacramental sign, for there are other signs which go with it to bring about incorporation into Jesus the Christ. Thus baptism and confirmation certainly belong together as two aspects – the bath and the anointing/ sealing – of the same prophetic event. Nor does baptism stand by itself as a community event. Baptism at the same time signifies the formation of the church. Therefore every individual baptism is at the same time an increase in the church. The Reformers rightly required that baptism should be celebrated 'in the midst of the community', i.e. at the Sunday service. We are seeing a welcome return to this practice in the Roman Catholic church, which is gradually gaining ground. The tradition of the early church which preferred to baptize on certain liturgical festivals (Easter, Pentecost, Epiphany) has again been commended to the churches in the baptismal agreement arrived at by Faith and Order. This puts the baptism of individuals, children or adults, in the context of the saving event in which the believing community participates by its commemoration.

There is one more point. The early church had strict rules about preparation for baptism, the catechumenate. The catechumenate was part of the life of the beliving community and was supported by the whole community. Over the course of time the baptismal catechesis was increasingly entrusted to individuals, and preparation for baptism was of importance only to those involved: those who were to be baptized, parents and close relatives of the children who were to be baptized. In this way considerable individualism developed in connection with baptism. When associated with an increasingly marked automatism of baptism – baptism was administered as quickly as possible with a view to bringing about liberation from original sin, and anyone who was presented was baptized – this individualism led to a marked devaluation of the significance of baptism in the community of believers. Those who strongly advocate the return of adult baptism have at all events made sure that the churches are aware of the close connection between baptism and faith, between baptism and the desire to be a lifelong disciple.

In practice this means that the whole reception of children into the community of faith is regarded as a task for the catechumenate. In this context, preparation for participation in the Lord's Supper (first communion) will increasingly mean a preparation for baptism, of children with their parents. In this way we shall gradually see the disappearance of the people's church with a local basis and of the distinction between those who are members by birth, those who are members by baptism, and confessing members, which can only be regarded as a theological monstrosity. We are not children of God or people of God by birth, though we are creatures of God and bearers of God's image by birth. It is the conviction of Jews and Christians that we only become the *ekklesia tou Theou* by allowing ourselves to be involved in God's initiative of grace. For Christians, baptism is the sign of this *par excellence*, a 'new birth' which presupposes choice and faith: God does not incorporate anyone into his *ekklesia* against their will. People only become 'people of God' through an explicit relationship to Abba-God, whose directions – whose kingdom – they want to follow.[8]

Baptism and the hesitations of modern men and women

What I have said so far is based on the presupposition that baptism into the churches of Christ is to some degree taken as a matter of course. However, for many people that presupposition is becoming increasingly less obvious. They find the symbol of baptism difficult.

Why are we still baptized? What is the meaning of this symbol in a secularized society, in which church involvement is constantly put to the test and in which churches regularly compromise themselves with the world? For example, the report on baptism produced by the Council of Churches in Holland states all too conveniently: 'In its actions, its liturgy and its instruction the church hands on from generation to generation the message of God's love and the breakthrough of his kingdom in Jesus Christ.'[9] Many people ask whether there is not a great gulf between what must be called 'the kingdom of God' and what the church actually is. What is the real purpose of the church? Is there not more of the gospel outside the church?

In what I have said so far I have described baptism as entry into the community of the church. However, the church as the people of God (*ekklesia*), the fellowship of the disciples of Jesus (*koinonia*) and the body of Christ (*soma tou Christou*), the instrument of God's rule (*basileia*), does not coincide with the institutionalized churches.

Participation in the Jesus movement – which can never be complete and will always remain partial as long as people are sinful disciples – takes on many forms. As we have seen, participation in the church – on the basis of a deliberate choice, and not just on the basis of birth – does not prevent the raising of serious questions, nor does believing mean the exclusion of all doubt and all the bitter riddles of life. It is precisely in connection with baptism that the fundamental questions of human life, to which God's gospel also relates, can be raised. How can we find a way through life for ourselves and our children? How can we continue to stand in the middle of anxiety and sorrow, mourning and death, love, sex, birth, possessions and power, conflicts and relationships which go wrong, careers which lead to heart attacks? Day by day we are 'baptized' into such questions which mark our lives. Here we are caught up in ambiguity, trapped between power, impotence and hope. Is that not what the theological tradition meant by original sin? And cannot baptism, as a 'bath of life', be seen as a turning point which makes us participants and sharers in the way of Jesus?

To be baptized 'in him' means taking a way which in the midst of the ambiguities of life that we inherited removes our human hesitations and is therefore wholesome and beneficent. To be baptized 'in him' means entering a group of people who know that they are 'fellow workers' in service and discipleship, and who allow the demands of the kingdom of God to serve as the principle of their action, as a guideline for their consciences. Following the way of the 'demands of the kingdom of God', this community makes its contribution to human welfare, to human salvation. Believers are convinced that human salvation is the rule of God in human life: where God is given his due, human beings also find theirs. This 'kingdom of God' is not achieved by limiting human self-fulfilment, but forms part of it. Salvation always means human wholeness. Christian salvation and redemption happen where people are healed, where they find a place in the whole of creation and history, where they can come fully into their own in their calling. Christian salvation means the healing of men and women, restored from isolation and alienation – as a result of sickness, broken relationships, prejudice, failure and misconduct – and being taken up into the wider whole, the community of contemporaries and companions, so that they can fully come into their own through care, dependence, another chance and forgiveness; so that they can ultimately know that they are secure in God and can experience the stilling of the deepest longings of their souls, the relationship which ultimately breaks through the basic loneliness of every man or woman. Baptism in Christ should allow people to feel at peace with themselves, with their fellows and God in that short time between cradle and grave in which they are to live meaningful lives. To bear witness to this is the gift of the Spirit through a living community. By that, baptismal practice stands or falls as a meaningful event. It will be clear that this common witness to the significance of baptism is particularly important for the fulfilment of this task in our days.

Therefore the invitation to discipleship must take a central place in proclamation, catechesis and the pastorate. But without honest solidarity with all this searching and questioning, with the anxiety and antipathy of those who are our contemporaries outside the church community, the invitation to become disciples will simply be understood as the cheap purveyance of religious certainties. Only those who, like Philip in the account in Acts 8, are on the way with their fellow men and women, but trained in the tradition of Israel and Jesus, will be able to help those who are seeking and one day will hear the words, 'See, here is water. What prevents me from being baptized?' (Acts 8.36).

7

The Lord's Supper: Communion with One who was Excommunicated[1]

One of the most decisive elements in the identity of Christianity and the church, if not the most decisive, which is at the same time a central aspect of Jesus' ministry, is table fellowship of and with Jesus, the Lord's Supper, the Eucharist, Holy Communion. Under these and other names – each of them a theological programme in itself and the fruit of historical developments and decisions – the New Testament and tradition speak of the sign *par excellence* of the messianic *koinoinia*. As eucharist (= thanksgiving) it represents the continuation of the Jewish *berakah*, but it is at the same time the new token of the conspiratorial *agape* (Origen) of the community, and lies at the heart of its meeting to remember the death and resurrection of the Lord (*O memoriale mortis Domini*). It is the supper that constantly 'actualizes' and 'confirms' the words and actions of Jesus at his farewell meal – 'This is my body, this is my blood'. The breaking of the bread (*fractio panis*) and the communion is the food of the pilgrim church (*viaticum*), the living bread which gives eternal life, the pledge of the future glory. It is the meal which prepares for the future of the day of the Lord and the kingdom of God. It is a divine liturgy (John Chrystostom), the radiance of glory from the heavenly liturgy before the throne of the lamb (Rev.19: *Ad coenam Agni providi*), the divine office, the sacrifice of the church of East and West (Mal.2.1) after the order of Melchizedek, the sacrament of the altar, holy mission, holy service (*missio, missa*, holy Mass).

The very multiplicity of names which the tradition gives us and from which individual traditions have often made a one-sided choice indicates that here we have a nucleus of Christian self-understanding, a 'structure' of our faith.

It is a basic datum of our Christian identity that on the basis of

whatever vision, and in whatever form, we meet on the day of
the Lord for the breaking of the bread (Acts 2.42), do this in
remembrance of him (I Cor.11.24; Luke 22.19), eat bread and drink
wine as he did with his disciples. This is rooted in the identity of who
Jesus was and what he wanted, in other words, in christology. That
is the basic discovery of ecumenism: the supper of *the Lord*, i.e. the
supper of the Kyrios, Christos, Messiah, is itself the confession of
the faith and hope of the Jesus movement. It is not just a sacrament,
a rite, an illustration for the sermon, one of many religious duties,
but is itself central proclamation, actually confession.[2] Catechisms,
handbooks, forms of the eucharist and liturgical rubrics have
together resulted in an unacceptable *reduction* of this central biblical
event which at the same time has led to the mutual alienation of the
traditions of East and West, and within the Western tradition, to
alienation between Rome and the Reformation. *A priori*, this
reduction has also hindered understanding of the eucharist for many
Western Christians, who meanwhile have left the church. And down
to the present day, in Africa, India and Oceania, the way in which
it is understood has caused difficulties for young Christians who
have entered the church from other religious traditions. Thus for
example the theology of the Eastern churches has stressed so much
that the divine liturgy of the Lord's Supper is a reflection of the
heavenly liturgy before the throne of God that its aspect as a
continuation of the earthly table-fellowship of Jesus with his disciples
has been neglected, and its link with *diakonia* has been excessively
spiritualized; in the long run the deacon is selected more for his
qualities as a singer than for his social involvement and skill in
providing help. In the West the emphasis came to lie so much on
the eucharist as having been 'instituted' by Jesus at his farewell meal
– *coena domini*, the Lord's Supper – that all attention was focussed
on the words of institution or consecration. For 'Rome' the chief
concerns are the making present and re-presentation of Jesus'
sacrifice on the cross and the real significance of Jesus' words over
the giving of bread and wine, 'This is my body', 'This is my blood'.
The presence of Christ as the living one among his own has been so
localized in the elements of bread and wine as a result of the doctrine
of transsubstantiation that all kinds of theological and catechetical
nuances are necessary to avoid the suspicion of magic and supranatu-
ralism. The Reformation associated the Lord's Supper as a celebration of the Last Supper so much with the memory of the death
of Jesus that in a long run the celebration took on more the character
of a memorial meal: it was celebrated rarely, for preference on

Good Friday, and the joyful element was strongly tempered. The forgiveness of sins announced in it – 'for the complete expiation of all our sins' became its central message – presupposed the sense of sin which had been instilled from youth upwards by preaching, catechesis and spirituality.

The most recent reduction, again in the West, has followed from the theology of secularization. Those who want to break with any explicit reference to God or transcendence, who want to confine themselves to the empirical and strip the experience of centuries of all 'mythical' conceptions, those who regard humanism – the humanizing of man – as the only honest alternative to theism, will also want to strip the sacramental practice of the church, and especially the celebration of the Lord's Supper, of all form and content that transcends or goes beyond the framework of a human meal of friendship. Thus agape and solidarity become the great key words in preaching about this sacrament. In that context many people have pressed for a return to celebrating the eucharist as a real meal, a time when the solidarity of the people of God can be expressed in action and reflection.

These reductions should not be looked at solely in a negative light. They may have over-stressed certain aspects, but at least they have safeguarded them, so that they can be incorporated into a broader vision. Moreover, it is legitimate to stress some aspects more strongly than others at certain times and in certain contexts, where one stress is all too often meant to correct other one-sided stresses. Did not the Reformation rightly correct mediaeval sacramental piety with its excessive emphasis on the almost physical presence of Christ in the elements and its emphasis on *worshipping*[3] rather than *sharing in* the gifts of bread and wine, by recalling the event on Golgotha and in the Upper Room at Jesus' farewell meal? And is not the recent concern for all that is human and the call for Christian solidarity at the Lord's table not a healthy correction of the ritualism and almost magical sacramentalism which had mummified the symbol of the meal, choking real life to the death with rubrics, regulations about admission and theological abstractions?

Within the ecumenical movement, a wide-ranging consensus has come into being over the meaning, the place and the form of the Lord's Supper in accordance with the apostolic tradition and Jesus' own intentions. This has come about through conversations with exegetes, historians and experts on Jewish rites and customs, and as a result of pressure from many non-Western churches who have to suffer most under the prevailing division of the churches.[4] This consensus has been matched by convergences in liturgy and praxis: the way in which we come together for the celebration of the Lord's Supper is increasingly a matter of mutual influence; the reciprocal hospitality which the churches extend to one another's members at the Lord's table is leading to increasing recognition of the way in which the eucharist is expressed and the eucharist itself is taking increasingly recognizable forms.[5]

Table-fellowship with Jesus, the crucified Messiah

What we celebrate when we meet for the Lord's Supper is not something that we have invented ourselves as Christians. We have received it (I Cor.11.23) from the ministry of Jesus. In his lifetime he ate with publicans (Zacchaeus) and sinners, with great crowds of people (the miraculous feeding of the multitudes) and in a very special and significant way with his disciples. The table fellowship with his disciples is one of comradeship, sharing and mission. That was a feature of any form of teacher-pupil relationship in Judaism,[6] but it acquires a special emphasis in Jesus' dealings with and choice of 'the Twelve'. In the circle of his disciples he forges together people with very different origins and very different politics and religious traditions into a real *ḥaburah*. Of course, to begin with this was limited to Jews, but in a very un-Jewish way. Women found a place in it, though not among the Twelve. That might have proved difficult, because for Jesus the Twelve were the patriarchs of the new Israel and in those days it would probably have been scandalous to envisage women in this role. The door was open to guerrilla fighters (the sons of Zebedee, Simon the Zealot and Judas Iscariot) and to collaborators with the Roman regime (Levi-Matthew). In a number of parables, sayings and commands Jesus discusses with them the meaning of this table-fellowship: it is a community of radical friendship in which there is no rank and status, and actions are governed by the ideals of God's rule: the kingdom of God. Table fellowship is the reflection of God's wedding banquet with Israel, the feast with the faithful of God on Zion on the day of the Lord.

At Jesus' farewell meal (Matt.26; Mark 14; Luke 22; John 13; I Cor.10;11) this table fellowship culminated in a new interpretation of Israel's passover and covenant: from then on memories of the mighty acts of God in Israel's exodus would be filled with recollections of the sacrifice of his life, his martyrdom for the imminent kingdom of God. This was also the turning point, the point of no return, for his disciples: could they worship one who had been crucified and accursed – according to Deuteronomy crucifixion always automatically meant excommunication from the *qahal YHWH* – and accept him as the Messiah, the Christ of God? Or did they have to leave him to his fate and abandon him? After his resurrection the choice was even more pressing, for the disciples on the Emmaus road (Luke 24) and the disciples with Simon Peter – who had returned in despair to their former occupations – by the Sea of Galilee (John 21).

In what we do now – in accordance with a centuries-old tradition in which people continually meet together for this meal of bread and wine, sometimes at the risk of their lives – the Jesus movement continues its communion with him, as an act of protest against his death and against all violent deeds, looking forward to the communion of grace with God and the new life of the Spirit which is breathed into us. Where this is not done there is no church, no 'body of Christ'. It is the eucharist received from Christ himself which regularly constitutes the church as people of God, body of Christ, temple of the Spirit.[7]

Here we have the heart of our confession as 'people of God', Jesus, confessed as the risen crucified one, the one present with us who was done away with, the one who was dead but now lives, who sits at God's right hand. Here we continue the tradition of Israel's exodus-covenant and celebrate the new passover, the pasch of God's new order.[8] God remains the saving, redeeming God who accompanies and guides his people according to the Torah, from generation to generation, albeit from now on in the footsteps of Jesus.[9] At a later time the church's tradition would constantly have to stress that we receive the eucharist as a gift of grace. Sometimes that led to misunderstanding, for example when Scholastic theology began to say that the power of the sacrament happens *ex opere operato* independently of the belief of the celebrant or the attitude of the participants. That does not mean that the faith of the church is superfluous at the celebration of the sacraments, as if the words over the elements made Christ present by some divine hocus pocus. What is meant, rather, is that by his grace and favour God himself is the 'author', the one who brings the eucharist about and takes the initiative, and that Jesus himself is the presenter, as the living Kyrios, and not simply the passive subject of the church's confession. In fact the *presentia realis* is a *presentatio realis* (an ongoing self-giving in the present), as de Lubac once put it.[10]

The eucharist is essentially the sacrament of the gift which God bestows on us in Christ through the power of the Holy Spirit. Every Christian receives this gift of salvation through communion in the body and blood of Christ. In the eucharistic meal, in the eating and drinking of the bread and wine, Christ grants communion with himself. God himself acts, giving life to the body of Christ and renewing each member.[11]

The Church confesses Christ's real, living and active presence in the eucharist. While Christ's real presence in the eucharist does not depend on the faith of the individual, all agree that to discern the body and blood of Christ, faith is required.[12]

In I Cor.10 and 11 Paul discusses what this 'discerning the body of Christ' means: communion with the crucified Messiah does not allow the community of believers, which is the body of Christ, to be divided again by conflicts over race and class, supremacy and poverty (I Cor.11.26-34); even less does it allow people of God to divide their worship between God and demons, God and idols (I Cor.10.14-22).

Thus the eucharist preserves the community of faith both from injustice and from idolatry by stamping us with the gift of life from the crucified righteous one who has fulfilled the will of the one God to the uttermost.

The Lord's Supper, the great prayer of praise

Exegetes are divided over whether Jesus' last supper on the evening of his arrest can be regarded as a passover meal.[13] Certainly the Synoptic Gospels place his passion – and within that his farewell meal – in the context of the Jewish passover and also make his farewell meal theologically significant by expressly referring to the covenant on Sinai. But in their picture of the course of Jesus' farewell meal (only Luke, perhaps, is an exception here), they leave out the essential passover rites – eating the lamb with the bitter herbs and the many blessings over the cup – and concentrate on the rites which introduce and round off each *seder* meal on the eve of the sabbath.[14] In this *seder berakah* (blessing) the head of the house or the host says a prayer of praise and thanksgiving to God at the beginning of the meal, taking a piece of bread and a cup of wine in his hand, of which those present partake after the prayer: this is an expression of participation in, assent to and solidarity with the faith expressed by the host in his prayer and the hope that is confessed in it. This rite is more extended at the passover meal. There it takes in the whole of the salvation history of the Jewish people and its hope for Zion. In the synoptic account Jesus also spoke this blessing, but at the same time he made it a prophetic action, filling the rite with a new content: his prayer to God became the gift of his life, his body and blood. And the disciples – patriarchs of the New Israel – took part in the thanksgiving and praise of God which Jesus – as their intercessor, spokesmen to God, the true host at their table – not only put into words but to which in fact he gave permanent form by offering up his life – as they discovered after the Passover.

Thus the Christian eucharist, too, is first of all assent to God's mighty acts: the Amen to God's *emunah*, his grace and trust even beyond the scandal of death. It is acceptance in joy of being accepted by God, the acceptance of sheer grace. At the same time the eucharist is a cry of prayer from the heart, from the depths of misery, with the 'bread of affliction' as the manna in the wilderness was called: a prayer of longing and endurance, of openness to God and living from promises. Thus the great prayer of praise – both our words and our eating and drinking – is simultaneously a sacrifice of praise and a beggar's cry of distress. As the Jesus movement and as the messianic community we offer to God the groaning of creation, the broken world of suffering, injustice, death and sin, but at the same time we pray and long in holy discontent and hope that his will may be done and kingdom come.

All the church traditions should put more stress on this character of the eucharist as prayer in which, in the midst of human limitation and contingency, we experience God's transcendent grace and truth in what M.M.Thomas calls a 'spirituality of combat' and in what the Taizé community sums up as 'lutte et contemplation'. We still have a good deal to learn in this area from the Orthodox churches. There, at any rate, the liturgy is one hymn filled with longing and trust which moves people to tears, and the eucharist can be experienced as medicine against death (*pharmakon athanasias*). Is not the death of people like Oscar Romero a contemporary indication of the power of this medicine in the struggle against death, even if, or precisely when, they are willing to give their lives for it?

Do this in remembrance of me

Our God – the Lord of Israel and the Father of Jesus Christ – is a God of history, who goes along with us; he is not an unmoved mover who remains permanently the same. In the history of God with man the event of Jesus of Nazareth – his life, his fate, his surrender to

God's will, his service to God's rule – has a central place. When we believe, we confess that this event has not remained barren and that God is effectively at work in history in the power of the Christ-event.

There are many so-called Christian conceptions of God's creative omnipotence which interpret what happened in and through Jesus of Nazareth simply as a demonstration of God's power. In that case God's real action is independent, independent even of any historical event or human action. The man Jesus and what he left behind, his disciples, the church, are simply the object and never the subject of redemption. The celebration of the Lord's Supper as what makes up the church resolutely goes against this approach, and where the approach has also penetrated ideas of the eucharist it must be rejected as heretical.

That is the abiding significance of the saying 'Do this in remembrance of me', which Luke and Paul have handed on to us as a saying of Jesus.[15] As a memorial celebration, like the Jewish memorial texts (*zikkaron*), the eucharist is the specific realization of God's effective activity in his Messiah. Just as the covenant that God makes with Israel is not some finished pact from the past that has been put on the statute book but a living and constantly new alliance, which has continually to be accepted and sealed by men and women with their hearts (Jer.31), so too the way in which Jesus 'with his heart' sealed the new covenant with his blood is continually actual and effective. 'The eucharist is the memorial of the crucified and risen Christ, i.e, the living and effective sign of his sacrifice, accomplished once and for all on the cross and still operative on behalf of all humankind. The biblical idea of memorial as applied to the eucharist refers to this present efficacy of God's work when it is celebrated by God's people in a liturgy.'[16]

Thus the eucharist cannot be some kind of *repetition* of the event of the cross, but is exclusively concerned with its effectiveness in history. It is concerned with God's effectiveness, the recollection in confession and action that we may rejoice in his care, through Jesus Christ our Lord. For this Vatican II uses the attractive term *perpetuatio*.[17] The memorial celebration of the eucharist, moreover, is not exclusively concerned with the event of the cross but with Jesus' ministry as a whole: his life and death, his resurrection and abiding presence to the end of time.

This recollection – *memoria, anamnesis* – is therefore more than imagining or remembering a fact from the past, more than the commemoration of a dead person or the memory of a heroic action.

Nor is it the same as meditation and concentration on the generosity of God, who forgives our sins, 'by means of' the symbol of bread and wine. Popular catechetics – not just from liberal Protestants! – is fond of giving this kind of rational explanation of the sacramental event. Memorial celebration means the encounter with the gracious God, who gathers people around the Messiah's table to be his covenant people. God takes possession of us as we offer our lives as a well-pleasing gift through, with and in Christ. 'Lord, in this sacrament we receive the promise of salvation... make us grow in faith and love to celebrate the coming of Christ our saviour.'[18] 'Lord, accept our sacrifice as a holy exchange of gifts. By offering what you have given us may we receive the gift of yourself.'[19]

In this remembrance, word and sign, preaching and sacrament go indissolubly together. Here preaching is more than an interpretation of the event; it is a proclamation of God's mighty acts and promises. And the sacrament is more than an illustration of the sermon; it is the form of the mysterious covenant, *mysterium fidei*.[20]

Thus the *whole* celebration has the character of remembrance and not just parts of it, like consecration or communion. It is celebrated within the framework of the church's festivals of remembrance and above all in the setting of the Lord's Day, as the community assembles on Sunday. Here the church community at the same time recalls God's gracious action in those who have preceded us in the communion of saints: confessors, martyrs, men and women who have given their lives as a sacrifice of praise so that we too might also hallow our lives with them. Here I am not referring to the human merits of saints from the past – that is a Counter-Reformation distortion of the veneration of the saints – but to the ongoing intercession of the risen Lord with whom the communion of saints knows itself to be united in prayer. Every reference that we make to those who preceded us in God's service thus presupposes that they are part of the community of the living God, although they are dead. So the celebration of the Lord's Supper spans the history of the church, which is the history of a 'community of discipleship' (J.B.Metz).

At the same time we know – in the same event of remembrance – that we are united with all who also truly renew the covenant with God in Christ in our time, 'from the rising to the setting of the sun' (Mal.2.1). However, this is not a triumphalist reference to worldwide piety, as the context in Malachi shows. Just as the prophet takes a critical view of Israel's worship and contrasts it with the religion and piety of other nations, which is often more honest than that of his own people, so too the church community, as it meets to remember, is a critical community. The remembrance of Jesus means the solidarity of those who have sworn to stand together, of a world-wide alliance against the powers of evil and a covenant of love which spans the earth in the service of God's rule. In the Catholic liturgy, as in that of the Eastern churches, this is expressed in the mention 'in remembrance' of the leaders of all the local churches with which the community is in communion: its own bishop, the bishops of the world church, the patriarch, the bishop of Rome. In almost all Christian churches, however, intercession for the whole of the people of God and for all sister churches plays an important part in the celebration of the Lord's Supper.[21]

The eucharist expresses the undivided longing of all the people of God in extremely concentrated form in the anamnesis. And in this way God remains a living God who remembers people as they remember him, who was and is and is to come.[22] In my view this transcends all earlier controversial eucharistic theology which damaged relations between East and West, Rome and the Reformation. Anyone who wants to call the eucharist a sacrifice can do so, provided that this is no infringement of the unique significance of Jesus' death in the saving work of God 'once and for all'. And provided that the real distinction between the Christian sacrifice of praise and both Jewish and pagan sacrificial practice is sharply observed, as it is in the tradition of prophetic criticism to which Jesus' activity bears witness and which is given to us as a guideline by Hebrews.[23]

Something comparable also applies to the age-old arguments about the 'real presence'. The first Christians lived in the awareness that the living Lord was himself the real host at the eucharist – as witness Luke's story about the people on the Emmaus road and John's story about the encounter with the disciples at the Sea of Galilee. Some communities kept a seat empty for the Lord at the time of the service as an indication of this. There was an awareness that the president of the community was acting in the name of the Lord as his representative: he was servant and not host. They experienced the presence of the Lord and his Spirit in word and sign, in liturgy and life, in the fact of the meeting and in everything that happened there: proclamation, prayer and actions. So they did not go on to enquire about the nature of this presence, any more than one goes on to enquire about the nature of the air we breathe or the light with which we see. We simply live by the air and the light, or we can celebrate it in poetry. That is what the classical liturgy and the theology of the church fathers also do. Thus the Syrian liturgy speaks of the glow of the spirit which warms our hearts through the bread and the wine just as the sun made the grapes ripen into wine and the warmth of the oven baked the wheat so that it became bread.

In later centuries Christians, and among them especially theologians, began to philosophize over the nature of the presence of Christ and the Spirit. How can the Lord who has left this earth still be with us in space and time? Here people developed concepts and images which got out of hand. Images of God's dealings with humanity usually go wrong. They give God human form – how else can it be? – and end up identifiying tangible earthly realities with the divine mystery: God with us adorned in gold and silver, localized in earthly elements. When this happens, images, however well intended, turn into their opposites and become idols. Philosophizing over the eucharist has not entirely escaped this fate. The presence of Christ among his people was sometimes so linked with the liturgical elements – the water of baptism, the oil of anointing, bread and wine at the eucharist, the hands of the bishop in blessing and even anything that comes into contact with these elements (the shell, the cup, the table linen, the tabernacle, the sanctuary) – that people began to talk in terms of a local, bodily and physical presence. This presence in, under or with the sacraments was isolated from the rest of the liturgy and from community life. The words of consecration were isolated from the rest of the liturgical action and people began to think about them independently of the actual eating and drinking of bread and wine, independently of recollection in word and sacrament, independently of the gathering together of the community. When that happened, in the words of consecration or institution, all the emphasis came to lie on two parallel sentences, 'This is my body, this is my blood', with the accent on *is*, which people began to understand as an equals sign ($=$). Thus the meaning shifted from the biblical dynamics of Jesus' prophetic action in the framework of the Jewish *berakah* and/or Passover celebration and simple believers began to think in terms of magical pronouncements. Like many theologians before them, the Reformers rightly protested against this development. But – and this is the remarkable paradox of history – precisely in order to keep this popular, exaggerated idea of a local, bodily and physical presence of Christ in check, in the eleventh century theologians began to use the word transubstantiation, on which the Councils of Constance and Trent later built their doctrines of the real presence. Bread and wine *are* the body and blood of Christ, as the early church unanimously testifies, and almost all traditions have maintained. But this copula, *are*, is not to be identified with a mathematical equals sign, as used in the natural sciences. Of course Semitic languages use no such copulas.

Later theologians began to say that the bread and wine *become* the body and blood of Christ. That makes the prophetic action a process of transformation. In that case one needed all kinds of qualifications to distinguish what happens here from other processes of change known to us. Precisely in order to achieve that, the early mediaeval theologians introduced the term transubstantiation. The way in which bread and wine become the body and blood of Christ, it was argued, differs from all other process of change known to us, especially from all chemical and natural processes. In contrast to these, the change which takes place here is a mysterious metaphysical change, of a kind unknown to humanity, a change of substance in entities in respect of all the properties that can be experienced empirically (the accidents remain the same but the substance changes, went the argument, in terms taken from Aristotle).

Later, already at Constance and Trent, the term, which was originally meant to rule out excessively materialistic conceptions of the mystery of the encounter with Christ, was used especially to challenge all kinds of spiritualistic conceptions which people thought they detected in the theology of Jan Hus, Wycliffe and the Reformers, and which brought with them the danger of reducing the sacramental symbolic action to something that worked like a rational symbol: just as the board outside an inn indicates the wine which is served inside, so the bread and wine at the eucharist indicate the life that Christ led for us. That is what Zwingli, for example, said in his eucharistic doctrine. In that case it is only the meaning that we give to them which makes the bread and wine the body and blood of Christ, and usage is the only difference between our daily bread from the baker, the Sunday eucharistic loaf and the remnants of it which are given to the pastor's chickens on Monday (to call the latter the birds of the air scarcely changes the intention). The Catholic tradition in East and West always opposed such rationalizations of the sacramental mystery by referring to the early church.

Modern theologians, however, are slowly beginning to agree that such views cannot be identified directly with those of the Reformers, Wycliffe and Hus, and that the accusations of Trent here are not always just. Insight into the history of the term transubstantiation which I have outlined above has also furthered understanding of the Catholic standpoint from the Reformation side. Catholic theologians have been able to relativize the use of the term: like all other theological terms it is an instrument for the better understanding of God's care for humanity. It is an auxiliary term in theology and the sacraments, and not the sacramental event itself, which exclusively comes into being through God himself by the liturgical action of the church.

Moreover, although Trent thought that this concept was *the* most suitable expression, or at least a very suitable expression, for understanding the sacrament, it does not exclude other imagery and expressions. In recent decades, for example, theologians have argued for terms like transfinalization or transsignification to express the fact that – by God, and not on the basis of human intentions and interpretations alone – this bread and this wine, in the context of the celebration of the eucharist, become effective remembrances, so that they are more than earthly food and drink and are in fact the food of eternal life which God himself gives to us in Christ. 'Under the signs of bread and wine, the deepest reality is the total being of Christ who comes to us in order to feed us and transform our whole being.'[24]

In the power of the Holy Spirit

Tradition attributes the fact that the living Lord can come and be present among us to the power of the Spirit of God. In the Western traditions this aspect is often forced into the background as the result of a one-sided christological basis for the Lord's Supper.

Yet it is the Father who is the primary origin and final fulfilment of the eucharistic event. The incarnate Son of God by and in whom it is accomplished is its living centre. The Holy Spirit is the immeasurable strength of love which makes it possible and continues to make it effective. The bond between the eucharistic celebration and the mystery of the Triune God reveals the role of the Holy Spirit as that of the One who makes the historical words of Jesus present and alive. Being assured by Jesus' promise in the words of institution that it will be answered, the Church prays to the Father for the gift of the Holy Spirit in order that the eucharistic event may be a reality: the real presence of the crucified and risen Christ giving his life for all humanity.[25]

This accent has been contributed above all from the side of the Orthodox churches. They have remained much more clearly aware of the 'epicletic' character of the eucharist: the eucharist as a whole has the character of prayer that God's Spirit will pour down upon the people of God, bedewing the gifts of bread and wine and making them fruitful, so that they can become the vehicle of God's grace.

This conception in fact avoids a whole series of misunderstandings about the real presence which have arisen in the West. It brings to our awareness the creative power of the living God. It reminds us of I Cor.12.3: 'No one speaking by the Spirit of God can ever say "Jesus be cursed!" and no one can say "Jesus is Lord" except by the Holy Spirit' (cf. I Peter 3.18; 4.6). In fact communion with the excommunicated Jesus is possible only 'in the Spirit' of God, who makes him the living Christ (John 6.63).

Koinonia-communion-fellowship

The eucharistic communion with Christ who nourishes the life of the Church is at the same time communion within the body of Christ which is the Church. The sharing in one bread and the common cup in a given place demonstrates and effects the oneness of the sharers with Christ and with their fellow sharers in all times and places. It is in the eucharist that the community of God's people is fully manifested. Eucharistic celebrations always have to do with the whole Church, and the whole Church is involved in each local eucharistic celebration. In so far as a church claims to be a manifestation of the whole Church, it will take care to order its own life in ways which take seriously the interests and concerns of other churches.[26]

We have already seen that the eucharist constitutes the people of God and is the visible expression of the communion of saints. The term communion is not so much a reference to the togetherness of a local group – although friendship and love (*agape*) are important aspects of this togetherness. Communion is a matter of *koinonia*.[27] This biblical concept needs to be looked at more closely, above all in connection with eucharistic communion. According to exegetes, the primary significance of the noun *koinonia* – with the genitive or dative – the verb *koinoneō* and the adjective *koinos/synkoinos* is not 'fellowship' in the sense of a bond between individuals but participation, sharing.

Hence the use of the genitive after the noun and the verb, indicating what people share in. Of course one needs others in order to share in something. Hence the biblical significance of *koinos*: friend, colleague, fellow, comrade. More clearly than the Jewish *ḥaburah* and the Latin *societas*, *koinonia* indicates that the found-ation of the community rests on something other than the bond between its members. Thus we find in the New Testament: participa-tion in the Lord Jesus Christ (I Cor.1.9); in the life of the Father and the Son (I John 1.3); in the Spirit (II Cor.13.13; Phil.2.1), on the basis of which fellowship in faith comes into being (Phil.6); in the gospel (Phil.1.5); in the Lord's Supper (I Cor.10.16); and in suffering and persecution (Phil.3.10; II Cor.1.7; I Cor.9.23; I Peter 5.1; Heb. 10.32). Fellowship with God (II Peter 1.4), fellowship with Christ (I Cor.1.9) and fellowship in the Spirit (II Cor.13.13) are thus the basis of church fellowship. It leads to mutual communication and solidarity (Acts 2.42; II Cor.8.4; Rom. 15.26; Gal.2.10); in the last text *koinonia* is the telling name for the church's collection for the poor in Jerusalem.

Thus the Jesus movement is at the same time a social movement, but not one which has its origin in common aims or a social contract. Consensus, communication, conciliar government all play a major role, but they are not of themselves constitutive of communion. So the nature of the church is not primarily determined by the institutions which it shares with all other patterns of organization (= *societas*) but by the dynamic participation of its members in the grace of God in Jesus Christ and the Spirit. That protects any view of the church both against hierarchical and legalistic distortions and against forms of congregationalism which regard the church exclusively as an association of believers (*associatio fidelium*).

When applied to the eucharist, the centre of Christian *koinonia*, this understanding means that the eucharist, too, is not primarily concerned with matters of human comradeship, with the exchange of ideas in a venerable kind of circle of associates or a structured assembly concerned for union. It is there to bind the 'people of God' to God himself and at the same time to one another as companions. Eating the *mazzoth* – the bread of affliction, rations for the journey – and drinking from the cup – a draught of longing for the promised land, strength for the way – turns pilgrims into fellow travellers, on the road from the wilderness to Zion. Thus the eucharist gives us a bond with martyrs and confessors, seekers and prophets of all times. However, the awareness of our destination also calls us to solidarity with our contemporaries, in order to overcome the oppositions between races, sexes and classes.

The eucharistic celebration demands reconciliation and sharing among all those regarded as brothers and sisters in the one family of God and is a constant challenge in the search for appropriate relationships in social, economic and political life (Matt.5.23f.; I Cor.10.16f.; I Cor.11.20-22; Gal.3.28). All kinds of injustice, racism, separation and lack of freedom are radically challenged when we share in the body and blood of Christ. Through the eucharist the all-renewing grace of God penetrates and restores human personality and dignity. The eucharist involves the believer in the central event of the world's history. As participants in the eucharist, therefore, we prove inconsistent if we are not actively participating in this ongoing restoration of the world's situation and the human condition. The eucharist shows us that our behaviour is inconsistent in face of the reconciling presence of God in human history: we are placed under continual judgment by the persistence of unjust relationships of all kinds in our society, the manifold divisions on account of human pride, material interest and power politics and, above all, the obstinacy of unjustifiable confessional oppositions within the body of Christ.[28]

Hence the eucharistic liturgy on the one hand summons us to the forgiveness of sins, conversion and a second chance, and on the other to radical love of the brethren. Communion means sharing, being the companion of the sick, the prisoners, those without rights. Sick communion and communion with prisoners is not just a liturgical service to those who cannot go to church; it is the confession of faith that the church cannot be called the church apart from the sick, the suffering, those imprisoned in Jesus' name. *Koinonia* implies solidarity in service 'in remembrance', 'acting like Jesus', as he teaches us when he serves his disciples in John 13 – that often forgotten account of the Last Supper.

Without honest striving for communion with all those who have broken off communion or who have been excluded from it, all eucharistic celebrations are wrong. Therefore in the eucharist, too, an open invitation to members of other churches – open communion – should really be the norm, and it is legitimate to exclude from the Lord's table only those who clearly do not share the basic confession of the *koinonia* of Christ. The very nature of eucharistic communion calls for the visible unity of the church as a *communio* of sister churches.[29]

The banquet of the kingdom of God

The eucharist opens up the vision of the divine rule which has been promised as the final renewal of creation, and is a foretaste of it. Signs of this renewal are present in the world wherever the grace of God is manifest and human beings work for justice, love and peace. The eucharist is the feast at which the church gives thanks to God for these signs and joyfully celebrates and anticipates the coming of the Kingdom in Christ (I Cor.11.26; Matt.26.29).[30]

The celebration of the Lord's Supper in the midst of the brokenness of our world and of fragile human relationships is a festival of joy, not a tense meditation on suffering. That is not in order to disguise or suppress the misery of our historical situation with candlelight and incense, comforting hymns and the sound of the organ, but to trace God's guidelines. It has not become any easier to find them, either inside or outside the church. This makes our gathering together on the Lord's Day to seek the kingdom of God all the more urgent.

A plea for the church is a plea for the restoration and the fullness of this sign of joy.

As to its form, that means the circulation of both bread and cup – the cup of the kingdom of God. As far as possible, all those present who are members by baptism of the body of Christ should share in the eucharist. The eucharist is clearly connected with the celebration of Sunday. That means that we need to think again about the frequency of eucharistic celebration. The Reformation never talked of 'avoiding the eucharist', but it did envisage less frequent celebration (three to six times a year). Moreover, in some churches children are excluded from the Lord's Supper. On the Catholic side its celebration is often privatized, and that obscures its character as the assembling of the community. One might ask whether in a secularized society, in which so many are alienated from the church, it is so natural to celebrate the eucharist on all kinds of occasions – marriages, anniversaries and funerals – when so many people no longer believe in it. At all events, this should indicate the need for a better understanding of the eucharist.

Serious questions have been put to the Catholic tradition by other churches about the reservation of the elements and the veneration of the 'Holiest of Holies'. The prime purpose of this practice is for the communion of the sick and others who are prevented from being present. The best way of showing respect for the sign of the presence of the Lord is its use, as is said in ecumenical conversations.[31] The worship of God, through, with and in Christ, is the task of all churches, and the veneration of the sacrament is a time-conditioned form which comes up against opposition from other churches as a result of the historical misunderstandings to which this practice has led.

The Lord's Supper is concerned with the form of the mysterious bond between God and humanity. The succession of gatherings of the people of God from Sunday to Sunday and from festival to festival is an effective way of working towards the sanctification of the world, a faithful confession of our baptism. The Letter to the Hebrews reminds us of that:

> Therefore, brethren, since we have confidence to enter the sanctuary by the blood of Jesus, by the new and living way which he opened for us through the curtain, that is, through his flesh, and since we have a great priest over the house of God, let us draw near with a true heart in full assurance of faith, with our hearts sprinkled clean from an evil conscience and our bodies washed with pure water. Let us hold fast the confession of our hope without wavering, for he who promised is faithful; and let us consider how to stir up one another to love and good works, not neglecting to meet together, as is the habit of some, but encouraging one another, and all the more as you see the Day drawing near (Heb.10.19-25).

8

The Ethic of the Kingdom of God

Confession and action, baptism and eucharist belong so closely together in any definition of the identity of the church and in the question of its credibility and attraction in history that rarely, if ever, is a separate discussion of Christian guidelines for behaviour thought to be a part of ecclesiology. Of course such guidelines are presupposed in the church's creed, but the creed gives no specific details. Naturally the nature of the Christian life-style is also discussed in the framework of the catechumenate as a preparation for baptism. The questions asked at baptism in the classical liturgy call on the candidates to abjure not only false convictions but also un-Christian behaviour. A penitential practice very soon grew up around admission to the eucharist within the framework of a system of disciplinary regulations. As the rules grew stricter, anyone who would not or could not live in accordance with the ideals of the new humanity was excluded from participation in the eucharist until his or her time of penance was over and the penance had been performed. Here the penance was regarded as a second chance, a second baptism, dependent on the judgment of the church leaders and especially the bishop. During later centuries a specific penitential practice, confession, appeared in both Eastern and Western churches, In it the individual spoke to a personal mentor - the confessor – who not only imposed penances for wrong behaviour but also gave counsel to help the penitent make good and grow in the Christian life.

The Reformation had a disciplinary system, above all over admission to the eucharist; it was administered by the local presbytery and only in exceptional cases by the organs of the synod. Alongside penance for the individual, the Catholic church of the West created a system of public discipline and public excommunication, in the form of the Inquisition and the Holy Office, developing a special official authority concerned with *fides et mores* which culminated in the authority of councils, the world episcopacy, assembled or dispersed, and in the last instance in the infallible, i.e. irrevocable, verdict of the bishop of Rome.

Just as admission to the community was accompanied by cate-chesis and penitential practices, so departure from it by death was celebrated sacramentally with careful pastoral guidance, focussed not so much on a humane death as on a peaceful and confident encounter with the Lord of all life, the judge of the living and the dead.

The practice of this church discipline, which could be adminis-tered in accordance with a very detailed system of obligations and prohibitions and also be backed by social sanctions – the state had to respect God's ordinances and carry out the church's sanctions, if necessary by using the sword of authority – has come under severe pressure in the Western world. Individual spiritual guidance has been overtaken by a whole system of secular counsellors: profes-sional therapists, the slogans of mass movements like the human potential movement, a thoroughgoing socialism or the civil religion of the welfare state: freedom, equality, fraternity, each with its ideological propagandists in literature and the media. Over the last two decades the frequent practice of penance has been decimated almost everywhere in the Western world. Where anything of it still remains, young people are not involved, or it is practised in such general terms – penitential celebrations – that there is hardly any difference between it and the regular liturgy – where paraenesis flourishes.

Much of what has disappeared has disappeared for good reasons, and attempts to return to the old ways seem hopeless from the start. For generations, Catholic penitential practice has involved people in anxieties and tabus from which many of them are glad to be freed. There is now protest in almost all churches, public excommunication of those with different convictions or deviant behaviour regarded as an infringement of human rights, as an incursion into the free conscience of human beings or a curtailment of freedom of thought and theology. The word 'discipline' – originally it simply meant what was required of disciples – has connotations of authoritarian structures of society, militarism and fascism. And the word 'ethics' has connotations of 'puritanism' or at least of a legalism which comes into conflict with the freedom of the children of God. Above all in Reformation circles – especially among Lutherans – ethics is a suspect word which is closely related to justification by works, asceticism and a struggle for perfection which threatens to remove the real sinfulness of humanity out of sight.

Have not the modern behavioural sciences taught us that human behaviour is unpredictable, untrustworthy and opportunist? That we are inclined to regard as normal what most people find normal? And does not the history of Christianity teach us how careful we must be in establishing a more or less circumscribed 'Christian' ethic? In a whole series of areas the churches have tended to prevaricate over human behaviour: in politics, in questions of war and peace, in the sphere of human relations, in the area of love, sexuality and procreation.

However, even if we concede all this, we cannot avoid the fact that the activity of Jesus, following on the tradition of Israel, is concerned with the human behaviour and conduct of affairs and not just with convictions and ideas. Jesus presents the kingdom of God as a principle of action and bases his ethic on it. The people of God should behave in accordance with the broad outlines of this ethic if they are to be the church of Christ. Therefore a plea for the church, too, cannot avoid ethics, and a chapter on ethics is an essential part of ecclesiology.

Is there such a thing as a Christian ethic?

The breakdown of the connection between Christianity and culture and the collapse of church discipline which I have just sketched out in broad outline compel us first of all to answer the question whether there is any sense in looking for a distinctive Christian ethic. There are respectable theologians who find that any attempt to derive ethical principles from the gospel of Jesus is rather a vicious circle: the ethical principles of Jesus are coloured by the current conception of the Jews of his time and moreover are known to us only through the views of the disciples and those after them who wrote the New Testament. A great pluralism prevails here, which is itself the echo of the different circumstances of the communities in Palestine, Asia Minor, Greece or Rome. A number of conceptions about marriage and sexuality, possessions and trade, slavery and the domination of the wife by her husband, behaviour towards those with other views and towards authority have been so overtaken by the cultural history of the West that the very authority of scripture has been put at risk. And on the other hand it seems that our ethical conceptions, whether at a personal or a social level, get so much in the way when we read the accounts of Jesus that we find in him what we are looking for. When the liberal Protestants of the nineteenth century went in search of the historical Jesus and his ethic, they found a liberal teacher in the fashion of the day who could have made a good career for himself in a business college. Nowadays, when liberation theologians paint a picture of who Jesus was and what he wanted, they show him as a partisan of the struggle for freedom, and his ethic seems to be that of the revolution of the dispossessed. For Rauschenbusch, von Harnack and Ritschl Jesus was a social and political moralist and super-deacon; for leftist theologians he is a Marxist ideologist. In the conservative political theology of Ultramontanist Catholicism he is above all the founder of a religion and a canon lawyer, who regulated church discipline down to the smallest detail, especially by establishing trustees to protect the natural laws, in the figure of church authorities: his ethic is an ethic of command, law, and obedience to authority.

One desperate argument has it that crusades were organized, heretics burnt, slaves exploited, colonies wiped out, world wars waged, population explosions defended and economic injustice praised, all with reference to Jesus. Then finally, after the Renaissance and the Enlightenment, when the eyes of man come of age were opened and he created his own autonomous principles of action – free democracy, solidarity among trade unionists and class warfare, personal conscience, experimental behaviour and the free play of social forces – the church reacted like a child whose toys have been put away. There was one great lament over the injustice done by secularization, a passionate defence of the remaining bulwarks like the Vatican State and the system of diplomatic representatives in the Catholic church, or the retention of the privileges of a state church in many Protestant nations. This put Christian ethics on a new course; with less influence and power over the lives of men and women in general, it resorted to an even more scrupulous discipline over members of the church communities.

Given all these misfortunes and the outrages committed by those who have defended a Christian ethic, it seems only reasonable to make a provisional beginning, like Vatican II, from the autonomy of earthly reality and the *humanum*. At all events, Jesus did not invent ethics, nor does the church have a monopoly of them. Even before Christianity appeared, right human behaviour was discussed along the lines of a number of 'anthropological constants'. As the action of a free subject, human behaviour seems to be neither the determined result of static human nature nor the arbitrary product of chance urges or reactions to the environment. Human freedom is a freedom in context, which in the very historical process of interaction with its environment leads to a sense of direction, to a sense of happiness, salvation, fulfilment, which is good, or to the experience of misery, disaster, regression and misfortune, which is evil. An infinite number of gradations and varieties is possible here, varying from individual to individual and from culture to culture. However, 'value centres' appear, clusters of values around particular spheres of life which form a framework of orientation and the beginnings of 'conscientious' action both in the sphere of direct interpersonal behaviour and in the wider sphere (short-term and long-term relations, micro- and macro-ethics, individual and social ethics).[1] Schillebeeckx[2] mentions six such constants as aspects of autonomous human reality which should be capable of being used to test a specific Christian orientation of values. Only if it emerges that there is no distinctive Christian behaviour at any of these points, or at least that the gospel of Jesus cannot provide an orientation which differs from other approaches, can it be said that there is no such thing as a Christian ethic.

Anthropological constants

The first group of values which seems to be constant through cultures and periods of history relates to physical life, our sheer existence. These are values which serve life and survival. They are the values connected with the satisfaction of our prime needs, basic needs like food, shelter, freedom of movement; health and physical welfare, ecological balance and the conservation of nature; a responsible distribution of population; a responsible use of technology as a means of producing food and equipment; a defence against disputes and ways of avoiding them; concern for health and combatting of sickness; respect for the life of children and the defenceless.

The second area embraces the values of human beings as those who achieve selfhood in relationship and partnership. Face-to-face communication, language, love, security in I-you relationships: a person does not need to be alone. A good deal of our emotional life, our love and the values connected with it belong in this area, and so too does tenderness, recognition, care for one another, being called by name, confidence in which personal identity can grow, especially in nurture.

However, people do not live only by I-you relationships. I-we relationships and the institutions which protect them and make them possible also belong among those things which determine our scale of values. Participation in structures of decision (democracy), peace and security in society, economic justice, respect for human rights, freedom of expression, welfare and recreation: all these social needs produce specific value-centres which, while differing from period to period and culture to culture – they largely determine culture – form just one area of values which together make up the object of social ethics.

A fourth system of values arises from the limitations to human life and the specific human capacity for remembrance. We allow our actions and what happens to us to be determined by the dialectic of past and future, memory and hope, tradition and prophecy. We live with very different kinds of memories: young and old, more educated and less educated people, conservative and progressive, people with more access to the past (those who study the arts) and those who work more with the potentialities of the future (scientists). We live by experiences of the past without wanting to bind ourselves to them and that creates tension in the ongoing learning process in which we find ourselves. This learning process includes values of its own: the transmission of culture, ideology, planning; we must act today in order to be able to live tomorrow. Much human work is preparation for the life of our children and the generations which will come after us, so a large number of values are not formed by the momentary needs of one generation alone. Thus tradition and experiment make their own contribution and have their own merits.

A fifth co-ordinate of the human value-system is formed by the permanent tension between theory and praxis, action and reflection. We do not just plan, we also control. Our life is one long exercise in cybernetics in which systems of thought and models of action are related: science and technology, social theory and politics, economics and trade. We are not simply controlled by the demands of history; we also impose our wishes on history. Thus values develop out of the practicability of our imagery, its practical use, the carrying out of ideals, the feasibility of science. This happens through direct reflection on compatibility with facts: it depends on whether technology and practice correspond to the starting points which we have found in other scales of values. Thus anything to do with meaningful work, careers, profession, circumstances of work, distribution of work, the relationship between productive work and the service sector belongs in this system of values.[3]

A last area relates to the values of religious awareness: the provision of meaning, utopia, hope, and belief in God or gods. Of course this system pervades all the previous ones – religion is not a sector of existence but a quality of existence – and it is equally true that religion is also governed by the other value systems. Yet it is a sphere of its own with a hierarchy of values of its own, evidently in a position to take over all other values: for the sake of religion people can give up their lives, behave unjustly, find meaning in suffering and death. An ultimate goal and ground of all life (Ground of Being, Ultimate Concern, to use Paul Tillich's terms; Omega Point [Teilhard de Chardin], Ultimate Righteousness [Hork-heimer], Principle of Hope [Bloch]) colours our existence and prompts values of its own: faith, surrender, basic trust, self-sacrifice, martyrdom, but also worship, desire for fulfilment, prayer in distress, praise, the glorious liberty of the children of God.

Each of us lives within these six co-ordinates all at once, in the dialectic of person and partner, individual and member of society, testator and heir, natural product and vehicle of culture. In synch-ronous and diachronous dialogue with our fellow human beings we form value-centres which are legitimated, but also constantly corrected and supplemented in the historical process, laid down in codes of behaviour (language, norms of behaviour, laws). Religion as an institutionalized system of meaning and the church as the continuum within which the Christian religion exists are related to these co-ordinates. Ethics, or rather, the ethos, is not just a sub-division of religion or a facet of the church, but a structure of it. Where religion and church became irrelevant for defining values and the criteria of behaviour which people impose on one another, they would be reduced to aesthetics – to a *view* of nature and history and to mere *interpretation* of human historical practice after the event. However attractive they might be, liturgy, gospel stories, sacraments and confessions would then ultimately prove to be no more than a commentary on an autonomous human practice.

The message and praxis of the kingdom of God: the ethic of Jesus[4]

That the gospel of Jesus is more than a commentary on human history seems to be rooted in his ministry, in which the theme of God's *basileia* governs his message and praxis. 'The time is fulfilled and the kingdom of God is at hand; repent and believe in the good news' (Mark 1.15). What is meant by *basileia tou Theou*?

Nowhere in the New Testament – nor in the Old – is there a definition of the term, though it is used 122 times, 90 of which are attributed to Jesus, and a large number of which seem to be authentic sayings.[5] Evidently Jesus presupposes that his contemporaries were familiar with the ideas, and so did his disciples. For its content we therefore have to turn to the context of its use in parables, miracle stories, sayings, and also in the activity of both Jesus and his disciples.

We usually translate *basileia* as 'kingdom', but it can equally mean kingship, rule, administration or government, sovereignty and lordship, and, given the Old Testament background, that would seem even more obvious. Of course we only find the Greek *basileia tou Theou* in the later writings of the Old Testament (Tobit 13.1; Dan.3.100; 4.31), but the idea of the kingdom of God (*malkut YHWH*) occurs much more often, both in the Pentateuch and in the historical and prophetic writings; YHWH as the leader of his people in Ex.15; YHWH as the real king who relativizes earthly monarchy and leadership in Judg.8.22; I Sam.8.4; 12.2; the earthly kingdom as a representation of God: I Kings 28.5; 29.23; II Chron.9.8 (Solomon on *God's* throne). For the prophets, YHWH is the Lord and shepherd of the people (Isa.6.5; 33.22; Obad.21; Zeph.3.15), who will eventually rule for ever (Isa.24.23; Jer.10.7; Micah 4.7; Ps.72; 103.19; 145.13; 146.10).

In Jesus' day this idea of God's rule over Israel and over the Gentiles had at least three current interpretations.

1. The restoration of the national political theocracy in Israel. We find this idea of a restoration of the kingdom of David in the Jewish apocrypha (Psalms of Solomon 5.18; 17.21-32; IV Ezra 13.35). It is naturally the interpretation which the Jewish resistance gave to the idea at the time of Greek and Roman domination, e.g the Zealots or the Sicarii, who were evidently also to be found among the disciples of Jesus (see Mark 11.10; Matt.20.21; Luke 19.11; 24.21; Acts 1.6; cf. Matt.11.12). The use of violence to establish this kingdom of God was not ruled out.

2. A transcendent eschatological and universal rule of God over all peoples. This is the conception in Jewish apocalyptic.[6] More or less in reaction to or in frustration over the nationalist and political slogans about fighting for God's kingdom, apocalyptic says that God himself will come on the day of the Lord. He will usher in a new paradise and found a thousand-year kingdom after he has judged the peoples and after the end of the world and the cosmos. Only a few initiates who know the signs and have prepared in constant expectation will escape the wrath of God. This is the dominant thought-pattern in the Qumran community.

3. A hidden rule of God in human hearts. That was the view of the rabbis and Pharisees. This *malkut YHWH* became possible through faithful fulfilment of Torah and Halakah, law and tradition. Conversion, repentance and observance of the law make the rule of

God in Israel possible again. They also hasten the universal lordship of God over all peoples who will accept belief in YHWH as the One God and thus take on themselves the yoke of the kingdom of God (Matt.10.29f.).

The New Testament talks of the kingdom that is coming (Matt.7.10; Luke 17.20), that is near (Mark 1.15; Luke 10.9-11) or that is to come (Mark 9.1; 11.10). People are asked to search and strive for it (Matt.6.33; 13.44f.; Luke 12.31), but more often there is talk of entering (being able to enter) into it (Matt.5.20; 7.21; 18.3; 19.23f; 21.31; Mark 9.47; 10.15,23-25; Luke 18.24f.; John 3.5; Acts 14.22). There is mention of being allowed to see, or of seeing, the kingdom of God (Mark 9.1; Luke 9.27; 23.51; John 3.3) and of inheriting it (Matt.25.34; cf. I Cor.6.9f.; 15.50; Eph.5.5; James 2.5) or of obtaining it (Matt.5.3,10; 19.14; 21.43; Mark 10.14; Luke 6.20; cf. Heb.12.28). The mysteries of the kingdom of God are revealed to the disciples (Mark 4.11; Matt.13.11). The keys of the kingdom are given to Peter (Matt.16.19). Others are excluded (Matt.25), while according to Matt.23.13 the scribes and Pharisees wrongly do this themselves.

Here Mark and Luke consistently use the term kingdom of God (*basileia tou Theou*), while Matthew usually uses kingdom of heaven (*basileia ton ouranon*),but that is a periphrasis to avoid using the name of God. At all events, the term does not refer to a kingdom of God outside this world. Almost all the texts clearly mean something important for this earth, our history, although it does not correspond to their structures (John 18.36).

However, it is difficult to derive the full meaning from the terminology alone: the important thing is the context in which the theme is discussed. Of course there is other imagery which seems to have the same meaning: gospel (the good news), year of grace (Luke 4.18-22), the time fulfilled, the day of the Lord, eternal life (John 6). All these terms describe a way of life in which God provides the criterion and sets the standard, where he is the guideline, so that he can come wholly into his own, win his case, implement his rule. Thus especially in the Sermon on the Mount (Matt.5-7) the kingdom of God and his will and work (John!) seem to be synonymous. Moreover, in the Lord's Prayer, 'Thy kingdom come' and 'Thy will be done' stand side by side. By using the Old Testament imagery about the rule of God, whose servant *par excellence* he seeks to be, Jesus characterizes both his career and the calling of the disciples as service to God's rule, as carrying out God's will for his creation. At the same time he corrects what we have seen to be views current in

his time. The violence of the Zealots gives place to the defencelessness and obedience of the cross, which will finally disarm everyone.
The great scandal, to begin with even for the disciples, is that he
becomes a crucified Messiah. The Jesus movement in the service of
the kingdom of God does not lead to any form of theocracy.

Future expectation in the apocalypses – God will come suddenly
to purify everything – gives place to a strong emphasis on what is
already happening (Matt. 9.1; Luke 11.20; cf. 17.20f.; 20.18-22) in
signs which differ from those forecast by the apocalyptists. The work
of God is not done through fire from heaven and devastation but
through healing, liberation, giving another chance to those who
have none, the advancement of defenceless children and the impure
(Matt.12.38f.; 16.1-4; 24.3; Mark 8.8-12; 16.17; Luke 11.29). Jesus
takes over the Pharisees' observance of the law and call to righteousness for the sake of God's rule, but removes their strong stress on
traditional observance. He makes a radical criticism of ritual purity,
cultic observance, and legalistic exegesis of the law, as is particularly
clear from the Sermon on the Mount.

Jesus' own interpretation of the way in which God will come into
his own is evident above all from the parables and from his practice
of healing and forgiving sins. Here he corrects the trend towards
forming an elite which was implied in the current views of his day:
Zealotism which can grow into a partisan dictatorship and the
sacrifice of people 'for God's good cause'; apocalyptic which aims
at a community of the pure in which only a small remnant will be
able to rejoice in God's love and peace; and legalism which seeks
to see the true service of God in the practice of virtue and formal
piety as ends in themselves (the Pharisee and the Publican, Jesus
and the Samaritan woman, the parables of the guests invited to the
feast). Jesus proclaims a rule of God without the formation of a
remnant.[7]

Thus there is no fanatical search for signs of God's rapid interven-
tion, no direct identification of nationalist political ideals with the
will of God, no moralistic calculation of obligations and fulfilment
of the law. The kingdom of God is a principle of action, the starting
point for thought and action, through which the person addressed,
and others, begin to look aslant across the way things happen in
society and act differently. How God will ever succeed in pushing
rebellious people so far that they live up to the expectations of the
first day is his secret and will be decided in his way and in his time.

The parables teach us that the kingdom of God comes unexpect-
edly and that we cannot calculate its coming. It is like a feast to

which God invites people from the streets and the byways and from which those who are not ready to come will be excluded (the parable of the unwilling guests, Matt.22.14); it has its own rules of conduct which contrast directly with what we human beings find usual (the parable of the prodigal son, Luke 15.11-32) and of the labourers in the vineyard, Matt.20.1-16); the kingdom of God is more important than anything else (the parables of the treasure and of the pearl in the field, Matt.13.44f.). To begin with it can hardly be seen, but its growth will be powerful (the parable of the mustard seed, Matt.13.44f.). It is not for us to stake its boundaries and to anticipate judgment (the parable of the wheat and the tares, Matt.13.24-30), but we are asked to be on the lookout; there is the threatening possibility that we might miss our chance (the parable of the bridesmaids, Matt.25.1-12).[8] Thus for Jesus the message and the praxis of the kingdom of God is that principle of action which makes him live in accordance with God's criteria of peace, righteousness and joy (Rom.14.17; Matt.6.33; Matt.5.20; II Peter 3.13; Rom.8.6; 2.10; Matt.5.4; Luke 6.21; I Peter 4.13; Jude 24; Matt.25.21) which are at the same time the gift of grace. Together they lead to eternal life (John 6, but also Matt.19.16-26).

Now if we put these ideas alongside the summary of coordinates of human action given above, we can answer the question I raised earlier. Is there a specific Christian ethic and a special discipline for the 'people of God', which they must observe if they want to belong to the Jesus movement?

As to *sheer existence and physical life*, it can be said that both the Jewish Torah, especially the Ten Commandments, and the gospel of Jesus show very great respect for human beings, who are created in the image of God, live by all good and joyful things and have freedom in their world. Life is more than food and the body is more than clothing (Matt.5.25-33). At this point the ethic of the kingdom of God calls for a life-style which leaves behind all compulsive 'heaping up in barns' and filling stores. Possessions are for serving life and indeed all who live. So those who suffer hunger or want, those who are excessively poor should have priority: in them we encounter God himself, who will judge by the criteria of his kingdom (Matt.25). And anyone who is sick, handicapped or ill-treated needs liberation, healing and acceptance: God is glorified in the healing of all who suffer. Every human life deserves respect and there are no untouchables: no one may become the victim of another; no one may be killed or cursed (Matt.5.21f.). The use of violence is rejected, even in a good cause. Peter's powers of the keys of the kingdom of God do not extend to violent use of the sword.

Therefore life, which, as we know and experience it, ends with death, has to be lived *sub specie aeternitatis*, as a chance and a calling given by God. It is not for us to judge the length of our days, far less pass judgment on whose life is still livable.

Christianity shares this boundless respect for all human life with Judaism, though it corrects Judaism and takes a more radical stand over the handicapped life (the parables about the cripples and those born blind). But are there not many other religions and ideologies which share this respect? If the church is to be faithful to Jesus, must it not revise its standpoint on violence and war? Must it not speak out more loudly against the death penalty? Must it not launch a more vigorous attack on the ill-treatment and martyrdom of men and women for the sake of national security or greater personal possessions?

On the question of *human partnership* Jesus preaches the equality of man and woman in the marriage relationship, referring to the kingdom of God (Matt.19), and denies the husband the *right* to divorce his wife (Matt.5.27,31f.). He commands us to forgive and offer another chance, seventy times seven, and to work for tolerance (Matt.5.38-42) and reconciliation (Matt.23-25). Love for outsiders – love for enemies – implies a readiness to listen and engage in dialogue and to forego lawsuits (Matt.5.25f.) or judging others (Matt.7.1-5). On the other hand, human connections – relations, family – are not the ultimate criterion. It is possible to give up everything for the sake of God's work (Matt.12.46-50; Mark 3.31-35; Luke 8.19-21; Matt.19.12), just as it is also possible to give up one's life for love of one's friends.

Thus the most important thing is not our own pleasure or self-fulfilment but the honour and welfare of others. The prime authority is not the law but the demand of love, not having one's own rights but leaving room for the standpoint of others.

The specific character of Jesus' ethic on marriage and relationships[9] has been submerged in legalism over the course of the centuries. His opposition to the *right* to divorce (which one person could impose on another) has been translated into a prohibition of divorce in all circumstances; his call for forgiveness, giving another chance and not condemning others has been translated into a system of church penalties and a casuistic morality which does not shy from excommunication; the power of Peter's keys has been developed into a criterion for judging all divergent behaviour. Here the

Christian churches have listened more to Roman and German law than to the order of righteousness which emerges from the gospel. However, for that very reason is not this specifically Christian order of righteousness, which runs counter to almost all existing codes of behaviour and legal regulations, vitally necessary, as an element in the Christian community of disciples and a really alternative canon law of the kind that is already being looked for, for example in the World Council of Churches?

The special character of Jesus' ethic of the kingdom of God emerges even more clearly in connection with *the individual and society*, i.e. social ethics. Of course the gospel does not outline any special view of society, nor does it discuss world problems. It is impossible to derive a social system like capitalism, social democracy or communism from the gospel, even indirectly. But there is a call – for the sake of the kingdom of God – to share possessions and riches, to rehabilitate the weakest members of society and to resist injustice and arrogance (John 8.1-11). It is impossible to say Amen to both God and money (Mammon): heaping up riches comes from the evil one (Luke 12). The command to love enemies certainly does not point towards war as a means of securing rights. Dictatorship is openly rejected as conflicting with what may happen among the disciples (Luke 22.24-30). Christians must act as the Lord did before them: everyone must be ready to be the slave of others (John 13). Hierarchical attitudes are contrary to the kingdom of God (Matt.23.5-8; Luke 14.7-14).

It is inconceivable that all this is to be rejected as a utopia, intended by Jesus as ethical advice for a short interim, after which the kingdom of God would break through definitively. We find the same ideas elsewhere in the New Testament, for example in the letter of James and in I John, and also in the paraenesis of Paul's letters. Like the law of Moses, the message of Jesus points to a specific way of living together in hope.[10] The fact that few people have taken this way consistently is no reason for shifting the frontiers or changing the route. The church community loses its identity if it ignores these ideals of the kingdom of God. However, that does not mean that such ideals can be incorporated into social structures like a law and applied with harsh sanctions. The real contribution of Christians to government by man in the city of man does not take the form of a theocratic system with the Sermon on the Mount as a basic law or of a specific church legislation set up alongside civil legislation. Far less can the church gratuitously identify itself with what is proclaimed as a democratic order on the basis of liberal ideals or the consensus of a majority of citizens. On the basis of the ethics of Jesus, Christians remain strangers in any land, but precisely in this way they become its inspiration, as the Letter to Diognetus tells us.[11]

I said that the fourth co-ordinate of human values lies in *human beings as vehicles of tradition*. Standing in the Jewish tradition, Jesus had great respect for the past of God's promises. Not a jot or tittle is to depart from the Torah. As one of the 'righteous', he himself observes the main lines of the Torah: the celebration of the sabbath, temple worship and daily prayer. His preaching is aimed at rediscovering the real intentions of the Torah in order to bring back the lost sheep of the house of Israel to the true worship of God. Contemporary Jewish scholars researching into the Jesus event[12] therefore rightly regard Jesus as a true Pharisee. At any rate he is not a rebel without a history who brings a completely new teaching. The course he chooses is to interpret and correct past orientations of faith and to use such interpretations – which are sometimes critical and innovative – in conversation with his contemporaries, in order to convince them. However, in doing this he does not follow the line of the current *halakah*, the hermeneutics of his day (Matt.7.20). When he talks 'according to the scriptures', he is not using a fundamentalist exegesis which can simply read texts from the past as though they had always been God's law. While faithfully continuing the Jewish Torah and prophetic endorsement of it, he nevertheless introduces a number of new perspectives precisely in order to safeguard its original orientation.

This also leads to a new pattern of behaviour, a new life-style. The earliest communities first had to fight a serious battle over it, but it nevertheless became a controlling factor in the spread of the Jesus movement in the Mediterranean basin and then later outside the bounds of the Roman empire and to other continents.[13] The ethic of Christianity is evidently capable of being adapted to changing contexts, though context itself is not the sole determinative factor. I have already mentioned many examples of decisive changes in the code of behaviour over the centuries: attitudes towards the state, slavery, dealings with money (Jesus himself never abrogated the prohibition against usury, but on the contrary said that it was unjust, Luke 16.1-9), the position of women in the church and society, the justification of war. Both in the development of this process of change and at those points where Christian ethics seems to be too close a reflection of prevailing cultural patterns – as in the sphere of sexuality – there is an unmistakable Christian trait in ethics: a reference to past experience of faith, a readiness to test personal values by the scriptures, and the insight that *sola scriptura*, interpreted literally at this point, does not offer any comfort. Between these extremes of tradition and innovation there is constant reference to the community of faith: its ethical orientation can be adjusted and implemented by a living authority in the living communication of faith at councils and synods. What other ideology or religion of our day is in a position to be subject to this hermeneutical process and conciliar control? Of course there is still much to be desired at this point – especially in the Catholic tradition. References to the history of the church ethos – what the church has taught universally and at all times – are often all too superficial and in any case a good deal more light needs to be shed on it. But as a hermeneutical principle, which can be used as creative remembrance, it is an irreplaceable and specifically Christian key to value-judgments from generation to generation.

Although human beings are determined by history, they also determine history. They are free in context. As we have seen, the kingdom of God does not come by itself, independently of human calling. Jesus preaches a calculating carefulness, not a complete carelessness (see the parable of the man who builds his house on sand or the general who goes to battle with too few troops, Matt.7.24-27; cf. Luke 6.47-49; 14.28-33). He wants interest on our talents (Luke 19.11-27). The kingdom of God itself implies a perspective on the future, though it cannot be identified with a future final state. On the basis of Jesus' own message and life-style, Christians continue to fight against all injustice and to work for a habitable earth. The Jesus movement is an opposition movement opposed to any fatalism or doomwatching. That holds for the individual – no one is ever written off; it also applies to people and to mankind as a whole.

To regard the ethic of Christianity as anti-revolutionary or in conflict with the interests of human progress and liberation therefore conflicts with the whole dynamic of the original Jesus movement. Only an ethic of justice and liberation corresponds to the deepest intentions of the whole of Jesus' ministry and his gospel of the kingdom of God. However, the way in which freedom and justice are fought for must correspond to the goal that we seek. Injustice can never be a Christian way to any just end. The end does not hallow the means, but holiness is the means to the end. According to the ethic of Jesus, God's right can triumph only by convincing people and winning them as disciples for God's cause. At the same time that is no condemnation of often inevitable violent revolution or of liberation fighters. But it does point the way for Christians: they are not to make the struggle an end in itself or to ignore its victims once violence has become unavoidable; they are to see that human lives are spared and that there is always constant readiness for negotiation. Christian legions of liberation are inconceivable. There can be no holy wars, no crusades against evil. And those who reject all weapons and opt for defencelessness in place of violence should be respected and held up as an example in the community and, where necessary, supported, as when they refuse military service.[14]

Finally, men and women are religious beings in search of a total reality by which their behaviour can be determined. As lived out by Jesus, the ethic of the kingdom of God finds its centre in his unique relationship to Abba-God. That makes all human life and all behaviour life in the presence of God (*coram Deo*) and for God's sake. Belief in God's creative power beyond death is an essential aspect of this. I Peter in particular gives a picture of Christian spirituality which is aware of the grace of God that overcomes death.

> As each has received a gift, employ it for one another, as good stewards of God's varied grace: whoever speaks, as one who utters oracles of God; whoever renders service, as one who renders it by the strength which God supplies; in order that in everything God may be glorified through Jesus Christ. To him belong glory and dominion for ever and ever. Amen (I Peter 4.10f.).

It will be clear that this ethic does not tolerate any discipline in the form of doctrinal processes, excommunications, harsh sanctions, and condemnation of those who do not observe the norm. It does not tolerate authoritarian action by church leaders. It is based on the conviction that like God, men must not use violence. Many of the forms of church discipline that we know from the past must disappear. Western men and women come of age will no longer tolerate being tied to apron strings. That seems to be in accord with the ethic of the kingdom of God.

As to church leadership and church government, the words of I Peter again still apply:

> So I exhort the elders among you as a fellow elder and a witness of the sufferings of Christ as well as a partaker in the glory that is to be revealed. Tend the flock of God that is your charge, not

by constraint but willingly, not for shameful gain but eagerly, not as domineering over those in your charge but being an example to the flock (I Peter 5.1-3).

9

Called to the Service of the One Lord

Classical ecclesiology paid a good deal of attention to a discussion of the place, the nature and the structure of the ministry. In this plea for the church it is being discussed towards the end, although it has constantly been touched on in previous chapters. What we call ministry is in fact an essential part of the structure of the event of the church, but it does not coincide with it. We can say that the ministry is part of the constitution of the church, but it is not all of it. Gospel, church and ministry are part of a hierarchy: the church serves the gospel and ministry serves the church. The 'people of God' live by God's initiative of grace and become the church on the basis of all the elements or structures of the community in Christ: the creed, baptism, the Lord's Supper, Christian discipline. Alongside the creed, sacramental praxis and the Christian life-style, the ministry is certainly a factor in Christian identity, but in the service of, and determined by the structures of *koinonia* which I have already mentioned.

The main question to be asked is whether ministry is serviceable, whether it deserves its name in every respect, *diakonia, ministerium*. The terms I have just mentioned are the most common and most comprehensive terms to be found in Latin and Greek theological terminology; the Latin term has found its way into the Romance languages (ministerio, ministère) and into English (ministry, ministerial). But in other languages (like Dutch and German) the ministerial functions of the church have been coloured by the more 'official' language: 'offices', 'functions', (Latin *munus*). And even the concept of 'service' can cause misunderstandings. This concept of 'ministerial service' is not identical with similar terms used in connection with belonging to the modern 'service sector'. Nor is it the same as being employed as a slave (= *douleuein*).[1] It is related to skills (= *charismata*) which are necessary for the steadfastness and purpose of the 'people of God' who as the Jesus movement adopt a way, seek a determination 'in the service of God'. It is related to people who form part of the group of the 'people of God' and who therefore are on the way, just as they are. That is the case only so long as the journey lasts, i.e. within the historical order. None of them is *pastor aeternus* (shepherd for ever) or *sacerdos in aeternum* (priest for ever).[2] These titles apply only to God, the shepherd of his people, and to Jesus, who extends God's pastorate over Israel to the nations (Heb.7).

Ministry, therefore, is service in the church with a view to God's service, calling and mission. It is not just there for good order, for resolving conflicts and organizing church life. All the ministries of the church must serve God's missionary charge: the continuation of his initiative of grace in the power of the *exousia*[3] of Jesus (Dan.7.14; Matt.28.19): his authority from God to determine the course of peoples everywhere, to direct them on the way to God and to guard, direct and judge them accordingly. In this sense any form of church ministry is essentially a missionary one and is concerned above all with 'messengers' (= apostles) and 'guides' (= *hegoumenoi*) of God's kingdom: his will, his guidance and his rule for humanity.

For all that I shall say later about differentiation in the ministry, about its structures in the local churches and its significance for the unity of the universal church, one thing must be paramount: the church's ministry is at the service of the divine mission. The local community – the parish, the basic community, the occasional community – can therefore never be the goal or the focus of a theology of ministry, nor is it, either in the New Testament or in later church history. The local ministry – the ministry as we come to know it first of all, with local pastors, bishops, presbyters and deacons – is the product of ministers engaged in mission, and if it is good, it continually stimulates such mission.[4] In fact, ministry is primarily a vocation and only after that the sphere in which it is exercised. The local communities are part of a historical movement. As *congregatio sanctorum* (the communion of saints) they form an ongoing community with other communities past and present. It is impossible to mark out any independent temple districts or to determine any welfare areas within which salvation is administered. Moreover there is no essential need for limiting the exercising of ministry by territory in any way. All kinds of groups and categories – people in a particular profession, students in a university association, gatherings of all kinds, those doing military service, those in hospitals – need guides just as much as those who live in a suburb or a village. Of course it is not long since people in the Western world lived all their lives in the same basic community. But in the long run, too great a stress on a 'grass roots' pastorate, in the sense of a pastorate for a fixed group of people, cripples the practice of the ministry, although as a correction to the constant threat of excessive centralization in the church there can be no harm in putting rather more emphasis on that aspect, following the ecclesiology of the Reformation and the Orthodox churches.[5]

Thus the nature and consequently both the unity and the plurality of the church's ministry lie in its missionary task. The gospel takes place in a context. The structures of the ministry are the result of a confrontation with this context. They are not the same in Jerusalem as they are in Antioch, Corinth, Ephesus or Rome. In the Roman empire after 313 they take their colouring among other things from the pattern of organization in the Roman empire, after 1000 from the feudal structure of Franco-German society and after 1517 from the social orders of peasants, middle-class citizens and nobility. Thus too in our day they are a reflection of the context of a complex society, based on the transmission of information, functional and oriented on communication.[6]

Thus differentiation within the one task is both legitimate and necessary. As early as the middle of the third century under Pope Cornelius the payroll included 46 presbyters, 7 deacons, 7 sub-deacons, 42 acolytes, 52 lectors, exorcists and *ostiarii*. If the bishop is included this amounted to eight different functions. It was not yet a matter of 'seven steps to the altar' of the supreme *sacerdotium* or a career leading to the highest jurisdiction; there were a variety of tasks, aimed at building up the body of Christ, and especially the catechumenate; it was a matter of gaining new disciples. No one had yet worked out a difference between 'higher' and 'lower' consecrations, between 'ministries' (*officia*) and 'services' (*institutiones*), clergy and laity (although we already find the beginnings of this in Tertullian and Cyprian). No one was yet thinking in terms of anything like the omnipresent 'threefold ministry'.[7]

Over the course of the centuries – and in a missionary context – new ministries constantly came into being, mostly because the patterns which had been accepted in the meantime were no longer or not completely adequate: apostolic vicars, catechists, *nuntii* (are they not also messengers?), apostolic delegates, generals and provincials of religious orders and congregations, abbots. It is by no means obvious that such functions fall outside the structure of the ministry – as is also evident from the history of the *ordinatio* of abbots and by abbots. The struggle between religious orders and congregations for 'exemption' is the eternal dynamic between the missionary character of the ministry and its local roots and presence in villages and cities. That also applies to the structure of what was later called the 'threefold ministry' of episcopacy, presbyterate and diaconate. The original deacons and presbyters had 'missionary' functions. The *paroikia* is literally a mission station in the midst of the *pagani* in the diaspora, served by the city centres, where the *episcopus* has his seat.

The churches of the Reformation and the Eastern churches also in fact differentiated: in addition to ministers of the word and the sacraments they had not only elders and deacons – connecting these with the presbyters and deacons of the early church and the New Testament was in fact theology after the event – but also catechists, pastoral workers, diaconal consultants, regional superintendents, secretaries and presidents of synods, deans and 'Probste' (as in Lutheranism).

Thus the one apostolic charge, the one *episcope* (Acts 1.19; cf. Ps.109.8), is divided into many tasks.

In practice this creates inevitable problems of demarcation and legitimation, both in connection with all kinds of tasks in the church which are not regarded as 'ministerial' and also in connection with the relationship of one ministry to another. We can formulate a responsible view of ministry for our time, too, only by a correct insight into New Testament intentions in this area. This will then also provide us with some ecumenical perspectives: the division in the churches always seems to have been most hopelessly rigid at precisely this point.

Problems facing the current view of the ministry

First of all, there is the inadequacy of the dogmatic distinction between 'ministers' and 'laity', which has led to confusion above all in the Catholic tradition. The inadequacy is already evident in the terms themselves. 'Ministry' has taken on the connotation of 'official function in the sphere of public service', though we have seen that the original content of the word was broader. Although the etymological derivation of the term 'laity' is from the most comprehensive of designations for all the members of God's people (*laos, laikos*), it has taken on narrower connotations of being ignorant and without competence. The tragedy of the use of both terms as opposite poles (ministers and laity) is that it produces a split in the church which is quite unbiblical, violates the universal scope of the gospel, and is unworkable in pastoral practice.[8] In *Lumen Gentium* (no.31) and in the Decree on the Lay Apostolate, Vatican II certainly extricated this split from the magical ontological connotations which attached to the earlier distinction between 'clergy' and 'laity' as between two states in the church.[9] But the Council did that by giving the 'laity' its own spheres of activity and its own right to initiatives, not by putting greater emphasis on the fact that the church's ministers also hold an essentially 'lay' position.[10] Vatican II did not take up the bold suggestions which Edward Schillebeeckx made at the time it was held, that the distinction between ministers and laity should be allowed only a functional significance.[11]

Being on the defensive against the danger of laicism, the Catholic view of the ministry has always attached more importance to jurisdiction and authority to preside at worship than to the manifold skills and forms of service which were originally denoted by minister and ministry. In the New Testament and in the tradition of the early church it was said of those who make their faith their work that they perform services, that they possess gifts, that they follow their calling and that they are sent. Reference to a formal mandate, to official authority or position, is alien to this view of the church's ministry. As *laikoi*, i.e. as members of the people of God, non-ministers have at least as much to say in the church (to teach, to prophesy, to instruct); look at the references to widows, to those who speak with tongues, to wonder-workers, martyrs, confessors, monks, virgins. And they have a prominent role in worship. Even in Hippolytus' *Apostolic Tradition*, which played a very large part in shaping the episcopal and sacerdotal character of the ministry in the Catholic church, confessors who had been imprisoned for their faith were considered to be presbyters without any form of laying on of hands or ordination.[12] Vincent of Lérins still regarded martyrs and virgins as the best guides to the faith. They ranked before bishops and councils in terms of authority.[13] This line has been continued in church history by founders of orders, church reformers, pioneering theological teachers and holy and pious men and women of all ages. Often they have maintained the true *paradosis*, handing on the gospel, in conflict with the 'official ministers'. And it seems that this should also be the case in the present day with workers in industry, scientists, welfare-workers, artists, members of groups critical of society, who as faithful *laikoi* show God's people the way of the gospel. To call this function in the church a 'charisma', and to include the exercising of the ministry in the multiplicity of such charismata

– albeit with an eye towards the ordering of them – is still only a partial recognition of a new revolutionary but essentially New Testament insight: that the people of God, the royal priesthood (I Peter 2.5-9; Rev.5.10) does not derive its access to God from mediators other than Jesus Christ; and that the whole community, with all its gifts, ministries and functions, is responsible for the *paradosis*, the handing on of the gospel, the mission and the programme of Jesus; for guarding the integrity of the faith, for carrying out the message and the life-style of the kingdom of God. See II Cor.1.21f.: 'But it is God who establishes us with you in Christ and has commissioned us; he has put his seal upon us and given us his Spirit in our hearts as a guarantee'; Rom. 15.14: 'I myself am satisfied about you, my brethren, that you yourselves are full of goodness, filled with all knowledge, and able to instruct one another.' The apostolic tradition is therefore the concern of the whole church and not just of its ministers.[14] The instruments of this paradosis, the scriptures, the sacraments, the ministries and the quest to lead the common life as disciples (*disciplina*), are instruments of the entire community of the church. The ministry is not the *sine qua non* of the church; rather, the church is the *sine qua non* of all ministries, in relation to the other instruments of the tradition.

In fact these fundamental insights have not been properly implemented in the church, even though they are subscribed to in principle. Time and again there is a tendency to mark out positions on the basis of mandate and ordination. We try to establish whether pastoral workers are laity or not.[15] Lay workers, for their part, are afraid that endorsement of their work in the church will result in their being incorporated into the ranks of the clergy, or at least being made a group set apart in the church. This would be a denial of the essential rooting of the ministry in the laity and the essential involvement of everyone in the one process of tradition.

A second cause of frustration is the excessive urge to split up the various forms or structures of tradition which build up the church. Message and life-style, worship and service form one event of paradosis in the New Testament, as is clear, for example, from Acts 2.42-46 and I Cor.11.17-34. The splitting up of ministries and functions leads to all kinds of irregularities. So at the moment catechetics, liturgy and the diaconate threaten to become a kind of delta, each looked after by groups of specialists. Catechists and 'pastoral workers for church and society' evidently have great difficulty in accepting official church involvement in their task. As far as they are concerned, consecration and ordination are reserved by higher powers for those who are authorized to celebrate the sacraments. We are learning to be content that catechesis should be given outside the sphere of activity of the ordained ministry, just as we are learning to be content that those aspects of belief which are concerned with service and society should be looked after outside the liturgy. Thus the idea of a sacrament is diluted if and when pastoral workers prepare people for baptism but do not baptize them themselves; escort dying people towards the presence of God but do not themselves give the sacrament to the sick; work on building up the church but are not allowed to preside at the eucharist. Depending on the ecclesiastical 'tone' of the diocese, minimal and maximal lists tend to be made of what falls within the competence of pastoral workers – or the laity. At the same time, pastors who have been ordained are increasingly being called upon simply because they are authorized to administer the sacraments. Not only is this difficult to cope with, even psychologically; it is also an internal threat to any understanding of the sacraments as sacraments which build up the church.

But in that case, is not all this an aspect of the highly-acclaimed 'differentiation of ministries'? Here we come up against a third cause of frustration. Not only within the Catholic church, but also elsewhere over the last few years, all kinds of auxiliary functions have come into being under the umbrella of 'differentiation', which have also been called 'services' or 'ministries'. This creates a new problem: it is very difficult to express the difference between 'official' and 'unofficial' ministries. Furthermore, the differentiation is only an apparent one: these are partial tasks within one and the same model of service in the ministry. In the Reformed Churches there are 'auxiliary preachers' or 'auxiliary elders' ('fellow workers in churchwork', who are not officially recognized as ministers). On the Roman Catholic side, the introduction of the diaconate as a kind of 'auxiliary priesthood', and of the role of 'lectors' and 'acolytes' as official 'institutions' has tended to lead to the formation of a class of 'levites' similar to those within the priesthood of the post-exilic temple.[16] A 'differentiation' of this kind tends to emphasize the existing cultic and sacerdotal colouring of the ministry rather than to connect it with other aspects of *paradosis*.

In that case, is it perhaps a solution to reserve the official term 'ministry' for 'the service of leadership',[17] with all other catechetical, pastoral, prophetic and liturgical functions in the church community becoming ordinary lay functions? Granted, they go along with the task of leadership, understood as *episcopē*, but they are not incorporated into it: they remain 'lay' services. While it may be true that this tendency in the present-day theological quest for a setting of the official ministry in the church offers some possible short-term solutions, does it fit the facts that we find in the New Testament? At all events, New Testament 'leadership' cannot be thought of apart from instruction and prophecy (cf. I Tim.5.17). It is not a form of management or diplomacy, nor a matter of legal or administrative positions, nor is it an early form of group dynamics. In the New Testament and the early church, leading the community does not stand alongside the functions of instruction in the faith, worship, the building up of community and the giving of service; the leadership itself consists in exercising these functions, directed by the Spirit, with apostolic authority 'in the name of Christ'.[18] Leadership of the commmunity is a matter of holding fast to the faith and carrying out of the work of mission. Mission itself is seen as the work of Jesus, which is continued in the Spirit. Mission is carried on in the life of the community. The structures of leadership and authority which gradually come into being with the formation of particular local churches are secondary compared with the permanent mission that is the reponsibility of all Christians. More 'official' terms (*presbyteros* in the Jewish-Christian world and *episcopos* in the Graeco-Roman world) come into use only gradually, and continue to contain the mystical and sacramental dimension of participating – in *diakonia* – in the Lord's mission along with the whole church. Thus to see 'leadership' or the 'service of leadership' as a specific element in the ministry at least calls for a closer specification of the nature of this leadership, and the leadership itself should not be made a separate function detached from the real instruments of the paradosis: proclamation, worship and service.

Finally, there is the problem of the 'vocational prohibitions' mentioned earlier. Is it not an intolerable anomaly for pastoral work to be detached from presiding at the eucharist and the administration of the sacraments, because of the sexual status of potential candidates for the sacrament of ordination? What conceptions of the ministry are cloaked by a refusal to admit women to the ministry of the church? Why does it remain such a problem for the Catholic church to admit married men to the ministry and to allow clergy to marry?

It seems to me that the basic cause of all the problems I have mentioned is an insistence on maintaining the sacerdotal character of the ministry.[19] When a large part of the tradition of the churches, both East and West, began to see the sacerdotal aspect as the specific feature of the ministry of the ordained clergy, the necessary consequence was clericalization and the emergence of 'levites'; here liturgy becomes the all-determining way of building up the church, and the functions of catechesis and diaconia run the danger of disappearing towards the periphery, as the sphere of the laity. In this way 'ordination', or rather 'consecration' (with its Germanic connotations), could be connected above all with being authorized to lead worship. At the same time, 'eligibility for ordination' and 'being unworthy of consecration' could be connected with sex and marriage. As far as this last is concerned, it is significant that the association of priesthood with celibacy has proved more persistent than people expected ten or fifteen years ago. Remarkably, theological and social developments have not in fact led to the abolition of priestly celibacy but to the dwindling of priestly ministry. There are theological reasons for this. The question of the celibacy of the priest was not just a question about his way of life; it was a question about the nature of his ministerial service. Now gradually, as more non-celibates perform pastoral tasks and women take their place alongside men – the only exception here being in the so-called priestly functions – we shall begin to discover that cultic priesthood has only relative value in the building up of the church, and that worship in a Christian sense is somewhat different from what is guaranteed by a priestly ministry.

It is not enough to criticize the sacerdotal character of the ministry. In the past, the Reformation protested fiercely against it.[20] But it overemphasized another paradigm of the ministry, that of preaching the word and teaching. The two paradigms of priest and teacher have only been corrected by each other in the context of the ecumenical movement.[21] Perhaps this is still not enough. In the light of what we find in the New Testament, must we not open up yet other paradigms if we are to overcome the problems raised above?

Ministry according to the New Testament[22]

The exegesis of the New Testament texts about the church's ministry provides important results for us at three points. We have come to understand more about historical development of the various structures of ministry that we encounter in the New Testament; the ecclesiological significance of the ethic of the New Testament ministry has been recognized more clearly, and the paradigmatic character of the various ministerial titles has been (re)discovered.

(a) The structures of ministry in the New Testament

The New Testament does not seem to be interested in uniform patterns of ministry. Very different structures of community organization are to be found side by side and in succession. There is no question of attempts at harmonization. Thus the structure of the community at Jerusalem is characterized by Jewish forms. The Twelve[23] are its theological and historical foundation. According to Acts 6, they are soon supported by the Seven,[24] but after the death of James (Acts 12) they are not replaced, nor are the Seven. They remain the prototype of all ministry in the church: disciples sent by Jesus (Mark 1.16-20; Luke 5.1-11; Matt.4.18-22; Mark 3.13-19; Luke 6.12-16; Matt.10.1-4; Mark 6.7-13; Luke 9.1-16; Matt.10.9-14; Luke 24.44-49; Matt.28.16-20; Acts 1.6-8; Mark 16.15-18); witnesses of the resurrection (I Cor.15.3-7; Luke 24.36-41; Acts 1.3,8-22; 2.32; 3.15; 5.32; 10.39-42; 13.31); preachers of the gospel (Acts 2.14-40; 3.12-26; 4.33-35); leaders of the community in prayer, *didache* and service (Acts 2.42-46; 6.2-4); patriarchs and judges of the new Israel that is coming (Matt.19.28; Luke 22.28-30; cf. Rev.21.14). However, as a group they are unique. They are 'succeeded' in Jerusalem on the one hand by an ordered government of elders under the direction of James, following the model of the Jewish Sanhedrin, and on the other hand by people with a new title (reserved by Luke for the Eleven/Twelve, but that is Luke's theology): the apostles. The latter are missionaries, ambassadors for the cause of Jesus.[25] They approach the non-Jews (Acts 11.19-22). As in Jerusalem, so too in Antioch and throughout the ancient church the ministry is to be characterized by a certain tension between the local church leaders with their way of ordering things and the travelling 'apostles', 'evangelists' and 'missionaries'; of course this tension may also be seen as a prototype for all later forms of ministry.

In Antioch, the most important missionary centre of the early church, the local leaders responsible for prayer, teaching and encouraging the community are called 'prophets' and 'teachers'.[26] People are 'delegated' from this group for the work of mission (Acts 13.1-3; cf. 14.26f.).

We also find apostles, prophets and teachers in Corinth and in Rome, along with all kinds of tasks which are characterized as gifts and services (I Cor.12.28), notably the gifts of prophecy, service, teaching and leadership (Rom.12.6-8). On the basis of other New Testament texts (Acts 11.27; James 3.1f.; Eph.2.20; 4.11;

Rev.18.20; 22.9) as well, we could call this structure of ministry the earliest 'threefold ministry' – although there is as yet no question of strict organization.

In Philippi, the local leaders are called 'overseers and helpers' (= Greek *episkopoi* and *diakonoi*, Phil.1.1). This is still a very general designation, which cannot directly be compared with the later 'bishops and deacons'. However, it is a foretaste of developments in the post-apostolic period, in which each community slowly seems to have formed its own system of ministries: in the Jewish-Christian communities following the traditional presbyteral pattern of building up the community (Acts 11.30; 14.23; 15.4,6,22,23; 16.4; 20.17-38), where a group of elders provides the leadership; in the new Hellenistic communities following the model of Antioch (as perhaps in Ephesus), or according to Greek models of community organization, in which a variety of names can be used: presidents (I Thess.5.12; Rom.12.8), administrators (I Cor.12.28), pastors (Eph.4.11), guides (Heb.13.7), overseers,[27] who are also called elders (Titus 1.5-9; I Tim.4.14; 5.17). Here emphasis gradually comes to fall on the local leaders, who communicate with the leaders of other local churches – see I Peter 1.1 and 5.1 – and force the missionary 'apostles' and itinerant 'prophets' into the background.[28] That is certainly the setting of the texts from Didache 15.1f. as compared with Didache 9 and 10. The old order based on the threefold ministry of apostles (Did.11.4-6), prophets (Did.11.7-12) and teachers (Did.13.2), who also have the leading role when the community meets for the eucharist, was supplemented and eventually gave way to an order made up of '*episkopoi* and *diakonoi*'. We can see the same thing happening in Corinth, in different circumstances, from I Clement (44.1; 65.1).

Although it is not possible to determine exactly the process of historical development, some important ecclesiological conclusions follow from this pluriformity of ministerial service in the early church which may also prove fruitful in ecumenical dialogue.

No norms can be derived from the New Testament for any model or organization of the ministry; neither the churches with a free, 'charismatic' ministry nor those who have opted for an episcopal-sacerdotal or a presbyteral-synodal order (Catholic and Reformed churches respectively) can appeal directly to the New Testament. Nowhere is there a plea for a completely free ordering; on the contrary, where this seems to exist, as in Corinth, rules for church order are applied (I Cor.12-14), while organization and the distribution of roles gradually win the field (with some polemic against deviant tendencies; this is to protect internal and reciprocal unity and solidarity). On the other hand, there is nowhere a strict demarcation of functions, while even the names of the ministries fluctuate. The one paramount factor is a conviction of the need to be faithful to the one *paradosis*, which must be safeguarded by the whole community, but which is the special concern of those who are chosen from the community to work within that community and to interact with it. Here they are more than democratic representatives; they are servants of Christ, themselves sent by Christ, stewards of the mysteries of God, grasped and seized by the Spirit.

Pride of place is taken by preaching the gospel, which consists in interpreting what happened in Jesus as the fulfilment of the Torah, as the coming of the kingdom of God, as salvation and redemption for those who are willing to go along the way of Jesus as the way of God. This interpretation is given in prophecy and instruction following the Jewish model, and in the quest for an authentic Christian life-style – the new life in the Spirit – in which the cultural situation of the transition to the Graeco-Roman world provokes the necessary tensions. The authority (*exousia, parrhesia*) of the apostolic ministry develops out of the commission to preach and the quest for the right course in accordance with the new law; in this mission it is sealed by apocalyptic, i.e. disclosure signs, which in turn call for interpretation 'in the Spirit'. Both then and now, the service of the ministry is therefore bound up with this event of the gospel ('*was Christum treibet*', as Luther put it). Ministry does not come first and then *euangelion* and *ekklesia*: gospel, church and ministry are fulfilled in accomplishing the mission of Jesus himself.

Finally, the New Testament itself does not put any obstacles in the way of the ministerial service of women. Romans 16.12; Acts 18.26f.; Colossians 4.15; Philippians 4.2f. preserve a recollection of women in leading roles in the communities; I Cor. 11.5 and Acts 21.9 explicitly also mention women in the role of prophets; I Cor.14.34f. is usually regarded as a later interpolation, just as I Tim.2.11f. is only the reflection of a gradually developing opposition to the role of women in the ministry. In this respect it is also too facile to assume that women simply performed subordinate roles. That is by no means clear in the case of the *diakonoi*; of the prophets it must be said that their ministry is part of the earliest structure of church life. According to Dautzenberg one of the characteristics of late Jewish and early Christian prophecy was that both men and women were involved.[29]

(b) The ecclesiological significance of the ethic of the ministry in the New Testament

Now it would be too easy a solution to put forward immediate proposals for reform on the basis of these fundamental New Testament facts. Even the pluriform structure of the ministry in the New Testament is not meant to be eternally binding. Later developments can also be legitimate, provided that they are seen against the criterion of the New Testament ethic of ministry. The evangelists and Paul derive this from Jesus himself. It is directly connected with the nature of the proclamation of the gospel, with the ministry of Jesus, with faith in the exalted Lord, and with the message and the life-style of the kingdom of God. This ethic is characterized by the key-words brotherliness[30] and service: *diakonia* is the most general term for the service of the ministry in the New Testament. Many further guidelines for service are spread over the parables and logia of Jesus in the Gospels: Mark 9.33-35 and 10.35-45 warn against rivalry and competitiveness; John 13.1-17, 31-35 and Mark 10.35-45 also show the christological foundation for these guidelines of service: the way the ministry is exercised is governed by the task of discipleship.[31]

We do not recognize sufficiently clearly the importance of this New Testament ethic of ministry if we read these guidelines only as providing practical advice about pastoral attitudes. This ethic must also affect structures and relationships. In fact it should become the core of ecclesiology rather than its spiritual corollary. The more the community of disciples around Jesus is considered to be constitutive for the specific character of Jesus' ministry and thus for christology, the more its ecclesiological significance grows. If the essence of ministerial service is located in the apostolic *exousia*, rooted in a post-Easter mission, without being connected with the *diakonia* of the historical community of the disciples around Jesus, who ate meals with him and shared in his ministry, the result must be ecclesiological monophysitism in the sense of ecclesiological docetism.

Of course the description of this community of disciples in the Gospel tradition already contains a theological element supplied by the early church, though the terminology is not as yet particularly ecclesiastical. However, precisely because they are addressed to already living communities, these accounts of the relationship between Jesus and his disciples try to establish the continuity of the life of the church with the historical ministry of Jesus and his specific 'way' among his contemporaries. The particular character of the Christian church, compared with the old law, is not so much that new functions and new authorities are created – the church inherits these from Judaism or itself sets up new ones according to its needs – as that there is brotherliness and service on the basis of a new relationship with God which is born out of sharing in the fate and destiny of Jesus.

(c) Paradigms in the New Testament

Even more important than the ecclesiological re-evaluation of the New Testament ethic of the ministry is the rediscovery of the abiding force of a number of New Testament paradigms of the ministry which underlie the various indications of function and which continue to be valid even after changes in organization. The names used in connection with the ministry are not arbitrary. They correspond with titles which were given to Jesus himself and thus have a christological basis. As Jesus was described as a servant, so too were ministers. As he was called apostle, evangelist, prophet, teacher and shepherd, so too were the servants of the church. For that very reason it should not be surprising that as he was also called 'priest' and 'high priest' (albeit by way of a contrast and at a late stage of the New Testament), the church began to apply this not only to its members (thus already within the New Testament: I Peter 2.5,9; Rev.5.10) but also to its servants (which the New Testament avoids; but cf. already Rom.1.9; 12.1; 15.16; Phil.2.17). However, it would distort the ministry if the choice of one paradigm obscured others. So although it cannot be said that the paradigm of priest conflicts with the New Testament – the Reformation was wrong in claiming this – fundamental criticism must be made of the way in which the Catholic tradition has made a one-sided choice of what from a scriptural point of view is a very secondary paradigm.

Vatican II has already come in for some criticism for using the title *presbyteros* alongside sacerdos in texts about the church's ministry.[32] However, it is at least as important to look for the contemporary content and usefulness of the other paradigms. Here it is not simply a question of whether the metaphors are usable – like the paradigm of 'pastor', which has been accepted remarkably quickly in Dutch-speaking areas. Also of importance is the christological and pneumatological depth of the metaphors and a contemporary interpretation of what is often the Old Testament experience that underlies them. What does it mean that those in the New Testament who made their faith their work and their hope their life-style are called 'servants' and 'apostles', 'prophets' and 'teachers', 'pastors' and 'guides'?

The translation 'servant' for *diakonos* and 'service' for *diakonia* is really too weak. The word describes serving at table (Mark 1.31; 15.41; Luke 8.3; 10.40; 17.8; John 12.2; Acts 6.2), and particularly caring service towards the poor and the needy (Rom.15.25,31; II Cor.8.14-19; 9.12-15; Acts 11.29; Heb.6.10). This is more than charity (*eleemosynē*) and different from servitude (*douleuō*). It is essentially being at the disposal of those who are sitting at table and fulfilling their needs.[33] For precisely that reason the term *diakonia* can also be used for the service of leaders in the community (I Cor.16.15f.; Col.4.17; II Tim.4.5; I Cor.12.28; Eph.4.11f.) and also for the office of apostle (Rom.11.13; II Cor.3.7-9; 4.1; 5.18; 6.3). However, in the last resort, for every Christian 'being available' is based on sharing fully in Jesus' own service, as shown for example in Mark 9.35; 10.42-25 (cf. Luke 22.25ff.) and John 13. This service, then, is no colourless 'helping'. All too often pastors understand service and being available in these terms: church members each get what they want and the customer is always right. However, the orientation for Christian helping is given by the gospel. Service is service of the gospel and of God and thus also of humanity. Ministerial service is there to provide appropriate help in the direction of God's kingdom. This includes message and life-style, preaching, worship and help in all kinds of distress. All the time, however, this happens for the sake of people who are God's own children and are therefore called 'brothers' by all who are involved in ministerial service.

The fact that some New Testament servants of the *paradosis* are called 'apostle' or 'evangelist' does not happen simply on the basis of a formal mandate or delegation. First of all they are 'sent', and as such are 'messengers', 'heralds', 'ambassadors' of the good news and of joy, and therefore liberators and proclaimers of the time of grace. They are messengers of joy after the model of Isaiah's messenger of joy (Isa.52.7, quoted and adapted in Rom.10.15), in the very footsteps of Jesus (Heb.3.1, following Luke 4.18-22; Mark 1.15; Matt.10.40). Their ministry is characterized by the Spirit of power, like the ministry of Jesus himself: their marks are healing, miracles, liberation. Thus the title of apostle helps a man to transcend his own individual capabilities and sets him in the history of God's salvation. Ministers of the church enter service along the way of righteousness and peace which God pursues with men. Thus the paradigm of 'apostle' or 'evangelist' comprises both service to the world and service to the community, but it has a marked emphasis on mission, on the centrifugal drive of all church ministries. It also has a sacramental component, in so far as it characterizes this human service as God's own initiative of grace: the apostle preaches God's own word (II Cor.5.20; cf. Rom.1.1; I Cor.1.1; Gal.1.15; II Cor.1.1; I Thess.2.13; Col.1.1) and the kingdom of God (Acts 28.31). The apostles are co-workers (*synergoi*) with God (I Cor.3.5-9), Christ's helpers, entrusted with the stewardship of God's mysteries (I Cor.4.1). For a long time the title of apostle was tabu. It was declared sacrosanct and unique by the Reformation, because no one in the church was to claim its authority for themselves, as some 'apostolic churches' still tend to do. Within the Catholic church it is reserved for those in positions of highest authority, the bishops. They alone are called 'successors of the apostles'. However, the widespread application of the term apostle in the New Testament now helps us to see better than ever that all functions in the church may be said to be apostolic, and that the servants of the church may rightly be called ambassadors, heralds and apostles (II Tim.1.11; I Tim.2.7; cf. Rom. 15.25).

In churches like those in Antioch and in Corinth, prophets and teachers are the main support and driving force. As prophets, they join the ranks of those who are called by God, who pledge themselves to fidelity to the covenant with Yahweh and a new life of discipleship. As prophets they interpret revelations of the Spirit (I Cor. 12.10; 14.29) which are given through texts, visions, and miracles, and so point the way towards the future willed by God.

Although the picture of the earliest Christian prophecy is not completely clear, there are so many parallels both with the emergence of prophets in Israel (cf. Eph.3.5) and with contemporary trends in late Judaism (cf. Rev.1.3) that we must accept that the phenomenon has Jewish roots.[34] Here Jesus himself is also a prophet (Mark 6.4 par.; Mark 6.15; Acts 3.22; Matt.23.31-34, 37, 62-68; Heb.1.1) who reveals the hidden things of God. He is not a member of the priestly groups and joins the prophetic movement of John the Baptist. It is characteristic of his ministry that 'he taught with authority, not like the scribes' (Matt.7.29). He is given the prophetic *exousia* of Dan.7.14, and his disciples also share in it. No wonder, then, that Jesus' prophetic ministry finds an echo in the young communities. It is the fulfilment of the vision of Joel 3.1-5 on which the church is built up on the day of Pentecost (Acts 2.16-21; cf. Heb.2.3f.). To call the leaders of the churches 'prophets' means to give them the role of indicating the way that the church has to follow.

The paradigm of prophet keeps the church from becoming fossilized, because prophecy is again and again the renewing force which interprets the tradition afresh in new situations. Prophets decipher the meaning of events, unveil the meaning of existence. Now, more than ever, a prophetic colouring of the ministry in the church along these lines is much to be desired.[35]

However, the first servants of all were also called 'teachers', just as Jesus' ministry was also characterized as that of a rabbi-*didaskalos*. *Didache* very soon became a description of the object of the paradosis. The nature of this teaching is exclusively concerned with instruction in the new law.[36] As teachers, the servants of the church have the task of leading the community along the path of righteousness, of shaping its conscience on the basis of already-existing traditions (I Tim.4.6; 6.3,20; II Tim.1.3; 2.2,14; 3.10, 14-17; Titus 2.1; II Peter 1.12, 19f.; II John 9). This also presupposes a life in accordance with what is taught (James 3.1,13).

In some passages in the New Testament the servants in the community are also called 'shepherd' (Eph.4.11), or their work is compared with that of shepherding the flock (John 21.26; Acts 20.28; I Peter 5.2). In precisely the same way, Jesus himself is described as a shepherd (John 10; Heb.13.20). Elsewhere they are called guides (*hegemones*[37]; Heb.13.7,17,24; Acts 15.22; cf. Luke 22.26). All the Old and New Testament connotations of 'shepherd' and 'guide' appear here: Yahweh the shepherd of his people (Isa.40.11; Jer.23.1-4; Micah 5.1; Ezek.34.11-22), Jesus the shepherd of his own (John 10.14f.). It is a matter of guiding the people along the way of salvation and righteousness to green pastures (Ps.23).

Why this stress on the paradigmatic character of the terms for the ministry in the New Testament? First of all, because they stress the personal and relational character of the exercising of the ministry. Those who make their faith their work are personally called upon to help and serve, to preach and evangelize, to interpret and to teach, to shepherd and to guide. They cannot hide behind their function. The authority that they have will depend on what they have to say. But above all, each one of these functions makes sense only in the context of the people, the community, the church. This seems to make two urgent demands on all forms of the ministry in our day. Furthermore, these paradigms – which the church of the New Testament evidently found to be an adequate definition of the place of the ministry – show that men *and* women can fulfil particular tasks within the church community. In fact the New Testament knows of women in the role of apostles and prophets. Why should they not also fulfil the functions of shepherds and guides? The rediscovery of these paradigms might provide local leaders – *episkopoi, presbyteres* and *diakonoi* with a better understanding of their ministry, which ensures that all exercising of authority follows the method and structure of the gospel. Perhaps they provide openings in ecumenical dialogue because they transcend the later episcopal-synodal and presbyteral-synodal forms. Or rather, they show that the true *paradosis* is not determined by the organization of the ministry, so that differences in the organization of the ministry need not of themselves prove schismatic.

The churches can encourage a stronger sense of the plurality of paradigms of the ministry by the correction of one-sided choices which have led to different types of ministry and churches: the priest in the Catholic tradition, the teacher-preachers in the Reformed tradition, the evangelists in the Pentecostal churches, the prophets or apostles in the independent and apostolic churches. The correction of the priestly paradigm and its tendency towards the making of levites is a particularly pressing problem for Catholics; this priestly paradigm is the origin of the exclusion of women from the ministry and the association of ministry and celibacy. Whether consciously or unconsciously, the levitical regulations for the Jewish priesthood – the motif of cultic purity- seem to have become conditions for admission to the church's ministry in the Catholic tradition. This has happened in correlation with views of the sacraments, and especially the eucharist, which overstress its cultic significance at the expense of its symbolic value in the service of building up the church, forming the community, achieving solidarity both inwardly and outwardly.

All this should and must lead to a reconsideration of the significance of ordination. The many facets of the tradition – service to the paradosis being seen as the specific feature of the pluriform ministry – call for a form of public endorsement and mission, and for sacramental participation in the mission of Christ in the Spirit. It would be a fatal development if ordination were reserved exclusively for priests and for deacons functioning as priests. It would be disastrous if the functions of teacher and prophet, of servant and pastor came to stand essentially outside the sphere of the ministry, as now threatens to become the case: theologians involved in the catechesis of the church, pastoral workers concerned with church and society, pastoral directors of faith and conscience in all kinds of thereapeutic and pastoral-training activities, who would rather not be paid by the civil authorities, but who at the same time no longer want to be governed by episcopal mandates (which is more than understandable in view of current circumstances). Thus in the last resort bishops come to stand apart from all the work that is being done for the sake of the kingdom of God. Who can be happy about this, if there is to be one flock and one shepherd?

Ecumenical perspectives

Above all on the basis of the exegetical rediscoveries which have been made in recent years, a large number of declarations of agreement over the ministry have been laid on the tables of church leaders. Can the main lines which emerge from this consensus also be of any help to the Catholic church in finding a way out of the problems posed by its own tradition of ministry?

A first line is the enlarged christological and pneumatological foundation of the ministry. Participation in the mission of Jesus and the preservation of the paradosis under the direction of the Spirit have now replaced the historical mandate or mystical-sacral representation as the essential feature of all church ministries. A recent text, the product of the dialogue between the Reformed World Alliance and the Secretariat for Promoting Christian Unity, begins its consideration of the ministry as follows:

> The church bases its life on the sending of Christ into the world and the sending of the Holy Spirit that men and women may be joined to Christ in his service; its authority is inseparable from its service in the world which is the object of God's creative and reconciling love. As servants of their servant Lord, ministers of the Church must serve the world with wisdom and patience.[38]

This implies a new view of the apostolicity of the church. The whole church shares in this apostolicity. The apostolic succession is not restricted to its ministers. It is broader than the succession of ministers and embraces the whole of the process of tradition directed by the Spirit, which is rooted in the divine initiative of grace and attested to by Jesus as messenger and witness, the apostle *par excellence*. It comes about through word and sacrament, the structures of remembrance and communion. As the Dombes Group put it in 1973:

> The fullness of the apostolic succession of the whole church implies continuity in the essential features of the church of the

apostles: witness to the faith, fraternal communion, sacramental life, service of mankind, dialogue with the world, and the sharing of the gifts which God has given to each member.[39]

As a result of more recent exegesis of I Peter 2.5,9, the relationship between the official priesthood and the priesthood of believers (see *Lumen Gentium*, no.10), a sore point in the controversy between Rome and the Reformed churches, is no longer a matter of dispute.[40] The ministry is not a special instance of that general priesthood, but lies on another level. The fact that the whole people is called a priestly people does not mean that now everyone becomes a priest (so that specific ministries are no longer needed), but that every form of priestly, i.e. vicarious, worship has been superseded: we have free access to God in the one great priest who has been set over God's house, although this will only be fully realized at the end of time (Rev.5.10).

There is also agreement over the essentially collegial and brotherly structure of ministerial service. This structure calls not simply for a collegial ministry – of the kind which Vatican II determined for the College of Bishops – but for synodical government within the local churches, for a conciliar constitution and 'sobornost'.[41]

We are seeing the development of a new shared insight into the significance of ordination or consecration. Here a variety of traditions from the New Testament and the early church are coming together: the secular-Greek usage of *cheirotonein* in the sense of indicating with the hand, appointing (e.g. in Acts 14.23; II Cor. 8.19); a widespread Jewish rite of appointment by the laying on of hands in the presence of witnesses, especially teachers in scribal circles (*šemika*); the use of *epiclesis* as a sign that the exercising of the ministry derives from the initiative of the Spirit; and finally *ordinatio* in the classical Roman sense: the appointment of office holders to an already existing *ordo*.[42] Here 'wijding' (German 'Weihe'), 'consecration', is a Germanic translation of this complex – a dangerous translation because it can so easily be sacralized, which stresses the sacerdotal character of the ministry and of those who are competent in the sphere of worship.

The multiplicity of New Testament paradigms which have been discovered through exegesis is already making its mark on the ecumenical consensus. The Canterbury Declaration of the international Anglican-Roman Catholic Commission of 1973 provides an example:

In the New Testament a variety of images is used to describe the functions of this minister. He is servant, both of Christ and of the Church. As herald and ambassador he is an authoritative representative of Christ and proclaims his message of reconciliation. As teacher he explains and applies the word of God to the community. As shepherd he exercises pastoral care and guides the flock. He is a steward who may only provide for the household of God what belongs to Christ. He is to be an example both in holiness and in compassion...

An essential element in the ordained ministry is its responsibility for 'oversight' (*episkope*). This responsibility involves fidelity to the apostolic faith, its embodiment in the life of the Church today, and its transmission to the Church of tomorrow.[43]

In this perspective, the ministry of word and sacrament essentially belong together. As the Canterbury Declaration points out:

> The part of the ministers in the celebration of the sacraments is one with their responsibility for ministry of the word. In both word and sacrament Christians meet the living Word of God.[44]

Thus the Agreed Faith and Order text on ministry[45] can produce this definition of the nature of the ministry, which has also been accepted in other bi-lateral dialogues:[46]

> The chief responsibility of the ordained ministry is to assemble and build up the body of Christ by proclaiming and teaching the Word of God, by celebrating the sacraments, and by guiding the life of the community in its worship, its mission and its caring ministry.

So according to most traditions of the church, the ministry is for confession and doxology, for the meeting and building up of the church which takes place through the celebration of the sacraments, and for acting in the service of the kingdom of God. For the sake of this whole, and with no other means than 'memory', 'counsel', and 'giving account of hope' the church comes to talk of *episkope*: authoritative care for the steadfastness and assurance of the Jesus movement.

This one *episkope* is divided into many forms and tasks and is realized in various functions which change with the times. However, for the sake of unity and the restoration of relationships between the churches a more or less equal building up of the churches is needed. In ecumenical dialogues there is a tendency towards a restoration of a threefold ministry: a ministry of bishops on a regional level and a ministry of presbyters and deacons on a local level. Precisely what is implied by 'regional' and 'local' is a matter of practical guidance and mature relationships and is not essential for consensus.[47]

The way in which all these ministries are practised serves to bear witness to a personal dedication, a collegial sense of responsibility, and readiness to speak on the part of the community of faith.[48]

It would be a welcome ecumenical development if, on the basis of the new interpretations which I have outlined above, contemporary problems related to the exercise of ministry which are arising in many churches could be overcome, and if at the same time that could lead to a recognition and reconciliation of the church's ministries in the service of the gospel of God and to the benefit of the 'people of God'.

10

A Universal Church?

In earlier chapters I have constantly spoken about *the church* as an undivided event rooted in Jesus, the Christ, and in the Spirit of God, in which people participate through faith and action, through sharing in the sacramental signs of the Christian community and recognition of the *episcope* of the ministry. Yet in fact the church is divided into many *churches* and denominations. Still, in the Nicene Creed, we confess the unity of the church, intended for all time and all places: one, holy, catholic and apostolic church. However, the specific 'people of God' are the bearers of these 'marks of the church', as they have been called from the sixteenth century onwards, and what I called the 'structures of *koinonia*' are the essential elements. If the church is one, holy, catholic and apostolic, then it is so on the basis of the unity, holiness, catholicity and apostolicity of its confession, the sacraments, Christian discipline and the ministry. In so far as churches can recognize these 'qualities' among one another, they may regard themselves all as sister churches within the one *koinonia*.[1]

Or must other conditions be fulfilled if we are to speak of the unity of the church? Sometimes churches give the impression that this is the case. The history of theology shows us that the unity of the church as formulated in the Nicene creed also has a historical connection with the deliberate concern of the Roman and Byzantine emperors to preserve the unity of the Roman empire. And all through history Rome has made the communion of the churches with its bishop, the first among the patriarchs, the condition for the unity of the church, among other things because of political factors. If we are to judge whether this claim is justified we must first investigate the history of a number of models of unity which appear within the ecumenical movement, so that we can then see what significance the primacy of the Bishop of Rome might have for the unity of the church.

And finally we must establish how far the one, universal church could in fact make a contribution to the unity of world society.

Models of unity within the ecumenical movement

It would be an arrogant falsification of church history to think that the ecumenical movement began only in the twentieth century.[2] Just as, almost from the beginning, there were differences of opinion in the church which led to divisions, so too, from the beginning, ways were sought to heal these divisions. The leaders of the churches, the bishops, had a special task here. The earliest synods and councils were often intended as forums for discussing and as a means of settling conflicts over belief and discipline in which churches, in the persons of their leaders, were in dispute – one example is the dispute between Pope Stephen of Rome and Bishop Cyprian of Carthage. Evidently the early church also had the power to bring people together time and again.[3]

Even after the great schism between East and West in the middle of the eleventh century, attempts were continually made to restore unity. The same thing also happened after the Reformation, especially through the 'Eirenists' of the seventeenth and eighteenth centuries who tried to heal the break between the churches of the West. Often, however, the initiatives were those of individuals (Lessing, Febronius) and were not taken up by church leaders; sometimes they were even condemned before a serious attempt had been made.

That is the great difference in the twentieth-century ecumenical movement, which from the beginning has been a movement supported by the official leaders of the church. Not all churches have become involved in it as quickly – for example, the Roman Catholic Church joined in only after Vatican II[4] – but when they are involved, they are involved as churches. However, that does not make it any easier to arrive at a consensus over the aim of unity and the way to achieve it.

In the discussions over reunion between East and West (Lyons 1274, Florence 1438-1452),[5] and above all from the seventeenth and eighteenth centuries onwards, under the influence of Romanticism and the Enlightenment (Lessing and Febronius, and in the nineteenth century Möhler and von Döllinger), the predominant ideal was that of the primitive church (the earliest church, earliest Christianity as a norm). This was seen by Old Catholics and Anglicans as the church of the first four centuries, by the Orthodox as the church of the seven Ecumenical Councils, and by Roman Catholics as the mother church in communion with Peter's see in Rome.

Of course this model of 'return' or 'reconciliation' has lived on in the background within the organized ecumenical movement, but it is really anti-ecumenical, because it produces an ecclesiological assymetry,[6] especially in relation to the churches of the Reformation, the nineteenth-century Free Churches and the younger, independent churches of the Third World. As long as churches maintained this model, and in so doing regarded themselves as the faithful continuation of the primitive church, so that they could set themselves up over other churches as the 'mother church' – and a mother of degenerate daughters at that! – they could hardly participate in the ecumenical movement, as was demonstrated above all by the Roman Catholic Church. The World Council of Churches, established in 1948, therefore rejected this ecclesiological asymmetry from the start, in the Toronto Statement of 1950:[7] all partners in the ecumenical movement which join the World Council of Churches may maintain their own sense of being the true church and their own vision of future unity, but they may not impose these views on anyone else, nor may they fail to recognize that the other partners are also the church. By the recognition of the other Christian communities of faith as instruments of the Spirit and of salvation (*Lumen Gentium*, no.8; *Unitatis Redintegratio*, no.3), Vatican II has also made the Catholic church of the West a partner in the ecumenical movement: it is also concerned to reflect on the model of unity without identifying this model exclusively with its own character as a church.

From the beginning, two main models have stood side by side within the organized ecumenical movement of the twentieth century: the model of organic unity and the model of union by federation.[8] Both derive from theological trends in the nineteenth century.

The idea of 'organic unity' derives above all from high-church Anglicans like F.D.Maurice (1805-1872)[9] and American 'episcopals' like William Reed Huntington (1838-1918).[10] Their ideas were accepted in Chicago in 1886 and in London in 1888, at the Third Lambeth Conference, in a four-point declaration which Huntington had already compared to the four sides of the city of God in Rev.21.16. It has therefore become known as the Lambeth Quadrilateral. The four points are:

1. Acceptance of the scriptures of Old and New Testaments as the revealed word of God.

2. Acceptance of the creeds of the early church, especially the Nicene Creed.

3. Acceptance of the two sacraments of baptism and eucharist as instituted by Jesus Christ himself.

4. Acceptance of the historical episcopate.[11]

Above all the Faith and Order movement – though since 1948 this has been part of the World Council of Churches – has taken this idea over and developed it further. In this model of church unity all the emphasis is laid on a visible church unity which incorporates all existing churches and denominations in a new comprehensive unity and which must be sought and striven for by the formation of a theological consensus and by the implementation of pastoral agreements in church life.

By the standards of this model, a good many 'church reunions' have in fact come about in the last fifty years.[12] Moreover, in this model the ecumenical movement is the overall church institution which integrates the separate traditions and prepares for them to die out as separate denominations. Alternatively – and this is a newer development, deriving especially from the young and often independent churches (independent, that is, of Western missionary societies and Western 'mother churches') – it becomes the setting in which these churches can incorporate themselves into the Christian, worldwide *koinonia*, the Christian family in six continents.

Now such ideas can be made specific in a wide variety of ways with a marked emphasis on unity and universality. For example, they could lead to an unhealthy centralism or uniformism, in which the dominant churches had the main say. The aim of 'organic unity' is not automatically identical, for example, to the church order of the 'Anglican Communion' (although that was the idea to begin with) or to that of the Roman Catholic Church (of whose participation in the ecumenical movement many people are still afraid). Therefore in the definition of organic unity which was prepared by Faith and Order, but taken over by the World Council Assembly in New Delhi, 'organic unity' is conceived of above all 'from below', from the local gathering of the 'people of God'. Following ideas from the early church about the unity of the local synaxis[13] and the links between local churches through members and leaders, New Delhi formulated the aim of unity as follows:

We believe that the unity which is both God's will and his gift to his Church is being made visible as all in each place who are baptized into Jesus Christ and confess him as Lord and Saviour are brought by the Holy Spirit into one fully committed fellowship, holding the one apostolic faith, preaching the one Gospel, breaking the one bread, joining in common prayer, and having a corporate life reaching out in witness and service to all, and whenever this community is so united with the whole Christian fellowship in all places and all ages that ministry and members are accepted by all, and that all can act and speak together as occasion requires for the tasks to which God calls his people.[14]

In Uppsala this stress on the local church community was extended to the unity of all Christians in all places, both because of the world-wide problems facing all the communities of Christ and also because a future general council of all Christian churches was envisaged.[15] Thus organic unity comes to be seen as a 'conciliar unity' of 'local' or 'sister' churches which in many respects are autonomous. In Nairobi in 1976 the World Council accepted the definition of the aim of unity as put forward at a meeting in Salamanca in 1973. This was again prepared by Faith and Order, above all at the request of the Orthodox and Roman Catholic churches.

The one church is to be envisioned as a conciliar fellowship of local churches which are themselves truly united. In this conciliar fellowship, each local church possesses, in communion with the others, the fullness of catholicity, witnesses to the same apostolic faith, and therefore recognizes the others as belonging to the same Church of Christ and guided by the same Spirit. As the New Delhi Assembly pointed out, they are bound together because they have received the same baptism and share in the same Eucharist; they recognize each other's members and ministries. They are one in their common commitment to confess the gospel of Christ by proclamation and service to the Lord. To this end, each church aims at maintaining sustained and sustaining relationships with her sister churches, expressed in conciliar gatherings whenever required for the fulfilment of their common calling.[16]

On this basis the aims of the World Council of Churches have been restated[17] and Faith and Order has been able to set up and put into practice its specific programme of consensus-forming. However, this already seems to be not without its problems. Also from the nineteenth century onwards, the ecumenical movement has been familiar with another model of unity, that of 'federal union'. As early as 1809,[18] Thomas Campbell, the founder of the 'Disciples of Christ', which was meant to be an ecumenical church, stressed that only revival and renewal in each separate church could lead to real spiritual unity. Unity would not be brought closer by negotiations, or the assimilation of traditions through organizational changes, but by reflection on their deepest intentions (*intentio fidei*, sympathy of feeling, cf. Acts.4.32). In organizational terms the model of federation would be more than enough for this. This idea was later taken over above all by American Lutherans like Samuel Simon Schmucker (1799-1903)[19] and at the end of the nineteenth century by the 'Social Gospel' movement of Rauschenbusch and his followers.[20] The Practical Christendom movement led by Nathan Söderblom, which was continued within the World Council of Churches after 1948 in the Church and Society Division (now Justice and Service in Church and Society) has always given priority to this model within the World Council of Churches. After Uppsala the model really took off as a result of the great emphasis on praxis throughout theology, specifically on the priority of justice and peace in the wider ecumene over unity between the churches in the smaller ecumene. There were two additional developments. On the one hand, some of the 'Free Church' traditions like the Quakers, the Pentecostal Churches and the Salvation Army were afraid that they were being drawn into too sacramentalist and episcopalian a current by the definition of unity made at Salamanca in 1973. If 'conciliar fellowship' also presupposes 'eucharistic fellowship', what of those traditions which have few or no sacraments? On the other hand, the representatives of the so-called 'Confessional Families', or, as they now call themselves, 'Christian World Communions', many of them older than the World Council of Churches and not incorporated into it in 1948, were afraid that there would be little room in the model of the 'organic unity' of local churches, bound together in a 'conciliar fellowship' (understand, e.g., the World Council of Churches) for the richness of confessions and for the distinctive identity of e.g the Lutheran World Federation, the Reformed Alliance, the World Council of Methodists, the Anglican Communion, the Pan-Orthodox Synod or the universal alliance of the Church of Rome. They have all developed their own ecumenical organs and their own programmes of unification, especially in a system of bilateral dialogues, which flourished above all after Vatican II. In 1973 this system had already born manifest fruit in the Leuenberg Concord,[21] which established eucharistic communion between Lutheran, Reformed and United-Protestant churches in Europe. In Germany, Holland and Belgium there have been more or less successful federations of churches. And from the beginning, in conflicts, the churches of the Reformation have followed the pattern of Erasmus: the restoration of relationships by the combination of confessions, standpoints and organizations in a federation and in 'Formulas of Concord', which demonstrate that people no longer feel particular expressions of the church to be schismatic.

On the basis of all these convictions, the Secretaries of the World Communions mentioned began to talk of the aim of unity as being that of 'reconciled diversity'.[22] The Lutheran World Federation accepted this model at its Assembly in Dar-es-Salaam in 1977. In the conversations between the Anglican Communion and the Roman Catholic Church a slogan from the previous century prevailed: 'United, not absorbed'. As early as 1931, Anglicans and Old Catholics entered into an agreement over intercommunion while each retaining their own independence. A number of Catholic theologians (W.Kasper, Y.Congar) and church leaders – including Cardinal Willebrands and Cardinal Ratzinger – hardly disguised their preference for this model: the separated churches could be regarded as *ritus* or *typoi* of the one church of Christ which is itself the mystery of God's love and union, in which the churches participate more or less completely.[23] The ecumenical movement strives for the integration of the riches of the separated confessions, not for their abolition, but through the restoration of communion between them as between sister churches.[24]

However, the supporters of the Christian World Communions cannot simply rely on a new variant of the nineteenth-century, low-church 'branch theory', which saw the existing confessions as so many facets of the one Jesus movement, with equal rights. That image looks good in a book of church history and at colourful meetings of church leaders of different styles. But the many tasks in everyday reality, in city and country, in mission and evangelization, in mixed marriages and in a variety of areas of social cooperation stand in the way: one can no longer see the wood for the trees. And no one can close their eyes to the widespread transconfessionalism, which seems to be increasing rapidly above all among the young, or to the specific questions of young churches from the Third World, who no longer want to bear the burden of their confessional past, tainted as it is by associations with Western domination, permanent dependence, ballast alien to their culture.

What tradition is a newly converted family in Africa or a village in India to join at this moment in time, when it has made the successsive acquaintance of Portuguese Catholics, Calvinistic Dutchmen, Anglican Britons, American Baptists, Electronic Church Evangelicals and Mr Moon's Unification Church? No wonder that there is a people in Botswana who approached Faith and Order in distress with the question whether people could still be ordinary Christians! And that Christians in all those European suburbs do not want to make their baptized children members of just one of the existing confessions.

These different standpoints were growing into convergence at a meeting of Faith and Order in Bangalore in 1978. The key concept at it was the model of *communio – koinonia*. Anyone who wants visible unity and at the same time a possible way to it must begin from local churches which are united with one another on the local level and are bound to one another as sister churches in a conciliar fellowship. This thinking in terms of the communion of sister churches is an echo of the Sobornost ecclesiology of the nineteenth-century Slavophiles, and the basis of the Orthodox theology of autocephalous (= independent) churches; it was also recognized by Vatican II as an important concept from Orthodox church doctrine (*Decree on Ecumenism*, no.14) and propagated by the Popes after Vatican II. In the meantime this terminology has also been taken over into other bilateral dialogues, for example in the Final Report of the Anglican-Roman Catholic International Commmission and in Lutheran-Catholic dialogue. The advantage is that *koinonia* is a dynamic concept, with many implications from biblical theology. It can be the cornerstone of an ecumenical ecclesiology. It takes the struggle for unity out of the sphere of administration and organization and legalism, into which it has often found its way, and restores it to the level of relations between churches, which – as always with relations – means between specific people. It cannot be limited to agreements on paper, but must relate to union in faith. Following the first forum of bilateral dialogues, which dealt with the conditions of the consensus process – Bangalore mentioned some elements or conditions for unity as communion: a common confession, common sacraments of baptism and eucharist, a common ethic, a mutually recognized ministry and common structures for decision.[25] This last point was made above all in connection with problems surrounding primacy and teaching authority, which Faith in Order had begun to discuss in 1976 (Geneva) and in 1977 (Odessa) and which Anglicans and Lutherans had also discussed bilaterally with the Roman Catholic church.[26]

Although the question of primacy and teaching authority is certainly of great importance for the actual realization of a universal communion of churches, I would not mention it in the same breath as the other conditions. It is auxiliary to them, and is not itself a quasi-sacramental condition for unity like confession, baptism, eucharist, discipline and ministry, which I have discussed above as 'structures of *koinonia*'.[27]

World-wide communion of sister churches and the role of the Bishop of Rome

The World Council affirms that the communion of sister churches is made visible and authenticated in ecumenical conversation, on the basis of the christological and pneumatological elements of the Christian community of faith, in a 'conciliar fellowship'. Although inevitably polemic flared up over this conception after Nairobi, it did indicate a structure of church organization which is accepted in all traditions. On the basis of Acts 15 (the so-called 'apostolic council'), mutual consultation by the 'people of God' is seen as the instrument of God's Spirit by which he can lead the church into truth. Both the churches of the East and the churches of the Western Reformation have made the synodal or conciliar principle the basis of visible church organization and the instrument *par excellence* for communicating faith and resolving conflicts. In principle that is also the case in the Roman Catholic tradition of the West. But this tradition bears within it the traces of a struggle lasting for five centuries over the relationship between the authority of councils and that of the patriarch of the West, the Bishop of Rome. The discussions over the primacy of the Bishop of Rome among his brother patriarchs of the churches of Jerusalem, Alexandria, Antioch and Byzantium (and later that of Moscow as the third Rome) are the sequel to this; so, too, is the conflict with the churches of the Reformation: at any rate, like the Old Catholic churches later, they arose as independent churches after their call for a general council was rejected by the bishops of Rome. So without an ecumenical resolution of this conflict, restoration of church communion will be extremely difficult, even if should be recognized that this point is not one of the essential features of church *koinonia*.

A rather simplified Catholic argument – current from the fifteenth and sixteenth centuries onwards, reinforced in the Counter-Refor-

mation, and apparently solemnly endorsed at the First Vatican
Council in 1870, runs as follows. By and large, Jesus himself willed
the church to be organized like the church of Rome. He appointed
apostles, who were followed by the bishops. He appointed Peter as
leader of the apostles. Peter was followed by the Pope, the leader
of the world episcopate. His role as leader was conferred on him by
Jesus himself – see, for example, Matt.16.18: 'You are Peter, and
on this rock I will build my church', Luke 22.30-32, where Peter is
commanded to strengthen the faith of the brethren – i.e. the local
churches – or John 21.15-23, where a special pastorate is entrusted
to him. So Peter and his successors become the touchstone of the
confession, the teacher of the faith, shepherd over the shepherds.
Hence his primacy, his infallible teaching office, his universal
jurisdiction.

The Orthodox churches of the East have never accepted this
argument, far less the churches of the Reformation. They counter
it with an equally simple argument: Jesus gave twelve of his disciples
a special role as the ancestors of the new Israel, the church. Peter
certainly had a striking role among them, but not the most important
one. This led the Eastern churches to stress the connection between
the local bishops, among whom a special role is played by the
patriarchs of the old 'mother cities' of the church: Antioch, Jerusalem, Alexandria, Rome and Constantinople. The Reformation
stressed that the role of the Twelve was once-for-all and unique, so
that it was illegitimate to speak of 'successors of the apostles', let
alone a 'successor of Peter' who was to occupy a central place within
the church. Some Reformation traditions, like those of Holland,
rejected the ancient episcopal organization from the sixteenth
century onwards, as conflicting with the basic structure of the church
and the 'universal priesthood of believers'. In that case any idea of
a special role for Peter and his successors would be a stumbling
block for them, a great obstacle to unity. Nor is it only the Dutch
Protestant alliance which constantly reminds us of this. Pope Paul
VI recognized the problem himself on his visit to the World Council
of Churches in 1970: 'My name is Peter. That is the greatest
stumbling block to unity.'

As so often in the ecumenical movement, at this point exegetical
and historical investigations[28] have contributed towards a breakthrough. Through them we have learned to see that a central
authority in the church grew up only gradually. The function of
Peter in the New Testament is not so much that of a supreme
authority as being the first of the disciples, the head of the brothers,

spokesman of the Twelve, apostle with the apostles. Peter, too, searched, and groped, and failed on his way to faith and his insight into what had to happen to the church in its transition from Israel to the Graeco-Roman world. So he is not the type of an infallible central leader in whom the power of universal jurisdiction is vested. But at the same time he is an outspoken intellectual leader, in Jerusalem, in Antioch and perhaps also in Rome. He was such a landmark for the young mission church that Paul himself had to take account of Peter's position, and according to Acts Peter also presided over the 'apostolic council' in Jerusalem. Could one call Peter's function as leader a 'Peter function' or a 'Peter service'? And can that ministry or this service of Peter be continued in a 'Petrine office' or a 'Petrine function' within the church? If the answer is yes, to whom does such a task fall? Is Rome to be regarded as the seat of such a function? In recent years a hopeful ecumenical dialogue has developed by means of these questions.[29]

As early as 1974, a report of the Lutheran-Roman Catholic dialogue group in the United States declared 'that the papal primacy, revised in the light of the gospel, does not need to be any hindrance to the reconciliation of our churches'. There is agreement about the different 'roles' which are assigned to Peter in the New Testament without any mention of a clear 'Petrine office'. It was also recognized that the later primacy of the bishop of Rome is a historical development which cannot directly be derived from the New Testament, but at the same time does not conflict with it. In other words, both the simple Catholic and the simple Reformed arguments mentioned above are rejected as being too simple. The same report says of the historical development towards the primacy of Rome that many social and cultural factors laid the foundation for it: in addition to this primacy many other 'principles of unity and truth' functioned, for example the canon of scripture, the councils, other local churches with particular authority (patriarchs, abbots of particular monastic centres, bishops of places like Tarragon, Tours, Lyons, Cologne, Trier, Worms), and confessional writings. People went on to formulate a number of principles for the contemporary exercising of the primatial 'oversight': the collegiality of the local church leaders, pluralism of the confessional traditions, and the relative independence (subsidiarity) of the local churches.[30] By and large these are the same principles as have also been mentioned within the Roman Catholic church as necessary if there is to be a healthy exercise of authority within the primacy of Rome. In 1976 the International Anglican-Roman Catholic Commission published the

Venice Declaration on authority in the church. Here, of course, all the emphasis was on the oversight exercised by the bishops of the local churches collegially and in a council or synod, as being the basic structure of the church. But within that there was the possibility of a universal primacy and also, for historical reasons, public recognition of the see of Rome in the service of church unity. The actual statement ran as follows:

> The bishops are collectively responsible for defending and interpreting the apostolic faith. The primacy accorded to a bishop implies that, after consulting his fellow bishops, he may speak in their name and express their mind. The recognition of his position by the faithful creates an expectation that on occasion he will take an initiative in speaking for the Church. Primatial statements are only one way by which the Holy Spirit keeps the people of God faithful to the truth of the Gospel.
>
> If primacy is to be a genuine expression of *episcope* it will foster the *koinonia* by helping the bishops in their task of apostolic leadership both in the local church and in the Church universal. Primacy fulfils its purpose by helping the churches to listen to one another, to grow in love and unity, and to strive together towards the fullness of Christian life and witness; it respects and promotes Christian freedom and spontaneity; it does not seek uniformity where diversity is legitimate, or centralize administration to the detriment of local churches.
>
> A primate exercises his ministry not in isolation but in collegial association with his brother bishops. His intervention in the affairs of a local church should not be made in such a way as to usurp the responsibility of its bishop.[31]

The *Final Report* goes one step further. Not only for historical reasons, it is said, but in principle, on the basis of the New Testament, the catholicity of the church demands a universal function of *episcope* – for the sake of its visible unity (and also to fulfil the conditions mentioned earlier).

> According to Christian doctrine the unity in truth of the Christian community demands visible expression. We agree that such visible expression is the will of God and that the maintenance of visible unity at the universal level includes the *episcope* of a universal primate. This is a doctrinal statement. But the way *episcope* is realized concretely in ecclesial life (the balance fluctuating between conciliarity and primacy) will depend upon

contingent historical factors and upon development under the guidance of the Holy Spirit.

Though it is possible to conceive a universal primacy located elsewhere than the city of Rome, the original witness of Peter and Paul and the continuing exercise of a universal *episcope* by the see of Rome present a unique presumption in its favour. Therefore, while to locate a universal primacy in the see of Rome is an affirmation at a different level from the assertion of the necessity for a universal primacy, it cannot be dissociated from the providential activity of the Holy Spirit.[32]

A statement to this effect has been included in the *Final Report.*[33]

There has also been increasing consensus in the dialogue with the Orthodox churches of the East on this point. From as early as the Council of Lyons in 1274 and then again in Florence in 1438, but even more after Vatican II, Roman Catholics and Orthodox have tried to establish mutual communion. The conflicts between these two 'sister churches' (Paul VI) are really more a matter of church order than of dogma, though theological differences of opinion also underlie the differences in church order. The East has often stressed the role of the local churches with their bishops, who only have supreme authority in the church as a college, meeting in council. The primacy of the patriarchs, even the patriarch of Rome, is only a primacy of honour. There are arguments over the hierarchy of the patriarchs – is Rome the first, or Constantinople, or Jerusalem? – but there is no mention of universal jurisdiction or of the infallibility of the Bishop of Rome. Hitherto there has still been no official dialogue on this point, but the bonds of friendship and of sacramental communion seem to have become so strong that there are prospects of a real reconciliation.

A reconciliation of this kind would mean at least a degree of decentralization in the church, with more scope for the different patriarchs. For the Orthodox it would mean the possibility of at last meeting together at a council, which the see of Rome could convene. In ancient times the convener was always the emperor of Byzantium. Who has taken his place: surely not those who give orders in Moscow? The restoration of unity with Orthodoxy, with its strong and distinctive traditions of liturgy and theology, could at the same time express the plurality and subsidiarity which is so desired by Lutherans and Anglicans too. It could be a safeguard against the excessive Western and bureaucratic centralism which seems to have been dominant within the Roman Catholic church since Trent.

However, these positive developments in dialogue with a number of Christian traditions are far from having solved all problems. Conversations with the Reformed, Calvinist and Free Church traditions have hardly arrived at this point. Granted, individual theologians – Cullmann, Vischer, von Allmen[34] – have made valuable beginnings. They have stripped the exegesis of the Petrine texts in the New Testament of confessional prejudices and prejudices born of controversy. They have recognized the significance of the see and the bishops of Rome for the unity of the ancient church. On this basis they are ready to acknowledge a new primatial function for the see of Rome – the church of Peter and Paul – as a step towards unity. But that is on condition that the basis shall clearly be the charismatic content of the ministry of the bishops of Rome, and not power and jurisdiction. This is to provide a safeguard for the other churches, in statement and counter-statement, just as Paul stands alongside Peter – and sometimes in opposition to him – and the other apostles. Lukas Vischer claims that Peter has successors in the many charismatic leaders of the church, people like Roger Schutz, Mother Teresa and Helder Camara. In the figure of John XXIII it is clear that such charismatic leaders can also sit on the cathedra in Rome. Thus Rome can best exercise a primacy if it can become in one way or another the model church of Christianity, if through a conciliar praxis – regular synods and councils – it can bring the many charisms in the church together and make them fruitful.

There are at least like-sounding visions within the Roman Catholic tradition of the future role of Rome's bishops within a purified Christian church. There have been, and still are, vigorous differences of opinion over the relationship between Pope and Council, which have not been sufficiently removed by Vatican I and Vatican II; there is also a permanent tension between the primacy of Rome and the right of the local, episcopal churches to their own initiatives. Moreover there are different options – extending even into canon law – in actually defining the place of the bishop of Rome. Must he first of all be 'pope', i.e. the one who guides, binds together, speaks for the universal church? We might see that role in a more 'progressive' light if we were to envisage someone from Africa or Asia performing such a function for a certain period and then giving place to someone else from another part of the world. It should be possible to have him chosen by the bishops of the world at the time of a Synod of Bishops. The other churches could be involved in the choice. After the restoration of unity the different traditions should take turns in providing such a president in the bond of love.[35] It might also be seen in a more 'conservative' light, as by those who think that the bishop of Rome, as Peter's successor, needs to exercise a universal episcopacy in the church, even over local churches and bishops. As such he is the leader of the central government of the universal church, which is represented in the different local churches by the local bishops.

There are others who want to connect his episcopal office more closely with the church and the see of Rome.[36] At all events, he is the local bishop of this particular church with which all are in communion but who also needs permanently to maintain *koinonia* with the local churches as with sister churches. His pastorate is first of all of the see of Rome.

Down to the eleventh century, moreover, he was chosen from and by the people or the clergy of that see, to oversee pastoral care in it. The College of Cardinals was appointed in 1059 to put an end to the corruption which influenced the choice of the bishop of Rome, especially through the influence of the Roman nobility. The cardinals are called 'cardinals of the church of Rome'. They are primarily advisors to the see of Rome. It is a modern notion to regard them as representatives of the world church who are meant above all to serve the needs of the world church in the choice of a pope. Only when the bishop of Rome is again a genuine pastor to the city, again truly cares for the needs of the people and the church in that place, could the primacy of Rome take on new content. It would be in keeping with this if his pronouncements kept closer to reality, were more pastoral in nature, sounded less like the pronouncements of a church politician. At the same time a similar approach should do away with the tendency of the administrative apparatus – the Curia – to divinize its pronouncements. For theologically the administrative apparatus is quite separate from the primacy. Over the course of the centuries it has taken many forms, and has constantly been modified, but further reform after Vatican II still leaves a good deal to be desired.

It seems to me that in the end the church and the churches have most to expect from the second approach: a bishop who is pastor of the church of Rome and as such is the centre of unity, stimulating the charisms in the church, one who convenes councils, a spokesman for the church, a conscience for the world. A review of his tasks in the spheres of government and administration, of his almost secular sovereignty, of his many representative duties (travel, audiences, receptions) would not only ease his inhumanly heavy task but also should avoid the centralism which is a continual threat. And it is precisely anxiety over centralism that prevents many churches from expressing the world-wide communion of the local churches within the one bond of love in church government, as well as in other things. It rules out the meeting of a truly universal council of all Christian churches, though there is such an urgent desire for it in order to tackle the enormous questions which face us as 'people of God' in the 'Spirit of God'.

The one universal church and its service in the renewing of society

Here we touch on an aspect of the church event which has permeated all the previous perspectives, but which has also become an independent topic for discussion within the ecumenical movement: the service of the fellowship of the church and its *koinonia* towards unity, righteousness and peace for all men and women in world society. All over the world Christians are also called locally to be the leaven in the loaf, the light on the lampstand, the salt in the food. However, they also have a quite specific ministry to fulfil together, as a universal church, through their mutual bonds which transcend the boundaries of nations and peoples. It can rightly be said that the unity of the church is in the last resort not an end in itself but necessary in order 'that the world may believe', namely in the sending of Jesus by the Father in the service of universal salvation. The church community is God's specific instrument of salvation, a universal and effective sign of the unity and togetherness of humanity, as the Uppsala Assembly and Vatican II put it.

The relationship between church unity and the unity of mankind has been the subject of a number of Faith and Order discussions and studies since 1971.[37] The theme will be taken up again in future years.[38] The themes of various WCC assemblies – Jesus Christ, The Hope of the World (Evanston 1954); The Light of the World (New Delhi 1961); The Life of the World (Vancouver 1983) – bear witness to one and the same spirituality.

In the footsteps of Jesus of Nazareth the church is thus characterized as a servant church. Seeking internal unity, the people of God have discovered that only the renunciation of power can lead to reconciliation and release from the vicious circles of evil and misery. Everything that tends towards theocracy, towards manipulation by church leaders, towards privileged actions by the churches, must disappear from church-state relationships. There is no ecumenical future for the system of diplomatic representatives which presents the see of Rome as the mini-state of the Vatican, though ways of performing the function of 'arbiter of the peoples', which falls to the leader of the universal church on a number of issues, and when its exercise is called for, must certainly be found

Living under the rainbow of God's grace, in ecumenical conversations the churches have also (re)discovered conversations with other religions. These conversations, too, will certainly have to be carried out at a universal level, now that migration and communication mean that not just Christianity but all religions are no longer geographically limited. Almost all societies are pluralist where religion is concerned.

The schism between East and West and the gaping abyss of poverty between North and South are both part of the countless legacies of the Christian past. There can be no hopeful conversation about the relationships of the economic systems which dominate our history without profound discussion with the universal church about questions of justice and peace, distribution of possessions and work, more equitable trade relationships. Here there is no need to duplicate the work of the United Nations. But should not the people of God in a world alliance – by virtue of their tradition of listening, their hallmark of sharing in Jesus' baptism and cup, their common discipline – be in a position to develop new models of peace and effective solidarity through programmes directed against hunger and hate? Is not the success of contemporary peace movements an indication that in the sphere of economic justice, too, a massive protest by universal Christianity against the present distribution of the prosperity of the world could make a dream come true?

In the year 2000, so the sociologists predict, two-thirds of Christians will live in the southern hemisphere. In that case the poor will determine the face of the church. Many of them have still to be born and many of them will already have died. As long as so many of us are in need, our *koinonia* lacks something, and we have not fulfilled God's mission to bring his gospel for the needy to the whole earth. Julio de Santa Ana wrote that the church cannot be fully the church as long as the poor do not recognize Christ in the church and the church does not recognize Christ in the poor.[39] However, we need a world communion for effective solutions to be found in which local churches can participate in such a way that they do not become disheartened by the immensity of the problems.

Finally, the universal church can serve humanity through the gospel of hope: that God is near men, supports them from cradle to grave and beyond. The mission of the church to the peoples is rooted in the remembrance of the crucified one as the risen one (I Cor.15.8; Matt.28.19f.; Luke 24.44-49; John 20.19-23; Acts 1.5-8). In this remembrance, doubt, denial, dispersal give place to hope, discipleship and gathering. Thus the *exousia* – the authority for the mission – derives from Jesus. Following him, men and women are to do the will of God (John 8.28; cf. Matt.11.2; 7.29; 8.8-10; 9.6-8) and to act in God's name (Mark 2.10; 3.15; 6.7; Luke 10.19; Mark 11.28). Likewise the disciples come forward with *parrhesia*, that is, boldly, with a good conscience, full of confidence that God himself is directing our efforts (Acts 4.29, 31; 9.27; 18.25; 28.31; I John 3.21; 5.14; Eph.3.12; 6.19; I Cor.3.12).

Thus the church event is rooted in God's own course through history, and the church itself can become the living proof of God's grace.

We know that in everything God works for good with those who love him, who are called according to his purpose... And I am sure that neither death, nor life, nor angels, nor principalities, nor things present, nor things to come, nor powers; nor height, nor depth, nor anything else in all creation, will be able to separate us from the love of God in Christ Jesus our Lord (Rom.8.28,38f.).

Epilogue
A Plea for the Church

At the highest point of the temple complex on the summit of Macchu Picchu, the university city of the Incas in Peru rediscovered in 1911, there is a kind of sundial. It is a massive block of granite with a perfect shape, which already for ten centuries has defied the ravages of the seasons. In the rarefied air of the Andes, and with nothing but the sound of the Urubamba, the holy river, and the cry of the condor, the bird of death, in the background, the Inca and his sons once waited here for their god: the sun, the light, the primal energy. By means of the hand of this sun-dial their scholars – priests?, theologians?, astrologers? – told them precisely how things were with their god, so that they could establish for the people the shortest and the longest days, the spring and autumn equinoxes, and thus the times of sowing and reaping, of sacrifices and feasts. What they offered, as in all world religions, was life itself: the first produce of the herd and of the harvest, given back to the earth and to the condor, the bird of the dead. In the temple complex of Macchu Picchu a condor has been sculpted in the rocky ground alongside the altar of sacrifice. The blood of the sacrificial animals dripped from the altar on to its stony beak, at the right time, the appropriate moment and the exact interval between the earth and the divine source of energy, the sun, as established by the seers of the people.

Is this the primitive religion of a people without writing, still bound up with the natural cycle, not yet enlightened as to mastery over cosmic energy? The 'minimal religion' of a people thinking in material and not in metaphysical terms, fighting for a harsh existence and ruled with iron discipline by the Inca dynasties and their hierarchical vassal system? Or is it a picture of the essence of religion: a prospect at the intersection of time and space of God who comes in the form of nature and history? Can we expect, in our place in the sun, anything other than a prospect of light and insight at the right time through observations given to us by faithful and skilled watchers on the basis of the co-ordinates accepted by the community, the language and symbolism of which are constantly refined?

It would already be an achievement if such a prospect and such an insight were to illuminate our dull earthliness and give colour to cradle and grave, bed and board. We should already be able to call ourselves 'people of God' because we would be living 'in the sight of God'. But that would not yet be what the Jewish-Christian tradition means by belief in God and *ekklesia tou Theou* (*qahal YHWH*). The religion of Israel and the Jesus movement have not just refined all the co-ordinates of the prospect of God by reading off the encounter with God from the lives of living men and women; they have declared the living man himself to be a participant in God's own life, indeed to have been so 'from the beginning', and at the same time in such a way that this sharing in God's own life can be freely accepted and grow over a lifetime.

The prospect of God is no longer simply read off the frightening and numinous side of nature; it is also read, rather, off the human desire for liberation, the human longing for justice, our questions about meaning and purpose. God does not only and primarily appear on the boundaries of time and space – where we fall off the periphery of the earth and disappear from the face of the living – but in living life itself; both in delight at his dynamism and in the threat of his power; in the faces of slaves who long for liberation, in the witness of martyrs at decisive points in their lives, in the fate of prophets who stood up for their cause; and also in the hope in which new life is born, children are constantly nurtured, nations develop and expand, and men and women give one another delight.

It is the conviction of Jews and Christians that the encounter between the living God and the human soul, the deepest mystery of the church, is rooted in God's own gift of himself to humanity, his initiative of grace, which culminates in Jesus of Nazareth, God's anointed, the servant of God, God with us and the man of God. The encounter with God by which we become what we are – people of God – therefore does not come about through our perception, our knowledge, our insight and our quest. We miss the heart of the church which we join in forming if we see the church simply as an optional instrument of faith, a help towards our knowledge of God, a pointer towards the ordering of our life – the rhythm of Sundays, the cultural pattern of the Christian year, the steeples amidst the bustle of the city which point to heaven like a warning finger and are monuments which bind us to the past. It must be said that many people do not get much further than this in their sense of the church.

In that case, they have got no further than the Incas, but as I have just said, that is at least something.

However, in two respects the church of Jesus Christ for which this plea is being made and which we share in forming, as 'people of God', is more and other than this. Moreover, these are the two facets of the church which are a specific feature of Jewish-Christian belief in God and are so essential to it that belief without the church or outside the fellowship of the church is virtually impossible.

The first point is connected with the more refined system of co-ordinates within which God comes into view for us. The structures of our belief which form the backbone of the Jesus movement, following in the footsteps of Israel's faith, and which determine our identity as Christians in the midst of many religions and many divergent convictions are in every respect dependent on the living subjects who are their vehicles. I have outlined these structures in earlier chapters: the confession of the apostolic faith according to the Word of God in the scriptures of Old and New Testaments; the sacramental sign of the messianic *koinonia* fellowship; the orientations for the way in which we are to behave as disciples, i.e. *disciplina*; the confidence in the directions that we are given by pastors, leaders, servants who are sent for that purpose and who are the interpreters of our common tradition of listening and prophets of our hope of the kingdom of God. All this is not a granite monolith in our midst, nor is it an institution at our disposal. Our confession according to the scriptures is more than swearing by texts; sacraments come into being only through active participation; Christian praxis is not guaranteed by a codex of disciplinary regulations, and the ministry is not service simply by definition of the authorities. A confession which lives by an active tradition of listening and a living proclamation are both needed if there is to be a confessing church; only where baptism and the Lord's Supper are allowed to determine the life of the community may we call on the name of the Lord who is in our midst; only when we sanctify one another into showing that service which is appropriate for disciples, will outsiders say, 'See how they love one another.' And only where the guides and leaders of the church are themselves trustworthy and stake their lives on what they do will 'people of God' follow them. That is why it can be said that the church must constantly be reborn. Unless the 'people of God' allow themselves to be incorporated into God's building as living stones, there will be no temple, no view with any prospect, no place to which we can look to find God.

The second facet, however, is even more important. Perhaps

some or even many people may succeed, either by following the way of the Incas or by personal assimilation of the holy scriptures or the most distinctive individualistic mystical experiences, in having a sight of God, in seeing and even keeping this vision. But does not the very nature of God, which we then begin to see, call for communication with others, for a consensus which becomes an orientation for society, mission and dialogue. God, whom we confess as the One who is above all, and his kingdom, which we seek to serve to the ends of the earth (Matt.24.14), cannot be reduced to a hypothesis which has validity for some and none for others. Scripture says that YHWH is a jealous God. What it means is that belief in YHWH, the one shepherd of his sheep, calls for a *qahal YHWH*, people of God, whose life and witness indicate from the start that they live for him. This witness itself constantly brings into being new groups which seek to share in the divine initiative and the course of the movement of Jesus, as he himself was impelled by that initiative.

That in this way, through the structures of our faith which determine the form of the church, we come together as 'people of God' to encounter God – now veiled and as in a mirror, but then face to face – nevertheless remains a project of faith, for us to note and freely accept. No plea for the church can end with conclusive proof. As I have said, the theology of the church is essentially provisional, even in that respect.

In the previous chapters I have tried to outline the essential facets of the phenomenon of the church:

1. The background of doubt about the mystery of God in our Western world;

2. Its roots in the tradition of Israel;

3. Its deepest concern, to lead people to live from God;

4. Its most authentic status, to stand in the service of God who in Jesus brings people deliverance and salvation.

Then I outlined the four pillars of our communion 'in Christ' which give form to our meeting for God's sake and by which, in our confession, we encounter God himself, who is our origin and destiny:

1. The confession of the apostolic faith according to the scriptures;

2. Immersion in the water bath of God's Spirit, in which Jesus too was baptized, and sharing in the supper of the crucified one who is alive;

3. Life in accordance with the standards of disciples of Jesus in the service of the kingdom of God;

4. Critical confidence in the course marked out for us by those who serve us as guides, pastors, overseers of our tradition.

Finally, I sketched out in broad outline the world-wide dimensions of all our searching and striving, in small groups, in parishes and comunities everywhere: the model of the one church, truly united locally in one community of faith and service, but bound together in love and consultation with all those within the same *koinonia*, of which communion with the shepherd of the church of Peter and Paul in Rome may be seen as the historical, albeit much disputed mark.

I hope that this provisional ecclesiology may provide building material for an ecumenical vision of the church, and that 'people of God' will find in this approach an invitation to learn to come together again as the church, so that finally the vision of God can shine out for all who seek him and there can be growth in the one true *ekklesia* which God himself calls to stand before his face.

Abbreviations

AvdK	Archief van de Kerken
BZ	*Biblische Zeitschrift*
ET	English Translation
EvTh	*Evangelische Theologie*
Greg	*Gregorianum*
KeO	*Kosmos en Oekumene*
KuD	*Kerygma und Dogma*
MySal	*Mysterium Salutis*
NF	Neue Folge (New Series)
NRT	*Nouvelle Revue Théologique*
NTS	*New Testament Studies*
QD	Quaestiones Disputatae
SC	Sources chrétiennes
TDNT	G.Kittel, *Theological Dictionary of the New Testament*
TQ	*Theologische Quartalschrift*
TTS	Trierer Theologische Studien
TvT	*Tijdschrift voor Theologie*
ZEK	*Zeitschrift für Evangelisches Kirchenrecht*

Notes

1. Alienation from Church and Religion

1. Karl Barth, *The Word of God and the Word of Man*, ET 1928, reprinted New York 1957, 104 and passim.

2. These facts are taken from David Barrett et al., *World Christian Encyclopaedia*, Nairobi-Oxford-New York 1982, 3-18.

3. W.Goddijn, H.Smets, G.van Tillo, *Opnieuw: God in Nederland*, Amsterdam 1979.

4. Ibid., 97.

5. Ibid., 65 and 33.

6. Ibid., 66.

7. W.Goddijn et al., *Hebben de kerken nog toekomst? Commentaar op het onderzoek 'Opnieuw: God in Nederland'*, Baarn 1981, 54; *Opnieuw: God in Nederland*, 33-8.

8. Ibid., 154.

9. *Hebben de kerken nog toekomst?*, 90-112.

10. W.Goddijn, 'Grenzen van kerkelijkheid en onkerkelijkheid', in *Handboek Pastoraat* 1, Deventer 1982.

11. 'Abwendung von der Kirche. Eine demoskopische Untersuchung über Jugend und Religion', *Herder Korrespondenz* 35, 1981, 443-6.

12. J.Peters, A.Felling, 'Kerkelijkheid en onkerkelijkheid: een onjuiste tweedeling', in *Hebben de kerken nog toekomst?*, (33-60) 44-50.

13. Ibid., 50-8.

14. For the term 'alienation', which is both a psychological and a sociological term, see R.Schacht, *Alienation*, London 1971; F.Johnson et al., *Alienation. Concept, Term and Meanings*, New York 1973. G.Baum, *Religion and Alienation. A Theological Reading of Sociology*, New York 1975. The great question is always 'who is alienated from whom?', because the term indicates a correlation. As far as religion and the church are concerned, the question is whether Christianity and the church alienate people from their authentic selves (Freud) or whether people are alienated from religion and the church by their choice of other aims in life; or whether this choice of other aims in life (prosperity, happiness, health) is something that finally alienates human beings from their deepest selves. In what follows, my starting point will be that in one way all these interpretations are contained in the use of the term. So they must all be brought out. These interpretations have not hitherto been tested, but are based on the theological literature of recent years.

15. L.Weimer, *Die Lust an Gott und seiner Sache*, Munich 1981.

16. The Dutch title of E.Schillebeeckx, *Christ*, ET London and New York 1979, see Part Four, 646ff. and especially 744-839.

17. A.Houtepen, *Theology of the Saeculum*, Kampen 1976, 15-52.

18. C. van Ouwerkerk, 'Is God toch in het gedruis...?', *Jaarboek Tenminste no.2*, Kampen 1981, 44.

19. J.B.Metz, *The Emergent Church. The Future of Christianity in a Post-bourgeois World*, ET London and New York 1981.

20. L.Grollenberg, *Jesus*, ET London and Philadelphia 1978; G.Theissen, *The First Followers of Jesus*, ET London 1978 (US: *The Sociology of Early Palestinian Christianity*, Philadelphia 1978); L.Schottroff and W.Stegemann, *Jesus von Nazareth – Hoffnung der Armen*, Stuttgart 1978.

21. A.Bittlinger, *The Church is Charismatic. The World Council of Churches and the Charismatic Renewal*, Geneva 1981.

22. K.Rahner, 'Brief an Mario von Galli', *Orientierung* 43, 1979, 206-7.

23. J.Thurlings, *De wankele zuil. Nederlands katholieken tussen assimilatie en pluralisme*, Nijmegen 1971; W.Goddijn, *De beheerste kerk*, Amsterdam and Brussels 1973.

24. H.Andriessen, *Religie en gezondheid. Toekomst van de Religie: Religie van de Toekomst?*, Nijmegen 1972 (congress paper, 4).

25. W.Berger, *Twee vragen: Religieuze behoefte? en: religieuze nood?*, ibid. (Congress paper, 1).

26. H.Küng, *Does God Exist?*, ET London and New York 1980, xxi.

27. *Rapport Maatschappelijke Dienstverlening – Levensbeschouwing*, 's-Hertogenbosch 1978.

28. K.Forster, *Religie zonder kerk?*, Baarn 1977, 22.

29. A.Vergote, 'Equivoque et articulation du sacré', in E.Castelli et al., *Le sacré*, Paris 1974, 471-92.

2. Living under the Rainbow

1. See e.g. Elmar Klinger, *Ekklesiologie der Neuzeit. Grundlegung bei Melchior Cano und Entwicklung bis zum 2. Vatikanischen Konzil*, Freiburg, Basle and Vienna 1978; Y.Congar, *L'Église de St Augustin à l'Epoque Moderne*, Paris 1970; id., *L'Ecclésiologie du Haut Moyen-Age*, Paris 1968; H.Küng, *The Church*, ET London and New York 1969; Eric Jay, *The Church. Its Changing Image through Twenty Centuries*, London 1977/78; J.Feiner and M.Löhrer, *MySal* IV, 1, Einsiedeln, Zurich and Cologne 1972, above all H.Fries, 'Wandel des Kirchenbildes und dogmengeschichtliche Entfaltung', ibid., 223-79; J.Ratzinger, *Das neue Volk Gottes. Entwürfe zur Ekklesiologie*, Düsseldorf 1969.

2. K.Becker, 'Articulus Fidei (1150-1230)', *Greg* 54, 1973, 517-69.

3. Cf. A.Houtepen, *Ontfeilbaarheid en Hermeneutiek*, Bruges 1973.

4. G.Philips, *De dogmatische constitutie over de kerk 'Lumen Gentium'*, Antwerp 1967.

5. U.Kühn, *Kirche*, Gütersloh 1980.

6. T.M.Schoof, *Aggiornamento*, Baarn 1968.

7. Karl Barth, *Church Dogmatics*, II/1 and IV/1.

8. K.Rahner, e.g. *Foundations of Christian Faith*, ET New York and London 1978; *Hörer des Wortes*, Munich 1963; *Theological Investigations* 4, ET London and New York 1966, 253-86; 10, ET London and New York 1974, 71-84.

9. J.B.Metz, *The Emergent Church* (see Ch. 1, n.19).

10. Y.Congar, *Diversity and Communion*, ET London 1984; J.Hamèr, *L'Eglise est une communion*, Paris 1962; P.C.Bori, *Koinonia. L'Idea della communione nell'ecclesiologia recente e nel Nuovo Testamento*, Brescia 1972; J.Tillard, 'L'Eglise de Dieu est une communion', *Irénikon* 54, 1981, 451-68.

11. H.Küng, *The Church*, 125f.; J.Ratzinger, *Das Neue Volk Gottes*, Düsseldorf 1969.

12. E.Schweizer, *Church Order in the New Testament*, London 1961; E.Käsemann, 'Paul and Early Catholicism', in *New Testament Questions of Today*, ET London and Philadelphia 1969, 236-51; W.Marxsen, *Der Frühkatholizismus im Neuen Testament*, Frankfurt 1964; R.Schnackenburg, *The Church in the New Testament*, ET New York 1965; H.Schlier, 'Ekklesiologie des Neuen Testaments', in *MySal* IV,1, 101-214; F.Hahn, K.Kertelge and R.Schnackenburg, *Einheit der Kirche. Grundlegung im Neuen Testament*, QD 84, Freiburg, Basle and Vienna 1979; J.Hainz, *Ekklesia. Strukturen Paulinischer Gemeindetheologie und Gemeindeordnung*, Regensburg 1972; id., *Koinonia. 'Kirche' als Gemeinschaft bei Paulus*, Regensburg 1982; H.Frankemölle, *Jahwebund und Kirche Christi*, Münster 1974; G.Lohfink, *Die Sammlung Israels. Eine Untersuchung zur lukanischen Ekklesiologie*, Munich 1975.

13. F.Malmberg, 'Naar een wezenlijk provisorische ecclesiologie?', *Bijdragen* 31, 1970, 33-53.

14. 'ekklesia', *TDNT* III, 504-13; J.Hainz, *Ekklesia*, 229ff.; id., 'Eglise', in *Dictionnaire de la Bible*, Supplement II, 487f.

15. Cf. A.Houtepen, 'De Kerk van God en het volk van Israël', *Ter Herkenning* 11, 1983, 38-46.

16. Cf. A.Houtepen, 'Lehrautorität in der ökumenischen Diskussion', in *Verbindliches Leben der Kirche heute*, Frankfurt 1978, (120-208) 142-6.

17. Vatican II, Dogmatic Constitution on the Church, *Lumen Gentium*, 9. Cf. B.Przewozny, *Church as the Sacrament of the Unity of all Mankind in 'Lumen Gentium' and 'Gaudium et Spes' and in Semmelroth, Schillebeeckx and Rahner*, Rome 1979.

18. H. van der Linde, *De kleine oecumene en de grote. De noodzaak van een nieuwe levenstijl*, Baarn 1981; H.Fiolet, *De kerk op de kruispunten van de geschiedenis*, Baarn 1982.

19. Vatican II, Decree on Ecumenism, *Unitatis Redintegratio*, 7.

3. Knowing God: A Way of Being

1. Hans Küng, *Does God Exist?*, ET London and New York 1980; J.Pohier, *Quand je dis Dieu*, Paris 1979.

2. Mary Daly, *Beyond God the Father*, Boston 1973.

3. G.Vahanian, *The Death of God*, New York 1961; T.J.J.Altizer and

W.Hamilton, *Radical Theology and the Death of God*, Indianapolis and New York 1966; T.J.J.Altizer, *The Gospel of Christian Atheism*, London and New York 1967. Cf. also the criticism of 'theism' in J.Moltmann, *Theology of Hope*, ET London and New York 1967, 116-72; D.Sölle, *Christ the Representative*, ET London 1967. Also E.Schillebeeckx, 'Life in God and Life in the World', in *God and Man*, ET London and New York 1969 (about J.A.T.Robinson, *Honest to God*).

4. H.Berger, *Zo wijd als alle werkelijkheid*, Baarn 1977.

5. H.Kuitert, *Wat heet geloven? Structuur en herkomst van de christelijke geloofsuitspraken*, Baarn 1977.

6. E.Schillebeeckx, *Jesus*, ET London and New York 1979, 262f.

7. Luther says: 'The trees of paradise provide the rods with which God will scourge those who want to know how he was before creation.' Cf. A.Dumas, *Nommer Dieu*, Paris 1980, 119.

8. B.D.Schilton, *God in Strength. Jesus' Announcement of the Kingdom*, Freistadt 1979; H.Merklein, *Die Gottesherrschaft als Handlungsprinzip*, Würzburg 1978; J.Schlosser, *Le Règne de Dieu dans les dits de Jésus*, Paris 1980.

9. H.Küng, *Does God Exist?*, 696f.

4. Through Jesus Christ Our Lord

1. H.Kuitert, *De realiteit van het geloof*, Kampen 1966, 202.

2. For what follows cf. e.g. H.Kessler, *Die theologische Bedeutung des Todes Jesu. Eine traditionsgeschichtliche Untersuchung*, Düsseldorf 1970; A.Grillmeier, 'Die Wirkung des Heilshandeln Gottes in Christus', *MySal* III,2, Einsiedeln, Zurich and Cologne 1969, 327-92; G.Bouwman, 'Gods gerechtigheid bij Paulus', *TvT* 11, 1971, 141-57; H.Wiersinga, *De verzoening in de theologische discussie*, Kampen 1972; L.A.Scheffczyk et al., *Erlösung und Emanzipation*, Quaestiones Disputatae 61, Freiburg, Basle and Vienna 1973; H.Berkhof, *Christian Faith*, ET Grand Rapids 1983, 200-22, 315-23, 451-64, 484-511; J.Moltmann, *The Crucified God*, ET London and New York 1974; id., *The Trinity and the Kingdom of God*, ET London and New York 1981; G.Theissen, 'Soteriologische Symbolik in den paulinischen Schriften', *KuD* 20, 1974, 282-304; H.Schürmann, *Jesu ureigener Tod. Exegetische Besinnung und Ausblick*, Freiburg 1975; K.Rahner, *Foundations of Christian Faith*, 228-93; W.Pannenberg, *Jesus – God and Man*, ET Philadelphia and London 1968, 21-37, 245-82, 365-98; K.Kertelge et al, *Der Tod Jesu. Deutungen im Neuen Testament*, Quaestiones Disputatae 74, Freiburg, Basle and Vienna 1976; E.Schillebeeckx, *Christ*, ET London and New York 1980; J.Sobrino, *Christology at the Crossroads*, ET New York and London 1978; R.Pesch, *Das Abendmahl und Jesu Todesverständnis*, Quaestiones Disputatae 80, Freiburg, Basle and Vienna 1978; R.Schwager, *Brauchen wir einen Sündenbock*, Munich 1978; John-Paul II, 'Redemptor Hominis', *Origins* 8, 1979, no.40, 625-43; M.Hengel, *The Atonement. A Study of the Origins of the Doctrine in the New Testament*, ET London and Philadelphia 1981; J.McCue, 'Ecumenical Reflection on Justification', *The Ecumenist* 18, 1980, 49-53; U.Kühn, 'Jesus

Christus, gestorben für unsere Sünden. Zur theologischen Deutung des Kreuzestodes Jesu', in *Die Frage nach Jesus Christus im ökumenischen Kontext*, Berlin 1980; O.Pesch, ' "Um Christi Willen..." Christologie und Rechtfertigungslehre in der katholischen Theologie', *Catholica*, 1981, 17-57; A.Dumas, 'La mort du Christ n'est elle pas sacrificielle? Discussion d'objections contemporaines', *Etudes theologiques et réligieuses* 56, 1981, 577-92.

3. E.Schillebeeckx, *Christ*, 477-511.

4. G.Theissen, 'Soteriologische Symbolik in den paulinischen Schriften', *KuD* 20, 1974, 282-304.

5. *Der Tod Jesu*, 205f.

6. E.Flesseman-Van Leer, 'De betekenis van Jezus' sterven in het hedendaags belijden', *Jaarboek Terminste* 3, Kampen 1982, 32-47.

7. G.Greshake, 'Der Wandel der Erlösungsvorstellungen in der Theologiegeschichte', in *Erlösung und Emanzipation*, Freiburg, Basle and Vienna 1973, 69-101.

8. W.Pannenberg, *Jesus – God and Man*, 39-47.

9. H.Berkhof, *Christian Faith*, 216.

10. P.Schoonenberg, *Het geloof van ons doopsel*, Part Four, 's-Hertogenbosch 1962.

11. H.Berkhof, op.cit., 218.

12. D.Sölle, *Christ the Representative* (see Ch.3, n.3).

13. K.Rahner, *Foundations of Christian Faith*, 285f.

14. J.Ratzinger, *Einführung in das Christentum*, Munich 1969.

15. A.Grillmeier, *MySal* III, 2, 371f.

16. J.Ratzinger, op.cit., 243.

17. J.Moltmann, *The Crucified God* (see Ch.4, n.1).

18. Id., *The Trinity and the Kingdom of God* (see Ch.4, n.1).

19. E.Schillebeeckx, *Jesus*, 274-317.

20. Ibid., 302.

21. Ibid., 310.

22. Ibid.

23. See especially G.Gutierrez, *Theology of Liberation*, ET London and New York 1974, 151f.; J.Sobrino, *Christology at the Crossroads*, ET London and New York 1978, 179-235; L.Boff, *Jesus Christ Liberator*, ET New York ³1981, 100-20.

24. R.Schwager, *Brauchen wir einen Sündenbock?*, Munich 1978.

25. R.Girard, *La violence et le sacré*, Paris 1972.

5. 'Hear, O Israel...': The Function of the Church's Confession

1. P.Steinacker, *Die Kennzeichen der Kirche. Eine Studie zu ihrer Einheit, Heiligkeit, Katholizität und Apostolizität*, Berlin and New York 1982; J.Dantine, *Die Kirche vor der Frage nach ihrer Wahrheit. Die reformatorische Lehre von den 'notae ecclesiae' und der Versuch ihrer Entfaltung in der kirchlichen Situation der Gegenwart*, Göttingen 1980; F.W.Kantzenbach, *Einheitsbestrebungen im Wandel der Kirchengeschichte*, Gütersloh 1979; Y.Congar, *Diversity and Communion*.

2. See Lukas Vischer, *Growth in Agreement*, Geneva 1984; M.Thurian et al., *Ecumenical Perspectives on Baptism, Eucharist and Ministry*, Geneva 1983.

3. J.C.Bennett (ed.), *Christian Social Ethics in a Changing World*, New York and London 1966; *Faith and Science in an Unjust World*, Vols. I and II, Geneva 1980 (Boston Report)

4. G.Gassmann, *Konzeptionen der Einheit in der Bewegung für Glauben und Kirchenverfassung 1910-1937*, Göttingen 1979.

5. E. Schillebeeckx, *The Understanding of Faith*, ET London and New York 1974.

6. W.Bühlmann, *Wo der Glaube lebt*, Freiburg im Breisgau 1974.

7. P.A.P.E.Kattenberg, *Credaal getuigen in kontekst*, Utrecht 1980; L.Vischer, *Reformed Witness Today*, Berne 1982; C.S.Song, *Confessing our Faith Around the World* I, Geneva 1978.

8. Lukas Vischer, 'An Ecumenical Creed?', *Concilium* 118, 1978, 103-17.

9. *Sharing in One Hope. Bangalore 1978*, Geneva 1978.

10. *Common Witness. A Study Document of the Joint Working Group of the Roman Catholic Church and the World Council of Churches*, Geneva 1980.

11. Cf. *Towards a Confession of the Common Faith*, Faith and Order Paper 100, Geneva 1980; and *Towards Visible Unity, Lima 1982*, Geneva 1982, I, 90f; II, 3-122.

12. F.Hahn, 'Bekenntnisformeln im Neuen Testament', in *Unterwegs zur Einheit. Festschrift H.Stirnimann*, Freiburg and Vienna 1980, 200-14; I. Havener, *The Credal Formulae of the Old Testament*, Munich 1976.

13. E.Schlink, 'Die Struktur der dogmatischen Aussage als ökumenisches Problem', in *Der kommende Christus und die kirchlichen Traditionen*, Göttingen 1961, 24-79; id., 'La signification oecuménique du symbole de Nicée-Constantinople et la structure des confessions de foi du christianisme primitif', *Positions luthériennes* 320, 1982, 137-56.

14. M.Lods, 'Les mots qui introduisent les confessions de foi dans le Nouveau Testament et dans l'Eglise Ancienne', *Positions luthériennes* 29, 1981, 97f.

15. *Verbindliches Lehren*, 142f. Cf. L.A.Hoedemaker, 'Oekumene en Paraklese. De identiteit van de gemeente in de leerschool van de wereld-kerk', in *Leren bij het leven*, Groningen 1981, 26-48.

16. Cf. R.Slenczka, 'Das ökumenische Konzil von Konstantinopel und seine ökumenische Geltung heute', *Una Sancta* 36, 1981/3. 198-209; Jung-mann, *Missarum Sollemnia*, Vienna 1948, 591f.

17. See *Towards Visible Unity. Lima 1982*, II, 51ff. Cf. *The Significance of the Early Creeds*, Bristol 1967; *The Council of Chalcedon*, Louvain Report 1971.

18. Lukas Vischer (ed.), *Spirit of God, Spirit of Christ. Ecumenical Reflections on the 'Filioque' Controversy*, London and Geneva 1981.

19. U.Duchrow, *Konflikt um die Oekumene. Christusbekenntnis – in welcher Gestalt der ökumenischen Bewegung?*, Munich 1980, argues for the expansion and deepening of this 'mini-creed'. However, he does not opt

for a return to Nicaea. Cf. H.Wegener-Füter, *Kirche und Ökumene. Das Kirchenbild des ökumenischen Rates der Kirchen nach den Vollversammlungsdokumenten von 1948 bis 1968*, Göttingen 1979.

20.*Confessio Augustana. Bekenntnis des eines Glaubens*, Paderborn and Frankfurt 1980.

21. Cf. the attempt made in Bangalore: 'A Common Statement of Our Faith', *Sharing in One Hope*, 244-6.

6. Baptism in the Name of Jesus

1. H.Spruit and H.van Zoelen, *Dopen... Ja, waarom eigenlijk?*, Kaskirapport 362, Hilversum 1980; cf. J.Straver, *Dopen? Wat een vraag!*, Hilversum 1975.

2. For what follows see e.g. E.Schlink, *Die Lehre von der Taufe*, Kassel 1969 (with a copious bibliography up to that date); G.Lohfink, 'Der Ursprung der christlichen Taufe', *TQ* 156, 1976, 35-54; L.Hartman, 'Into the Name of Jesus', *NTS* 20, 1973, 432-40; J.Moltmann, *The Church in the Power of the Spirit*, ET London and New York 1977, 226-41; F.Hahn, 'Die Taufe im Neuen Testament', in *Taufe*, Calwer Predigthilfe, Stuttgart 1978, 1-20; P.Pokòrny, 'Christologie et baptême à l'époque du christianisme primitif', *NTS* 27, 1980, 368-80; K.Blei, *De kinderdoop in diskussie*, Kampen 1981.

3. J.Becker, *Johannes der Täufer und Jesus von Nazareth*, Neukirchen 1972.

4. 'Oecumenisch Dooprapport', *AvdK* 32, 1977, 573-84.

5. For texts relating to the recognition of baptism see *Heel de Kerk. Een oekumenisch Werkboek*, Hilversum 1977, 167-74; 'Oekumenisch Dooprapport' (n.4); the agreed Faith and Order texts, *Baptism, Eucharist and Ministry*, Faith and Order Paper 111, Geneva 1982.

6. L.Spruit and H. van Zoelen, *Dopen... Ja waarom eigenlijk?*, 31f.

7. For this section see E.Schlink, 'Das Verhältnis von Taufe, Glaube und christlicher Kindererziehung', *ZEK* 21, 1976, 114-18; K.Blei, *De kinderdoop in diskussie*, Kampen 1982.

8. The Dutch practice of a compulsory registration of the allegiance of the child, religious or otherwise, at birth and the inclusion of this fact on birth certificates – often long before the date of the baptism and any use of this registration, even when people are not baptized and have no connection with the church – is a typical relic of a national established church. This practice should be abolished not only because of the possible abuse to which it is open in fully automated data bases – for example declarations of not being a Jew – but also because there are theological objections to it. Such a change would compel the churches to register their members in a healthier and more pastoral way.

9. *AvdK* 32, 1977, 113.

7. The Lord's Supper: Communion with One who was Excommunicated

1. For this chapter see e.g. J.Jeremias, *The Eucharistic Words of Jesus*, ET London and New York ²1966; M.Thurian, *L'Eucharistie. Mémorial du Seigneur. Sacrifice d'Action de Grace et d'Intercession*, Neuchâtel and Paris 1959; R.Feneberg, *Christliche Passafeier und Abendmahl. Eine biblisch-hermeneutische Untersuchung*, Munich 1971; G.N.Lammens, *Tot zijn geda-chtenis. Het commemoratieve aspect van de avondmaalsviering*, Kampen 1968; F.Hahn, 'Zum Stand der Erforschung des urchristlichen Abend-mahls', *EvTh* 35, 1975, 497-524; R.Pesch, *Das Abendmahl und Jesu Todesverständnis*, QD 80, Freiburg, Basle and Vienna 1978; J.Blank, 'Das Herrenmahl als Mitte der christlichen Gemeinde im Urchristentum', in J.Blank et al., *Das Recht der Gemeinde auf Eucharistie*, 1978, 8-29; E.Schillebeeckx, *Jesus*, 200-28, 305-11; F.Hahn, *Herrengedächtnis und Herrenmahl bei Paulus'*, *Liturgisches Jahrbuch* 32, 1982, 166-77; P.Fiedler, 'Probleme der Abendmahlsforschung', *Archiv für Liturgiewissenschaft* 24, 1982, 190-223.

2. J.Tillard, 'Confesser aujourd'hui la foi apostolique', *NRT* 114, 1982, 22-33. Compare the developed catechesis of the 1979 eucharistic prayer of the French bishops: 'Il est Grand, Le mystère de la Foi', Kattenberg, 132f.

3. A. van Bruggen, *Refléxion sur l'Adoration eucharistique*, Rome 1968, shows that before the ninth century (*Ordo Romanus* V) the elements were not venerated but simply respected, reserved for the communion of those who were not present and to serve as a mutual demonstration of *communio*. The eucharistic bread was brought by deacons from the bishop's church; the people in the local churches shared it and mixed it in the chalices. The development of a separate 'sacramental devotion', separate from the celebration of the eucharist, only came in the thirteenth century, especially through the celebration of the Feast of Corpus Christi.

4. *Baptism, Eucharist and Ministry*, Faith and Order Paper 111 (= Lima); *Das Herrenmahl. Gemeinsame Römisch-Katholische/Evangelische-Lutherische Kommission*, Paderborn and Frankfurt 1979; *Gemeenschappe-lijke Verklaring over de Maaltijd des Heren*, Commissie Intercommunie en Ambt, Nederland, Amersfoort 1976; *Agreed Statement on the Eucharist*, Anglican Roman Catholic International Commission (Windsor Statement), London 1972 (now in *The Final Report*, London 1982, 11-16; Elucidations, 17-25); *Accord Doctrinal sur l'Eucharistie*, Groupe des Dombes, Taizé 1972. Cf. N.Ehrenström and G.Gassmann, *Confessions in Dialogue*, Geneva 1975, 165-79; J.Puglisi, *A Workbook of Bibliographies for the Study of Interchurch-Dialogues*, Rome 1978; H.Meyer and L.Vischer, *Growth in Agreement*, Geneva 1984.

5. See A.Houtepen, 'Wederzijdse eucharistische gastvrijheid: model voor groeiende eenheid tussen de kerken', *KeO* 15, 1981, 29-39; id., 'Doop, eucharistie en ambt. Naar een consensus over ambt en sacramenten', *KeO* 16, 1982, 50-7; W.Boelens, *Tafel en gastheer. Toenadering bij interkom-munie en ambt*, Baarn 1979.

6. See M.Hengel, *The Charismatic Leader and his Followers*, ET Edinburgh 1981, 50-7.

7. Lima, nos.19 and 26.

8. L.Dussaut, *L'eucharistie. Pâques de Toute la vie*, Paris 1972.

9. Lima no.1: 'The meals which Jesus is recorded as sharing during his earthly ministry proclaim and enact the nearness of the kingdom of God, of which the feeding of the multitudes is a sign. In his last meal, the fellowship of the kingdom was connected with the imminence of Jesus' suffering. After his resurrection, the Lord made his presence known to his disciples in the breaking of the bread. Thus the eucharist continues these meals of Jesus during his earthly life and after his resurrection, always as a sign of the Kingdom. Christians see the eucharist prefigured in the Passover memorial of Israel's deliverance from the land of bondage and in the meal of the covenant on Mount Sinai (Ex.24). It is the new paschal meal of the Church, the meal of the New Covenant, which Christ gave to his disciples as the *anamnesis* of his death and resurrection, as the anticipation of the Supper of the Lamb (Rev.19.9).' It can hardly be put in a terser form than that.

10. E.Schillebeeckx, *The Eucharist*, ET London and New York 1968, 110f. H. de Lubac's position dates from as early as 1938 (*Catholicisme*, Paris 1938, 56-74), and was later taken up by G.Bacchiocchi, e.g. in 'Les sacrements, actes libres du Seigneur', *NRT* 83, 1951, 681-706. We have already almost forgotten how much these ideas from the 'new theology', arising out of the rediscovery of patristics, reformed Roman Catholic thinking on the sacraments, just as the studies of Thurian and Leenhard gave support to liturgical reforms on the Protestant side.

11. Lima, no.2.

12. Lima, no.13.

13. Cf. G.N.Lammens, op.cit., 41-6. Those who opt for a passover meal include J.Jeremias, *The Eucharistic Words of Jesus*; R.Pesch, *Das Abendmahl und Jesu Todesverständnis*; those against include G.Dix, *The Shape of the Liturgy*, London 1954; G.Delling, *Der Gottesdienst im Neuen Testament*, Göttingen 1952.

14. Cf. S.de Vries, *Joodse Riten en Symbolen*, Amsterdam 1968, 64-6.

15. Lammens, op.cit., 66-85; for *zkr* and *zikkaron* cf. ibid., 34-41.

16. Lima, no.5.

17. Constitution on the Liturgy, no.47.

18. Communion Prayer from the Roman Missal, Fourth Sunday in Advent.

19. Offertory Prayer from the Roman Missal, Twentieth Sunday after Trinity.

20. *L'Esprit Saint, L'Eglise et les Sacrements*, Groupe des Dombes, Taizé 1979, no.93, p.60. Cf. Vatican II, Constitution on Divine Revelation, no.21; Lima, 7 and 8.

21. Cf. the Ecumenical Prayer Cycle of the World Council of Churches, *For the Whole People of God*, Geneva, 1978; L.Vischer, *Intercession*, Faith and Order Paper 95, Geneva 1980.

22. Cf. the Joint Declaration on the Eucharist, 1976.

23. Lima, nos.4 and 8; ARCIC, *Final Report*, no.5 and Elucidations nos. 3-5.

24. Lima, no.13, commentary. For this whole question, E.Schillebeeckx, *The Eucharist*; L.Smits, *Actuele vragen rondom de Transsubstantiatie en de Tegenwoordigheid des Heren in de Eucharistie*, Roermond and Maaseik 1965. Cf. *A New Catechism*, ET London 1967, 163-70, 332-347 and the reactions to it in *Onze Verhouding tot de rooms-katholieke kerk. Heroriëntering en appèl*, The Hague 1969, accepted by the General Synod of the Dutch Reformed Church, 3-41.

25. Lima, no.14.

26. Lima, no.19.

27. What follows is based on P.C.Bori, *Koinonia. L'idea della communione nell'ecclesiologia recente e nel Nuovo Testamento*, Brescia 1972; J.M.McDermott, 'The Biblical Doctrine of Koinonia', *BZ* NF 19, 1975, 219-33; F.Hahn,K.Kertelge and R.Schnackenburg, *Einheit der Kirche. Grundlegung im Neuen Testament*, QD 84, Freiburg, Basle and Vienna 1979; J.Tillard, 'L'Eglise est une communion', *Irenikon* 1981, 451-68; Y.Congar, *Diversity and Communion*.

28. Lima, no.20.

29. Cf. A.Houtepen, 'Wederzijdse eucharistische gastvrijheid', 36-9.

30. Lima, no.22.

31. Lima, no.32.

8. The Ethic of the Kingdom of God

1. L. van Bladel, *Christelijk geloof en maatschappij kritiek*, Antwerp and Amsterdam 1980, 117-45.

2. E.Schillebeeckx, 'Questions on Christian Salvation of and for Man', in David Tracy et al., *Towards Vatican III*, Dublin 1978, 27-44. Cf. id., *Christ*, 734-43. Schillebeeckx uses this system of co-ordinates for analysing Christian salvation for human beings. My search for a Christian ethic is much more limited. The suggestion that Christian salvation is 'simply' an ethical code of behaviour is thus avoided from the start. For that reason I have also left out of account Schillebeeckx's seventh co-ordinate – the synthesis of the previous constants as the reality which heals human beings and brings salvation.

3. In Schillebeeckx this aspect is completely absent. Moreover, nothing is as complex as the theme of 'meaningful work' or 'the right to work'. For example, all the values connected with it which are defended in the West are looked at quite differently in the Third World. In many situations there, 'work' is much more connected with the basic needs of life. Perhaps that is also becoming increasingly the case in the West.

4. For what follows I have used e.g. H.Merklein, *Die Gottesherrschaft als Handlungsprinzip. Untersuchung zur Ethik Jesu*, Würzburg 1978; E. Schillebeeckx, *Jesus*, 140f.; B. van Iersel, *Met betrekking tot Jezus*, Bilthoven 1974, 140f.; F.Zehrer, *Die Botschaft der Parabeln*, Klosterneuburg 1972; B.D.Schilton, *God in Strength. Jesus' Announcement of the*

Kingdom, Freistadt 1979; J.Schlosser, *Le règne de Dieu dans les dits de Jésus*, Paris 1980.

5. K.L.Schmidt, *basileia*, *TDNT* 1, 579-90.

6. D.S.Russell, *The Method and Message of Jewish Apocalyptic*, London and Philadelphia 1964, 285-302.

7. E.Schillebeeckx, *Jesus*, 146.

8. ' "Uw Rijk kome, Uw wil geschiede". Verklaring van de Raad van Kerken', *KeO* 14, 1980, (243-8) 245.

9. Cf. A.Houtepen, 'Huwen in de heer. Kerken op zoek naar gezamenlijke visie', in *Oecumenisch huwelijkspastoraat. Praktijk en achtergronden*, Amersfoort 1982, 10-22.

10. L.Grollenberg, *Jesus*, ET London and Philadelphia 1978.

11. *À Diognète*, SC 33, ed. H.Marrou, Paris 1951.

12. Cf. C.J. den Heyer, 'Joodse visies op Jezus van Nazareth', *KeO* 15, 1981, 3-8.

13. M.Hengel, *Acts and the History of Earliest Christianity*, ET London and Philadelphia 1979, 71-126.

14. G.Lohfink, 'Der ekklesiale Sitz im Leben der Aufforderung Jesu zum Gewaltverzicht (Mt.5, 39b-42/Lc. 6, 29f.)', *TQ* 162, 1982, 236-53. Cf. G.Theissen, *Studien zur Soziologie des Urchristentums*, Tübingen 1979, 160-97; W.Lienemann, *Gewalt und Gewaltverzicht*, Munich 1982; J.Blank, 'Gewaltlosigkeit-Krieg-Militärdienst', *Orientierung* 1982, 157-63, 213-16, 220-3; Knut Willem Ruyter, 'Pacifism and Military Service in the Early Church', *Cross Currents* 32, 1982, 54-70. Lohfink, op.cit. 243: 'I suppose that we do not take Jesus' call to renounce violence seriously and cannot take it seriously because the social context, namely the kind of society or community for which this demand was once meant, has slipped away.' We do not take the ethics of the Sermon on the Mount seriously any more because we regard this ethics either as an unrepeatable norm for the individual or as a utopian perspective for the whole of society. In that case we have forgotten that Matthew and Jesus are concerned with a specific discipline for the *ekklesia*; ibid., 248: 'Jesus understands the people of God who are to be brought together, from which the church later took shape, as a real critical community. I.e., he did not regard it as a state or as a nation, but as a community which forms a distinctive sphere of life, a community in which people live differently and deal with one another differently from what is usual in the world. We could describe the people of God, whom Jesus means to bring together, as an alternative society. This world's power structures are not to prevail there, but reconciliation and fraternity. The radical ethic of the Sermon on the Mount is not addressed either to the invidivual or to the whole world, but specifically to this people of God which has been shaped by the good news.'

9. Called to the Service of the One Lord

1. J.Kahmann, 'Ambt en dienst in de kerk van het Nieuwe Testament', in *Ambt en Bediening in Meervoud*, Hilversum 1978, 39-55.

2. K.Rahner, *Minister Christi*, Hilversum 1968, 43; C.Janssens, 'Kerkopbouw en Ambtsbeleving', in *Kerk, Ambt, Kommunikatie*, Breda 1978, 11.

3. W.Foerster, *exousia*, *TDNT* II, 559-71.

4. P. van Leeuwen, 'Bijbelse achtergronden van het kerkelijk ambt en vorming van het kerkelijk ambt in de oudste kerk', in *Intercommunie en Ambt. Bijbelse achtergronden en kerkelijke perspectiveven*, The Hague 1976, 9-43.

5. E.Schillebeeckx, *Basis en Ambt*, Bloemendaal 1979.

6. E.Schillebeeckx, 'De sociale context van de verschuivingen in het kerkelijk ambt', *TvT* 22, 1982, 24-59.

7. Letter from Cornelius to Fabius of Antioch (251), reported in Eusebius of Caesarea, HE VI,43,11. Cf. P.Martimort, *L'Eglise en Prière*, Tournai 1962, 500ff.

8. L.Karrer, 'Ist der Priestermangel durch die Auffächerung der kirchlichen Dienste zu beheben?', in *Der Priestermangel*, 53: 'The current distinction between laity and clergy has ceased to be useful either theologically or structurally because it is oriented on a system which once worked (status) but must now be transformed into a new understanding of the church and into new social conditions. If it maintains the pattern of priest and layman, the church cannot develop any pastoral programme which gives specific form to its mission and its task and which clarifies the problems and the questions in connection with leadership of communities, the ministry of church and priest, co-responsibility, developing points of contact, and so on. Above all, it can no longer do justice to the multiplicity of new forms of community and co-responsibility which have already come into being, and the many new forms of ministry in the community which may be honorary, part-time or full-time. Conceptions which remain closely caught up in a pattern that made sense earlier (substitute curates, all-round service, strictly segregated training) are in the last resort regressive models.' Cf. also J.Neumann, 'Die wesenhafte Einheit von Ordination und Amt: Priester und Laien im Dienst der Kirche', ibid. 95-128.

9. In *Lumen Gentium*, no.31, laity are defined as *omnes christifideles praeter membra ordinis sacri et status religiosi in Ecclesia sanctii*, but in no.32 there is stress on the equality of all people in the church ('*Nulla igitur in Christo et in Ecclesia inaequalitas...*', with a reference to Gal.3.28; Col.3.11).

10. Thus already in *Lumen Gentium*, no.31: '*Laicis indoles saecularis propria et peculiaris est... Laicorum est, ex vocatione propria, res temporales gerendo et secundum Deum ordinando, regnum Dei quaerere. In saeculo vivunt... Ibi a Deo vocantur...*' This is developed further in the Decree on the Lay Apostolate, nos 2 and 23.

11. E.Schillebeeckx, 'Dogmatiek van Ambt en Lekestaat', *TvT* 2, 1962, 258-94: 'Thus being a layman or a priest is not something in itself: there are no defining characteristics which could introduce a distinction in actually being a Christian; these are terms denoting *functions within the church*' (267).

12. *Traditio apostolica* 10; '*Habet enim honorem presbyteratus per suam confessionem*' (SC 11, Paris 1968, ed. B.Botte). Cf. J.Martin, *Die Genese*

des Amtspriestertums in der frühen Kirche, Der Priesterliche Dienst III, Quaestiones disputatae 48, Freiburg 1972.

13. Vincent of Lérins, *Commonitorium*, chs. 2; 3; 5; 24; 28; 30-32: PL 50, 640, 641, 644, 679, 680-3.

14. 'Die apostolische Sukzession und die Gemeinschaft der Ämter', *Reform und Anerkennung kirchlicher Ämter*, 123-62 (with bibliography).

15. Thus, for example, G.Greshake, 'Priester und Pastoralreferenten', *Lebendige Seelsorge* 19, 1978, 18-27; H.J.Pottmeyer, 'Thesen zur theologischen Konzeption der pastoralen Dienste und ihrer Zuordnung', *Theologie und Glaube* 66, 1976, 313-31; id., 'Die pastoralen Dienste in der Gemeinde', 3.1.1, in *Gemeinsame Synode der Bistumer in der Bundesrepublik Deutschland*, Freiburg 1976. Because they are not ordained, pastoral workers cannot represent the theological symbolism in which Christ stands 'over against' the community in the way that ordained ministers can. Quite apart from the question whether Christ does stand 'over against' the community (why does not the community stand 'around' him?), this is the 'transvaluation of all values'; the relationship between Christ and the church is thus evidently dependent on prohibitions expressed in canon law.

16. A.Deissler, 'Der Priestertum im Alten Testament: Ein Blick vom alten zum Neuen Bund', *Der priesterliche Dienst I, Ursprung und Frühgeschichte*, QD 46, Freiburg 1970, 9-80 (the quotation comes from p.45); A.Cody, 'Priesthood in the Old Testament', in *Sacerdoce et Prophetie*, Studia Missionalia 22, Rome 1973, 309-29.

17. Thus W.Veldhuis, 'De plaats van de pastorale werker in de rooms-katholieke kerk', *Praktische theologie* 1979, 99-112, also following G. Groener, *Dienst van de leiding*, Nijmegen 1976, and in the light of mainly German tendencies: see the recommendations in the Memorandum of German Ecumenical Institutes, *Reform und Anerkennung kirchlicher Ämter*, 18-19.

18. Thus Kahmann, op.cit., 41-9; W.Thusing, 'Dienstfunktion und Vollmacht Kirchlicher Ämter nach dem neuen Testament', in *Macht, Dienst und Herrschaft in Kirche und Gesellschaft*, Freiburg 1974, 61-74.

19. Cf. R.Laurentin, 'Lumières du Nouveau Testament sur la crise actuelle des ministères', *Concilium* 8, 1972, 10, 13-23 (not in the English edition). For discussion in recent years see M.Houdijk, 'A Recent Discussion about the New Testament Basis of the Priest's Office', *Concilium* 80, 1972, 137-47. For the historical background to the focussing of all ministry on the priesthood, which can hardly find support from the New Testament, see G.J.Pinto de Oliveira, 'Signification sacerdotale du Ministère de l'Evêque dans la Tradition Apostolique d'Hippolyte de Rome', *Freiburger Zeitschrift für Theologie und Philosophie* 25, 1978, 398-427. A.Closs, 'Priester', in *Sacerdoce et Prophétie*, Studia Missionalia 22, Rome 1973, 1-14, points out that priest figures appear only in settled communities, and not among nomads, hunters or foragers, among whom – medicine apart – stress is laid more on the role of the father of the house. We can see this also in the history of Israel. To begin with, there is 'ni idole, ni temple, ni sacerdoce'. Only from the time of the monarchy does a priesthood begin to develop. This presupposes temple worship, an 'amphictyony', a life of

faith centred on the temple. Temples are only of use to people to whom the possession of land is important for their existence. They symbolize the connection between God and the land which is cultivated, the fruits which are offered, and the forces which lead to prosperity. They are full of symbols of prosperity. From a sociological point of view, temple worship and priesthood belong to the sphere of sedentary culture. It is not surprising, therefore, that the introduction of the titles *sacerdos* and *pontifex*, taken over first by the bishops and popes, and later by the leaders of the prosperous Roman suburban churches and country parishes who were subordinate to them, is connected with the growing link between church and state. That the New Testament does not think in these terms emerges from its specific remembrance of Jesus, who died in conflict with the temple cult, and from the fact that the church expanded at the time when temple worship came to an end, moreover in an area – the Jewish diaspora – in which Jewish tradespeople – once again nomads – had no message for the temple in Jerusalem. The fact that Acts 6.7 also mentions converts among the priests and gives a graphic account of the polemic with the high priest also points along the same lines and is typical of the departure from the priesthood which the New Testament indicates. Here Rom.12.1 is in fact the fulfilment of the prophetic criticism of the priesthood from the Old Testament. In later centuries *sacerdotium* and *imperium* again went hand in hand. It is hardly surprising that the ministry, thus conceived of in sacerdotal terms, again began to claim rights on the land, introduced the anointings of kings – as was already the practice of the line of Zadokites after the exile - and made prebends or benefices a condition of bestowal of office.

20. A. Ganoczy, ' "Splendours and Miseries" of the Tridentine Doctrine of Ministries', *Concilium* 80, 1972, 75-86 (esp.82f.).

21. E.g. in the 'Common Declaration of the Dutch Churches on the Ministry in Connection with the Celebration of the Lord's Supper', Dutch text in *Intercommunie en Ambt*, 120.

22. For this section cf. *Concilium* 8.10, 1972; K.Kertelge, *Gemeinde und Amt im Neuen Testament*, Munich 1972; *Le ministère et les ministères selon le Nouveau Testament*, Paris 1974; *Kirche im Werden*, Munich 1976; E.Schillebeeckx, *Basis en Ambt*, 43-78; id., *Ministry*, ET London and New York 1981, 5-37; J.Kahmann, op.cit.

23. G.Schmal, *Die Zwölf im Markusevangelium*, TTS 30, 1974; F.Hahn, 'Der Apostolat im Urchristentum', *KuD* 20, 1974, 54-77; M.Sheridan, 'Disciples and Discipleship in Matthew and Luke', *Biblical Theology Bulletin* 3, 1976, 235-55. Before this, see the pioneering study by B.Rigaux, 'Die "Zwölf" in Geschichte und Kerygma' (1961), in *Das kirchliche Amt im Neuen Testament*, Wege der Forschung 189, Darmstadt 1977, 279-304; R.Schnackenburg, 'Apostolicity, the Present Position of Studies', *One in Christ* 6, 1970, 243-73.

24. A.George, 'L'oeuvre de Luc: Actes et Evangile', in *Le ministère et les ministères*, 215-17.

25. A.Lemaire, 'Les ministères', 16-18. J.Delorme, 'Diversité et unité des ministères d'après le Nouveau Testament', in *Le ministère*, 289-02, attacks Lemaire (290 n.6) over his view that the name and the concept of

the 'apostolate' derive from Antioch, the centre of the mission; perhaps a Jewish origin, for example from Jerusalem, is also possible. However, in Acts 11 the 'missionaries' from Jerusalem are called 'prophets'.

26. See *Le ministère*, 292-4; Lemaire, op.cit., 18f.

27. Apart from Acts 20.17, 28; Phil.1.1, above all in the Pastoral Epistles, I Tim.3.1-7; Titus 1.7.

28. See the interesting survey of names for ministry in H.Bruders, 'Existenz eines christlichen Amtes', in *Das kirchliche Amt*, 86f.

29. G.Dautzenberg, *Urchristliche Prophetie*, Stuttgart 1975, 257-73.

30. Matt.5.22-24, 47; 7.3-5; 18.15; 23.8 and parallel passages; the term has a christological foundation: the Lord makes the disciples his brothers: Matt.12.49f.; 25.40; John 20.17; Rom.8.29; Heb.2.11-18.

31. H.Frankenmölle, *Jahwebund und Kirche Christi*, Münster 1974; id., 'Amtskritik im Matthäusevangelium', *Bibl* 54, 1973, 247-62; S.Legasse in *Le ministère*, 188-206; J.Delorme, ibid., 164-80.

32. The terminology is not very consistent. In *Lumen gentium* we find: no.10: *sacerdotium, sacerdos, sacerdotalis*; no.21: *presbyteri, sacerdotium, sacerdotes*. In the Decree on the Episcopate, no.15: *sacerdotes, presbyterium, sacerdotalis*; no.16: only *sacerdotes*; no.28: *presbyteri* and *sacerdotium, presbyterium* and *sacerdotes*. The Decree on the Training of the Ministry and the Life of the Priest mostly uses *presbyteri* and *presbyteratus*, but sometimes (nos.4,6,7,9,13,17) also *sacerdotes*, and usually the adjective *sacerdotalis*; also *sacerdotium* (no.5).

33. Kahmann, op.cit., 50-5.

34. Dautzenberg, op.cit., criticizes the current concept of prophecy drawn from kerygmatic theology, which lays too much stress on the kerygmatic aspect of the Christ event. Prophecy on the Jewish model is not simply connected with the proclamation of the word but equally with visions, dreams and signs. In this sense the glossolalia of I Corinthians is nothing strange, no more so than Paul's attempt at interpretation through prophets.

35. F.Haarsma, 'Kerkelijk ambt als profetisme', *TvT* 10, 1970, 179-202.

36. K.H.Rengstorf, 'Didache', *TDNT* II, 163-5.

37. C.Perrot, *Le ministère*, 123-8. The translation 'leaders' is therefore too weak. These are 'pioneers', 'patrol leaders'. The term has the connotation of guiding people on the march.

38. *AvdK* 33, 1978, 1160.

39. *Modern Ecumenical Documents on the Ministry*, London 1975, 95.

40. For an almost complete survey see E.Schüssler Fiorenza, *Priester für Gott*, Münster 1972, esp. 4-67; J.Tillard, 'What Priesthood has the Ministry?', *One in Christ* 9, 1973, 243-69.

41. Report on the Reformed-Catholic Dialogue 102 (n.35), 1162f.

42. Faith and Order, *Accra Consensus 'A Mutually Recognized Ministry'*, nos.40-43. For the derivation of the New Testament laying on of hands from the Jewish *šemika* cf. G.Kretschmar, 'Die Ordination im frühen Christentum', *Freiburger Zeitschrift für Theologie und Philosophie* 22, 1975, 35-69.

43. *AvdK* 29, 1974, 4, nos.8-9.

44. Ibid. 5 (no.11).

45. *Baptism, Eucharist and Ministry*, Faith and Order Report 111. Geneva 1982.

46. Ibid., no.13; *The Ministry*, Lutheran Roman Catholic International Commission, no.31.

47. *Baptism, Eucharist and Ministry*, nos.19-31.

48. Ibid, no.26.

10. A Universal Church?

1. J.M.R.Tillard, 'Towards a Common Profession of Faith', in *Sharing in One Hope, Bangalore 1978*, Geneva 1978, 22-232.

2. See Ruth Rouse and S.C.Neill, *A History of the Ecumenical Movement 1517-1948*, 1-216; F.W.Kantzenbach, *Einheitsbestrebungen im Wandel der Kirchengeschichte*, Gütersloh 1980, 1-103.

3. Y.Congar, *Diversity and Communion*, 23-7.

4. H.G.Stobbe, 'Lernprozess einer Kirche. Notwendige Erinnerung an die fast vergessene Vorgeschichte des Oekumenismus-Dekrets', in P.Lengsfeld et al, *Oekumenische Theologie. Ein Arbeitsbuch*, Stuttgart, Berlin, Cologne, Mainz 1980, 71-123.

5. Heribert Mühlen, *Morgen wird Einheit sein*, Paderborn 1974, 66-78.

6. R.Beaupère, 'What Sort of Unity? The Decree on Ecumenism Ten Years Later. A Roman Catholic View', *One in Christ*, 10, 1974, 237-55; A.Houtepen, '15 jaar oekumene na Vaticanum II: Hoe verder?', *KeO* 13, 1979, 283-90.

7. 'The Church, the Churches and the World Council of Churches', in *Minutes and Reports of the Third Meeting of the Central Committee, Toronto (Canada) 1950*, Geneva 1950, 84-89: 'The World Council cannot and should not be based on any one particular conception of the Church. It does not prejudge the ecclesiological problem... Membership in the World Council of Churches does not imply that a Church treats its own conception of the Church as merely relative... Membership in the World Council does not imply the acceptance of a specific doctrine concerning the nature of Church unity.'

8. G.Gassmann, *Konzeptionen der Einheit in der Bewegung für Glauben und Kirchenverfassung*, Göttingen 1979.

9. *The Kingdom of Christ*, 1838.

10. *The Church Idea. An Essay towards Unity*, Boston 1870.

11. Chicago Quadrilateral 1886: 'As inherent parts of the sacred deposit, and therefore as essential to the restoration of unity among the divided branches of Christendom, we account the following, to wit:

    1. The Holy Scriptures of the Old and New Testaments as the revealed Word of God;

    2. The Nicene Creed as the sufficient Statement of the Christian Faith;

    3. The Two Sacraments – Baptism and the Supper of the Lord – ministered with unfailing use of Christ's words of institution and of the elements ordained by Him;

    4. The Historic Episcopate, locally adapted in the methods of its

adminstration to the varying needs of the nations and peoples called of God into the unity of His Church' (*Journal of Proceedings of the Bishops, Clergy and Laity of the Protestant Episcopal Church in the USA, Assembled in a General Convention*, Boston 1886, 79ff.).

Lambeth Quadrilateral 1888:

1. The Holy Scriptures of the Old and New Testament, as 'containing all things necessary to salvation', and being the rule and ultimate standard of faith (= Article VI of the Thirty-Nine Articles);

2. The Apostles' Creed, as the Baptism Symbol; and the Nicene Creed, as the sufficient statement of the Christian faith;

3. The two sacraments ordained by Christ Himself – Baptism and the Supper of the Lord – ministered with unfailing use of Christ's words of Institution, and of the elements ordained by Him;

4. The Historic Episcopate, locally adapted in the methods of its adminstration to the varying needs of the nations and peoples called of God into the Unity of His Church.'

12. Surveys in Rouse/Neill, *History of the Ecumenical Movement*, 445-508; R.Groscurth et al, *Kirchenunionen und Kirchengemeinschaft*, Frankfurt 1975.

13. Cf. Council of Chalcedon, canons II, IV; Lateran Council, canon 9.

14. *The New Delhi Report*, London and New York 1961, 116 (Section on Unity I,2).

15. *Uppsala Report*, Geneva 1968, 17: 'So to the emphasis "all in each place" we would now like to add a fresh understanding of the unity of all Christians in all places. This calls the churches in all places to realize that they belong together and are called to act together. In a time when human interdependence is so evident, it is all the more imperative to make visible the bonds which unite Christians in universal fellowship... The members of the World Council of Churches, committed to each other, should work for the time when a genuinely universal council may once more speak for all Christians, and lead the way into the future.'

16. *Breaking Barriers, Nairobi 1975*, London and Grand Rapids 1976, 60.

17. Ibid., 317: 'The World Council of Churches is constituted for the following functions and purposes:

(i) to call the churches to the goal of visible unity in one faith and one eucharistic fellowship expressed in worship and in common life in Christ, and to advance towards that unity in order that the world may believe...'

18. *Declaration and Address*, 1809. Cf. Gassmann, op.cit., 34ff.

19. *Fraternal Appeal to the American Churches. With a Plan for Catholic Union on Apostolic Principles*, 1838. Cf. Gassmann, 510ff.

20. Rouse and Neill, *History of the Ecumenical Movement*, 510f.

21. D. von Allmen et al., *Zeugnis und Dienst reformatorischer Kirchen im Europa der Gegenwart*, Frankfurt 1977, 13-22. Cf. *Konkordie und Kirchengemeinschaft*, Frankfurt 1982.

22. H.Meyer, 'Theologische Grundanliegen konfessioneller Weltfamilien', *LWB-Report 5*, August 1979, 14-41.

23. See *La Documentation Catholique 1970*, 265-9, in *Materialdienst des Konfessionskundlichen Instituts Bensheim*, 28, 1977, 63.

24. J.M.R.Tillard, 'L'Eglise de Dieu est une Communion', *Irénikon* 54, 1981, 451-68.

25. *Sharing in One Hope*, 237: 'The Faith and Order Commission is committed to keep before the churches this vision and goal. It is its constitutional task to contribute to the creation of conditions which will make it possible for the churches to enter into full communion. They will then recognize each other's ministries; they will share the bread and the cup of their Lord; they will acknowledge each other as belonging to the body of Christ in all places and at all times; they will proclaim together the Gospel to the world; they will serve the needs of humankind in mutual trust and dedication; and for these ends they will plan and take decisions together in assemblies constituted by authorized representatives whenever this is required.'

26. Cf. A.Houtepen, 'Eigentijds leergezag. Een oecumenische discussie', *TvT* 18, 1978, 26-48.

27. So too the ARCIC Final Report, no.12, p.86: 'Being in canonical communion with the bishop of Rome is not among the necessary elements by which a Christian community is recognized as a church.' Cf. J.Tillard, op.cit., 463: 'So the local church of Rome has a "privileged position" which makes it the "perpetual and visible principle and foundation of the unity of faith and communion" (*Lumen Gentium* 18). In this sense it "presides in love". It is not the church on which all the others must depend, as a kind of guardian, but that on which the health and well-being of the *koinonia* depends. As a consequence its bishop is charged by the Spirit with a personal ministry but one which is in the service of the *communion* of all the churches.'

28. R.Brown, K.Donfried and J.Reumann, *Peter in the New Testament*, Minneapolis 1973; *Petrus und Paulus. Pole der Einheit*, Quaestiones Disputatae 76, Freiburg, Basle and Vienna 1976; J.M.R.Tillard, *L'Evêque de Rome*, Paris 1982, 134-54.

29. *KeO* 16, 1982, no.9, 'Het Petrusambt'.

30. *AvdK* 1974, 777-808.

31. *Authority in the Church* I, nos.20-22. Final Report, 63.

32. *Elucidations* 1981, no.8, 76.

33. *Authority in the Church* II, nos.6-7, 83f.: 'The New Testament contains no explicit record of a transmission of Peter's leadership; nor is the transmission of apostolic authority in general very clear. Furthermore the Petrine texts were subjected to differing interpretations as early as the time of the Church Fathers. Yet the church at Rome, the city in which Peter and Paul taught and were martyred, came to be recognized as possessing a unique responsibility among the churches: its bishop was seen to perform a special service in relation to the unity of the churches, and in relation to fidelity to the apostolic inheritance, thus exercising among his fellow bishops functions analogous to those ascribed to Peter, whose successor the bishop of Rome was claimed to be. Fathers and doctors of the Church gradually came to interpret the New Testament data as pointing in the same direction.

This interpretation has been questioned, and it has been argued that it arose from an attempt to legitimize a development which had already occurred. Yet it is possible to think that a primacy of the bishop of Rome is not contrary to the New Testament and is part of God's purpose regarding the Church's unity and catholicity, while admitting that the New Testament texts offer no sufficient basis for this.'

34. O.Cullmann, *Peter. Disciple, Apostle, Martyr*, Philadelphia and London 1953; H.Stirnimann-L.Vischer, *Papsttum und Petrusdienst*, Frankfurt 1975; J.J.von Allmen, *La primauté de l'Eglise de Pierre et de Paul*, Fribourg and Paris 1977.

35. G.Denzler et al., *Papsttum heute und morgen*, Regensburg 1975. Cf. K.Rahner, *Vorfragen zu einem ökumenischen Amstverständnis*, Quaestiones Disputatae 65, Freiburg, Basle and Vienna 1974, 19-32.

36. Thus especially Tillard and also von Allmen.

37. See G.Müller-Fahrenholz, *Unity in Today's World*, Geneva 1978.

38. *Towards Visible Unity, Lima Report 1982*, Geneva 1982, II, 123-230.

39. Julio de Santa Ana, *Towards a Church of the Poor*, Geneva 1979.